BOLLINGEN SERIES LXI · 3

ESSAYS OF ERICH NEUMANN

VOLUME 3

Editorial Committee

Renée Brandt†
William McGuire
Julie Neumann†

PUBLISHED IN JOINT SPONSORSHIP WITH THE
C. G. JUNG INSTITUTE OF SAN FRANCISCO

† deceased

ERICH NEUMANN

The Place of Creation

SIX ESSAYS

Translated from the German by
Hildegard Nagel, Eugene Rolfe,
Jan van Heurck, and
Krishna Winston

BOLLINGEN SERIES LXI · 3

PRINCETON UNIVERSITY PRESS
Princeton and Oxford

Published by Princeton University Press
41 William Street, Princeton, New Jersey 08540
99 Banbury Road, Oxford OX2 6JX

press.princeton.edu

GPSR Authorized Representative: Easy Access System Europe -
Mustamäe tee 50, 10621 Tallinn, Estonia, gpsr.requests@easproject.com

First published in 1989
New cloth, paperback, and e-book Bollingen Recollections editions, 2026

Cloth ISBN 9780691279183
Paperback ISBN 9780691279190
ISBN (e-book) 9780691279206

This is the third volume of number sixty-one in a series of works
sponsored by and published for Bollingen Foundation

The Library of Congress has cataloged a prior edition of this book as follows:

Neumann, Erich.
[Essays. English]
The place of creation : six essays/ Erich Neumann; translated
from the German by Hildegard Nagel ... [et al.].
p. cm.—(Essays of Erich Neumann ; v. 3) (Bollingen series ; LXI, 3)
Essays originally presented as lectures at the
Eranos conferences 1952 –1960
Bibliography: p. Includes index. Contents: The psyche and the
transformation of the - reality planes—The experience of the unitary
reality—Creative man and the "great experience"—Man and
meaning—Peace as the symbol of life—The psyche
as the place of creation.
ISBN 0-691-09965-0 (alk. paper)
1. Creative ability. I. Tite. II. Series. Ill. Series: Neumann, Erich.
Essays. English. Selections.
BF408.N374 1988   153.3'5—dc19   8S.88-25297

CONTENTS

v

EDITORIAL NOTE

The six essays in this volume originated as lectures at the Eranos Conferences, in Ascona, Switzerland, and were first published in volumes of the *Eranos-Jahrbücher* (Zurich). Erich Neumann lectured at Eranos every year from 1948 to 1960. After C. G. Jung's retirement from the platform in 1951, Neumann was regarded as the dominant figure among the Eranos lecturers. He gave what proved to be his final lecture, "The Psyche as the Place of Creation," in August 1960, four months before his death at the age of fifty-five.

All but the first and last essays in the present volume were collected, with some revision by the author, in a volume entitled *Der schöpferische Mensch* (Zurich, 1959), which also included two essays that have been translated in previous volumes of the present series—"Creative Man and Transformation" (1954), in *Art and the Creative Unconscious*, and the study of Georg Trakl, in *Creative Man* (1959)—and Neumann's preface, which is published here.

Three of the essays were translated by Eugene Rolfe (1914–1986): "The Experience of the Unitary Reality," "Creative Man and the 'Great Experience,'" and "The Psyche as the Place of Creation." "The Psyche and the Transformation of the Reality Planes" was translated, with some abridgment, by Hildegard Nagel (1886–1985), in the annual *Spring 1956*; the translation was completed and revised by Inge Roberts in consultation

vii

with William Goodheart. "Man and Meaning" and the preface were translated by Krishna Winston, and "Peace as the Symbol of Life" by Jan van Heurck.

The analytical psychologist Renée Brand, of San Francisco, who took the initiative that resulted in the continuation of this publication of Neumann's essays under the cosponsorship of the C. G. Jung Institute of San Francisco, reviewed the translation of the second essay with the assistance of Stanford Drew. After Dr. Brand's death, in 1980, in her eightieth year, Dr. Goodheart, on behalf of the Jung Institute, assumed the responsibility for reviewing the translations, except for that of the third essay, which Andrea Dykes dealt with in consultation with Mr. Rolfe.

The author's widow, Julie Neumann, also an analytical psychologist, who participated in the planning of this edition, died in 1985 in Tel Aviv, as a result of being run down by an automobile.

•

Works of Erich Neumann in English translation are listed under the Abbreviated References. In the footnotes, brackets enclose contributions by the editor and the translators.

For quotations from translations in *Johann Wolfgang von Goethe: Selected Poems*, copyright © 1983 by Suhrkamp Publishers New York, acknowledgment is made to the publishers. For research help, I am indebted to Gerhard Adler, William Alex, Mark R. Cohen, Ralph Freedman, John E. Grant, Kathleen Raine, Rudolf Ritsema, and Theodore Ziolkowski.

WILLIAM McGUIRE

PREFACE

The thematic unity of the essays collected in this volume revealed itself gradually as they were being written. The essence of creative man, as I have attempted to capture it here, does not manifest itself exclusively in the artist, although his example is perhaps the most convenient for illustrating many aspects of creativity.

While working on the problem of portraying man as the creative being par excellence, I found it necessary to expand the concepts of analytical psychology and to establish certain new emphases. My more comprehensive definition of the archetype and my attempt to develop the concept of "unitary reality" must be seen in this context.

Above and beyond all theoretical considerations, it was my intention to focus on the inseparable creative link that unites the individual, the immediate background to which he himself belongs, and the world that surrounds him and that he creates. Man as *homo creator* is the decisive concern of our times, and whether he can be restored to health and continue to evolve will depend on whether the individual comes once more to experience himself as creative, that is, in touch with his own being and the being of the world.

All the Eranos lectures published here have been ex-

Vorwort to *Der schöpferische Mensch*. Translated by Krishna Winston. See the editorial note, above.

panded, and, I hope, thereby made clearer. The essay on the poet Trakl attempts to illuminate by way of a concrete example the nexus between the personal and the transpersonal that is portrayed in more general terms in the other papers.

Tel Aviv, February 1959　　　　　　ERICH NEUMANN

ABBREVIATED REFERENCES

B.S. = Bollingen Series (New York and Princeton).

The I Ching, or Book of Changes. The Richard Wilhelm translation into German, rendered into English by Cary F. Baynes. New York/Princeton (B.S. XIX) and London, 3rd ed., 1967.

CW = The Collected Works of C. G. Jung. Edited by Gerhard Adler, Michael Fordham, William McGuire, and Herbert Read. 20 vols. Translated by R.F.C. Hull. New York/Princeton (B.S. XX) and London, 1951-1979.

EJ = *Eranos-Jahrbücher*. Edited by Olga Froebe-Kapteyn (until 1960). Zurich.

Neumann, *Amor and Psyche: The Psychic Development of the Feminine. A Commentary on the Tale by Apuleius*. Translated by Ralph Manheim. New York (B.S. LIV) and London, 1956.

Neumann, *Art and the Creative Unconscious*. Translated by Ralph Manheim. New York (B.S. LXI:1) and London, 1959.

Neumann, *The Child*. Translated by Ralph Manheim. New York and London, 1973.

Neumann, *Creative Man*. Translated by Eugene Rolfe. Princeton (B.S. LXI:2) and London, 1979.

Neumann, *Depth Psychology and a New Ethic*. Translated by Eugene Rolfe. New York and London, 1963.

Neumann, *The Great Mother: An Analysis of the Archetype*. Translated by Ralph Manheim. New York (B.S. XLVII) and London, 1955.

Neumann, *The Origins and History of Consciousness*. Translated by R.F.C. Hull. New York (B.S. XLII) and London, 1954.

Neumann, U. d. M. = Umkreisung der Mitte. 3 vols. Zurich, 1953.

PEY = Papers from the Eranos Yearbooks. Translated by Ralph Manheim and R.F.C. Hull. 6 vols. New York/Princeton (B.S. XXX) and London, 1955-1968.

THE PLACE OF CREATION

I

THE PSYCHE AND
THE TRANSFORMATION OF
THE REALITY PLANES:
A METAPSYCHOLOGICAL
ESSAY

1

It is with some misgivings that I am addressing you now, for I am well aware of the problematic nature of my material. I am offering here tentative interpretations, neither facts nor proofs, more questions than answers. All that I have to say may well be called into question. Still, I decided to present this essay, since I keep bumping into people for whom these same problems have created a headache similar to my own. And this term, headache, is really an understatement.

My endeavor concerns the premises for a theory of the psyche that includes data and experiences which I am not going to prove here, but which I assume to be proven. This theory must encompass parapsychic phe-

---

"Die Psyche und die Wandlung der Wirklichkeitsebenen: Ein metapsychologischer Versuch," *Eranos-Jahrbuch 1952*, on "Man and Energy." Translated by Hildegard Nagel, *Spring 1956*; revised by Inge Roberts in consultation with William Goodheart.

nomena, but also the anticipatory character of childhood and initial dreams, the validity of the *I Ching* oracle,[1] and the synchronistic phenomena discovered and made partially intelligible by C. G. Jung.[2] Once established, these concepts ought to extend to and benefit the field of biology and, indeed, life as a whole.

It is a question of determining the unity of a reality which can be no longer (or rather, which can be no longer exclusively) divided into an outer physical-biological world and an inner psychic world by means of the polarization of our consciousness.

The work of C. G. Jung gave me courage, especially "The Spirit of Psychology"[3] and "Synchronicity." But let me add that I am responsible for everything I am going to say: at this point one must risk one's own skin.

I am unable to adhere to scientific modesty, supposedly a great virtue in our day, and to remain within the confines of what has been proven. It seems to me of crucial importance today to have the courage to compromise oneself in this respect. This entails asking anew the question of meaning for humanity, and attempting to sketch a unified image of the human being's position in the world. Even though it may be necessarily an imperfect one, such an image would counterbalance the atomization of our outer reality. In this sense, my attempt yet again has its source in daily psychotherapeutic work and circles back to end in it.

1. *I Ching*. See Abbreviated References.
2. Jung, "Synchronicity: An Acausal Connecting Principle," CW 8. [Orig. 1952. A brief version was given as a lecture at Eranos 1951.]
3. *Spirit and Nature* (PEY 1, 1954; orig. 1947). [Revised as "On the Nature of the Psyche," CW 8.]

Scientific caution, which does not take into account the human soul's hunger for orientation, tries to appease with stones instead of offering the staff of life. This leads human beings to go wherever they can to find bread, even if it is of the cheapest kind. Since science refutes the human quest for meaning, it drives us to search for it in collective movements, even though in reality these hollow us out from within or destroy us from without.

Our essay is based on the various kinds of "knowing" [*Wissen*] we encounter in one and the same individual. The concept of knowledge most familiar to us is that of conscious knowledge, i.e., an ego-centered form of knowing. Its contents are linked to the ego and form a more or less closed system. Also part of the ego-centered knowledge are those contents which have become unconscious (i.e., those which had originally been linked to the ego, but became subsequently unconscious by dropping out of consciousness): contents which we have at the disposal of our memory or have forgotten, suppressed, or repressed. Classification becomes dubious when the contents of "perceiving consciousness" are concerned, i.e., all those contents which, for instance, hypnosis can transfer to consciousness, such as subliminal perceptions and experiences. These are capable of becoming conscious without having been linked to the ego.

Here we encounter the reality of an uncentered system of knowledge. This means we must assume that a system—here the perceiving system—has at its disposal a complicated knowledge with manifold contents. And yet this knowledge is not centered, not linked to the ego for instance. The question arises, whether we must still

5

designate the contents of this system as contents of ego-consciousness. In all cases, however, these are contents that can easily be linked to the ego and filed into the conscious system. We might even have to designate the knowledge of such contents as knowledge beyond the ability of the ego, or as *extraneous knowledge*. It follows that all knowledge that is not primarily linked to the ego-complex must be considered as being extraneous knowledge. Therefore, a forgotten or repressed content is unconscious but not extraneous, while a subliminal perception, in a more general sense, ought to be called conscious but extraneous, if there is no initial linkage to the ego-complex.

When we speak in figurative terms of the differing intensities of consciousness, we usually refer to the contents being at different "distances" from the focus of ego-consciousness. Those contents which are in the focus of consciousness are light, the others are less light to dark, and ego-consciousness turning toward a previously unknown or unconscious content lifts the latter into the light of consciousness.

All ego-centered contents of conscious knowing can (and do, to a large extent) determine the ego's reflected and consciously meaningful behavior. We usually with good reason call only these conscious contents "knowledge." When considering, however, the concept of an "unconscious knowing," it becomes obvious that there ought to be different degrees, steps, or kinds of knowledge. And the question arises: what are the relations between these different degrees or kinds of knowledge and in what manner do they constitute our picture of the world?

Here we encounter an important and, in our eyes, highly problematic and familiar association, namely that of knowledge and consciousness. This corresponds to the equally untested association of ignorance and unconsciousness. Because it seems self-evident, we assume that the evolution of life, leading to human consciousness, represents a development from unconsciousness and ignorance to consciousness and knowledge. But unconsciousness signifies merely unconsciousness of knowledge, not its absence. There are various forms of unconscious knowledge, and ego-consciousness only represents one particular form of knowledge whose clarity, precision, and applicability to the ego is dearly paid for with its one-sidedness. Just as the ego represents only one specific yet leading complex among the manifold psychic entities, so also is its associated knowledge a specific and restricted knowledge in which the multiplicity of other forms of knowledge is renounced.

The fact that we associate knowledge exclusively with the system of ego-consciousness is the result of our obsession with the ego-complex , with which we habitually identify our total personality. This identification was historically significant and necessary for our development, but it is nevertheless false and responsible for a dangerous narrowing of our horizon and of our "knowing."

Recognition of the incompleteness of our ego-consciousness and of the non-identity of the ego with our total personality has led to the concept of the "unconscious" in depth psychology. The misleading idea that ego-consciousness is synonymous with knowledge, and unconsciousness with ignorance, is understandable, since such an idea is correct for the ego-complex, which knows about the contents of the conscious mind but which is ignorant about those of the unconscious mind. Matters take on a new aspect, however, if we proceed from a psychological system where an ego-centered ego-consciousness represents merely one sector, next to which there exists as unconscious mind a far-reaching psychic realm, encompassing infinite contents and forms of knowledge.

Ego-consciousness is the distinguishing characteristic of the human species. It is one of the most significant instruments or organs that enabled human beings to develop a nearly unlimited capacity for adaptation to every possible earthly environment in contrast to most other living creatures. An essential achievement of this ego-consciousness has been the construction of the picture of a so-called objective "real outer world." In general, living creatures are closely linked to a specific environment, "their" world, together with which they form a unified field. They are bound to this field, fitted and adapted to definite, species-related segments of the world. Their functioning and their very existence depend largely on the invariability of their specific environment. If there is any radical change in the section of the world which had formed their field, they perish. It is true in a certain sense that living creatures are capable of changing and of adapting to new situations, but biology has taught us that those instincts of living creatures which are part and parcel of their field are largely rigid and can only to a very small extent be varied by the individual animal. Thus, non-human creatures are largely field-determined and unfree. The extent of their adaptation to their particular field, the one applicable to them, allows their existence, just as it excludes their freedom, that is, their existence under different living conditions.

Thanks to the development of the conscious mind in connection with the ego-complex, the human situation is different. For the conception of an outer world, as it is presented by the conscious mind, is based on the fact that this world appears as something objective, in which we are not enclosed as in a field, but which we confront at a distance and handle by means of developed instrumental techniques. This constitutes human adaptability and freedom in contrast to the restriction of the non-human creation. But at the same time it constellates our feeling of isolation and our alienation from that world for, unlike animals and plants, we are not embedded in this world, which appears to us as the real world outside. Instead we confront it.

Ego-consciousness represents a specifically restricted field of knowledge in which the world-continuum is broken up into constituent parts. But we must not say "into *its own* constituent parts," since this breaking up of the world-continuum by the conscious mind into things, attributes, and forms as separate realities which exist side by side is not even what we as total personalities directly perceive. It is the world of our ego-consciousness, artificial in a sense, that makes the world appear thus to our rationally cognizing ego. As experiencing totalities, in heightened or lowered states of consciousness, we experience the world as something altogether different. We are only just beginning to recognize that different psychic constellations are associ-

9

ated with different experiences of the world, and that the world experience associated with our ego-consciousness is only *one* form, and not necessarily the one that is most comprehensive and closest to reality. But since we habitually identify ourselves with ego-consciousness, we assume its corresponding experience of the world to be "the" correct world experience per se.

Just as we have learned to associate animals with their specific environments, so we must ascribe to human beings an experience of the world that is specific to them alone and that is, moreover, dependent on the psychic situation in which they and their cognizing system exist. The ego-associated conscious mind and the world cognizable to it form an interrelated unity that has become a historical fact, just as, for instance, the world of early humans with its emphasis on magic was a fact—a world where cognition was not centered in ego-consciousness as it is in modern human beings. But in neither case can that which cognizes, or that which is being cognized, be deduced one from the other. Neither the subjective nor the objective approach is adequate. For the cognizing system itself evolved only in the context of the world to which it is related. Knowledge of this world, the one it is related to, is built into the organic basis of the cognizing system.

If we start from the conscious system, we detach subject and object from the field of mutually conditioning entities and view them as forces opposing one another. In so doing we easily forget that this polarization is but a product of our cognitive system, and not a property of the world-field that forms its basis. This separation into an inner and an outer world, which is so self-evident to our ego, is conditioned only by our cognitive system. There are other forms of cognition for which this polarization is not valid but which are evident to ourselves as totalities, though they are not evident to our ego-centered conscious system. In ourselves as totalities, extraneous psychic systems are active which to our egos initially pass for unconscious cognitive systems.

With this audience I may assume that the concept of the archetype is a familiar one. I need only to point out that the development of human consciousness is directed by archetypes. These are psychic entities or systems which, like the entire extraneous psyche, are characterized—among other properties—by being directive and orientative. And they behave as well as if they had knowledge, or as if knowledge were incorporated in them. In this sense the ego-complex is the offspring of the totality, or of the self; and the knowledge commanded by ego-consciousness is only a variety of extraneous psychic knowledge which is fostered in a development specific to humanity. This is taught by child as well as by adult psychology, and by the symbolism of the neuroses as well as by the symbolism of the imagination.

The extraordinary difficulty of even approximately coming to terms with these problems, a difficulty which has often made me despair of ever succeeding to clarify those matters concerned in this essay (either for myself or for you), is due to a fact already touched upon by Jung in his work on synchronicity. It is a question of a psychological "indeterminate relationship," a concept analogous to that in physics. In physics the term is used to describe the fact that there are situations where basically only one part of the phenomenon under investigation can be studied, while simultaneously another part becomes thereby indeterminable, and vice versa. In the psychic realm the cognitive systems are similarly related. When we are identical with the ego as the center of the conscious mind, the extraneous systems of cognition, which we call the unconscious, are lost to our cognition to a large extent. We can do little more than transmit some of their contents to the conscious system with its tendency to polarize, to concretize, and to causalize. This means that we are not actually able to realize extraneous knowledge and its supposedly pre-logical form of cognition by way of the categories of our conscious mind. When, on the other hand, we are in a situation in which extraneous knowledge dominates, we speak of an *abaissement du niveau mental*, and we say that we have become "unconscious," despite the fact that we may know much more in this state than in the state of consciousness. The most familiar example of this is hypnosis, during which a person may remember an immense amount of data of which the conscious ego is ignorant, or which it is unable to remember. The makeshift names used by the conscious mind, which speaks—not without reason—of an unconsciousness, a subconscious, an approximate consciousness, and a superconsciousness, indicate in themselves that our Western conscious system, which is specialized for other tasks, remains in fact a stranger in relation to this extraneous cognition of the psychic realm.

It is important to note that the experiences we have during a state not centered in ego-consciousness are bound up largely with this state. These experiences appear to be "invalid" after we have returned to the state of ego-centered consciousness, and we find it difficult or are entirely unable to get hold of them by the means available to us within this state of consciousness. There is even a marked tendency on the part of the system of ego-consciousness to repress the extraneous knowledge. This is the natural expression of the tendency toward self-preservation which impels the conscious system, as every system and every entity would be impelled, to ward off all disruptive forces and contents.

Experiences that stem from a world-field other than that of the conscious mind, and that belong to a situation of our total personality not centered in ego-consciousness, cannot be controlled by ego-consciousness, since they are outside its area of focussed vision. The conscious mind is a cognitive system whose emphasis on clarity and discrimination tends to sunder the world-continuum into opposites and at the same time to eliminate systematically the emotional component of all that is alive. Thus, the world's aspect of unity and continuity, as well as its liveliness and significance, graspable for instance through feelings and through intuition, must be renounced and is lost in the presence of the ego's restrictedly specialized conscious cognition. These same excluded elements, however, play an emphatic and leading role in extraneous psychic cognition. Just as we, as conscious egos, are capable of clear if restricted knowledge—with all the losses that this restriction involves—so are we unable to maintain the controlled definition and unemotional discrimination of conscious cognition while in the state of extraneous cognition. Assertions resulting from cognition are always field-related; they are only applicable to the cognitive system that is actualized at the time of cognition.

In *participation mystique*, which we—not, to my mind, too accurately—describe as an "unconscious" state, there is the experience of an abundance of connections and relationships of unity between humans, between humans and animals, between humans and the world which does not agree with the experiences that apply to conscious cognition and its field of reality. *Participation mystique* is more than merely "subjective" impressions, especially since during this situation the subject itself has dissolved into a field-situation where the boundary between subject and object is blurred, if not suspended. The conscious mind—only partially comprehending—describes the relationships that are valid for this reality as illusory. But ego-consciousness is not fully competent to deal with phenomena relating to a reality-field other than its own. And the reality to which *participation mystique* refers therefore must not be labelled illusory, i.e., false, although it too is only a relative reality, as is that of the field of the conscious mind.

We shall elucidate this with the help of the concept of projection, so important in this context. We are accustomed to explaining *participation mystique* as a state resulting from the presence of projections. Conversely, we say that projection is—or rather constructs—a part of that unconscious identity and thus leads to a *participation mystique*.

When a primitive man says he obtains his knowledge from a bird that told him a secret, we call this a projection. This theory could be stated as follows. We claim that this knowledge was present "in him" but "unconscious," that he, however, experiences it as coming from outside, and that the connection with the bird is accidental. Hence we say that he has "projected" something inner to the outside. However, all these assertions of our conscious mind are not really correct, even though they are convenient for our ego-centered cognizing. The inaccuracy begins with the statement that the knowledge has been present "in" him. We further assume, in opposition to this inner dimension, a separate outer dimension which we associate with the bird; thereby this bird, which is the essential factor for the primitive (he calls it the "doctor bird" for this reason), is excluded from our interpretation as an "accidental" phenomenon.

When we try to improve the interpretation by using the term "exteriorization," we emphasize, it is true, the primary "outwardness" of the experience, while the concept of projection presupposes its primary "inwardness." But this outwardness, too, is thereby understood not as something real, but only as something phenomenally outward. The correct description of the facts would be to say that the knowledge imparted to the primitive by means of the bird is field knowledge, extraneous knowledge, present or emergent in the living field, enclosing both bird and primitive.

The field character of that which pertains to the psyche has been stressed in Gestalt theory.[4] And Heyer, too, pointed out the field character of archetypes and instincts.[5] To contrast or to complement these conceptions,

4. For example, John Cohen, "Analysis of Psychological 'Fields,'" *Science News* 13 (Harmondsworth, 1949), 145ff.

5. G.-R. Heyer, *Vom Kraftfeld der Seele* (Stuttgart and Zurich, 1949).

I am interested in the attempt to emphasize the meta-psychical unitary character of this field, which is not merely a psychic one. And furthermore I want to stress the quality of this field's knowledge which leads us to speak of field-knowledge. The knowledge was not present "in" the primitive—for he didn't find it within himself—nor was it, in the sense of consciousness, "outside," for it was not an objective part of the bird, which for us is part of the outer world. Rather, the knowledge emerges as part of a reality-field in which something happened between the primitive and the bird, as if this knowledge itself, like the primitive and the bird, were a part of the field.

This description may at first sound odd. In a sense it is a conception that is difficult to follow, since we assume knowledge to be something real and in the same category as we assume human and bird to be. But strange as it is, the extraneous knowledge appertaining to that which we term unconscious seems best characterized—at least relatively—by the image of a field-content. Depth psychology as well as biology have shown that there exists a knowledge connected with neither the cerebrospinal nervous system nor with any nervous system whatever. It follows that we must learn no longer to regard as self-evident that all knowledge is "inner," that is, in our consciousness, in our psyche, in us, in a living creature. This becomes especially clear when we remember that inner and outer are categories of our conscious system and are competent only for its own reality, but not for the reality, for instance, of *participation mystique*, nor consequently for the reality of projection. The reason why we find it so difficult to understand the phenomena presented by biology, depth psychology, and parapsychology is simply that they cannot be grasped or even described by the concepts familiar to our conscious minds.

The findings of depth psychology bring us closer to an extraneous knowledge pertaining to the psyche, a knowledge which—though not bound to the ego or to consciousness—is nevertheless of decisive importance for human life, possibly even more so than the knowledge of ego-consciousness with is primary orientation toward the outside world. I should like at this point to refer to the passages in "Synchronicity" in which Jung, while tackling similar problems as we do here, speaks of an "absolute and prior" knowledge of the unconscious mind.

The necessary inclusion of borderline phenomena in psychology forced Jung himself to formulate new concepts, even though these as well call into question anew the established image and system of depth psychology and the theory of the unconscious.

My proposition now is no more than an attempt to construct an altered model for the position of humanity, and especially our psychic personality, in this world. I have been much encouraged in this by conversations I had with Professor Knoll[6] last year. He explained to me that it is customary in modern physics to outline model images on the express understanding that the concepts for those models may be false, are subject to constant changes and are to be replaced by different ones which

6. [Max Knoll (1897-1971), physicist, philosopher of science, professor at Princeton and Munich, lectured at Eranos 1951 and later.]

may be more appropriate. I therefore ask you to consider my model as a groping attempt in this sense—and in this sense only—an attempt for which my remarks furnish a text, the validity of which is equally tentative.

The first sketch of our diagram (a) refers to the normal situation of the conscious mind. There is the customary "personality sphere" with the field of ego-consciousness and with the operative self as center. Right and left of this sphere we have the world of ego-consciousness, divided into psychological "inner" and physical "outer." The angled corner position of these worlds indicates that this polarization becomes invalid already in the deeper layers of the personality. There, through the phenomena known as *participation mystique* and projection, outer is experienced as inner and inner as outer, and those differentiations and polarizations familiar to our conscious minds cease to operate. Below and outside this personality sphere are two fields; the upper one I have termed the "archetypal field," and one below the "self-field."

I propose to subdivide my remarks as follows:

To begin, we must consider the nature of the "archetypal field" which contains the collective unconscious. In doing so we must clarify the transgressive character of this field in its metapsychical and its metaphysical structure. Then we must elucidate the alternative character of this field, a field which appears either as an effect of energy or as form [*Gestalt*]. Some of the laws concerning the processes of formation and dissolution of this field can aid us in grasping the parapsychological phenomena. In this context we must also consider the tritemporal nature of our conscious minds and the different

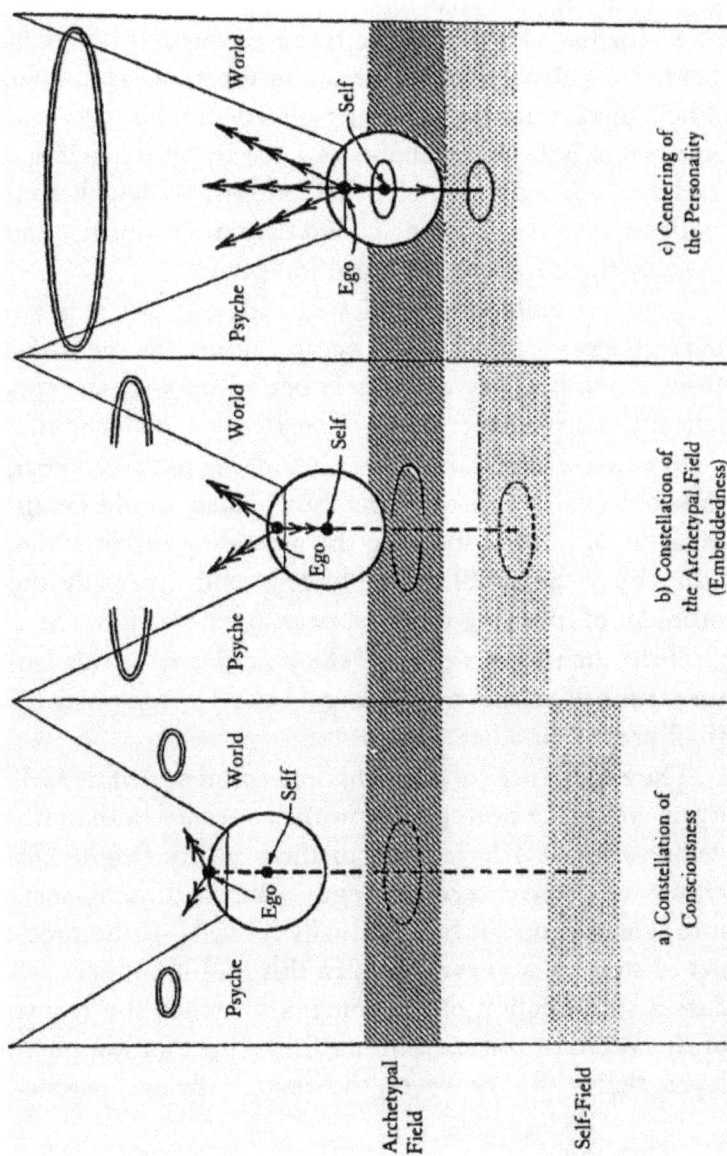

a) Constellation of
Consciousness

b) Constellation of
the Archetypal Field
(Embeddedness)

c) Centering of
the Personality

Archetypal
Field

Self-Field

orientation to time which seems to be characteristic of certain archetypal structures.

A further chapter ought to be devoted to the self-field, a regulatory field superior to the archetypal field. The connection between the self-field and ego-consciousness is brought about, as I see it, by the self-ego and ego-self axis; namely, the central axis which constellates the regulating phenomenon of form, and thereby the possibility of cognition per se.

Developments connected with this ego-self axis are part of the specific human nature, insofar as we differ from animals. They are closely bound up with the specifically human experiences of creativity and freedom.

In a final chapter, no longer belonging in this context, the concepts and distinctions thus gained would be applied to an outline showing the ascending order of life, whereby some problems of biology and especially the problem of meaning might appear in a new light.

Since such a plan exceeds the boundaries of this lecture, I must confine myself largely to references which I shall present at a later date.

The experiences of our conscious mind and of its reality as well have been gained in the course of human development. As I have tried to show in my *Origins and History of Consciousness*,[7] the ego—like the consciousness into whose center it has gradually moved—is the product of step-by-step evolution. In this evolution there occurs a stratification of phenomena in which the reality of the Western conscious mind forms the topmost outer layer. Below this, however, the biologically and psycho-

7. [Orig. 1949.]

logically deeper layers of alternate realities, of alternate experiences and forms of knowledge, are alive in every personality.

To the extent that we leave the reality-world of the conscious mind and enter regions where a unitary world is the operating reality, and where psychical and physical matters are no longer polar opposites, the firm outline, defining a person or form, becomes blurred. Not only do collective phenomena emerge as the distance from ego-consciousness increases (hence the term "collective unconscious"), but the formations achieved by the unconscious become increasingly indefinite, ambiguous, and formless as we move away from consciousness. Unambiguousness is lost in ambiguity; definition is superseded by an abundance of overlapping and indistinguishable symbols until at last the "archetype itself" must be recognized as something without form, something that only under certain conditions is disposed to crystallize into form or forms.

The total reality of our conscious minds cannot be experienced in a single unified act, but consists of polarized worlds. To ego-consciousness, the physical reality of the outer world and the psychical reality of the inner world are given facts. Each is characterized by a series of causal connections which are ostensibly relatively unified and independent of one another. While this consciousness situation prevails, the ego perceives archetypal structures, as we have suggested in the first sketch, sometimes in the world outside and sometimes inside the psyche. And yet no connection between them, let alone their identity, is or can be experienced by ego-consciousness.

In a certain sense there exists in all of us the notion that the archetypes and the collective unconscious represent a layer that we encounter "within" us by introversion, just as by extraversion we come up against the world as something "outside" ourselves. It is true that we speak of the collective unconscious as of an objective psychic dimension. And yet the inner archetypal character is so self-evident to us that it was only in his later works that Jung spoke of the transgressive character of archetypes (when he was discussing exceptional cases of synchronistic phenomena) as being an option in which the archetype's inner phenomenon also appears outside by affecting the outside world.[8]

Since the concept of archetypes and of a collective unconscious was based on experience gained by observing the psychological events in individual people, it would be natural to attribute to the self, if to any subject at all, that extraneous knowledge which exceeds the knowledge that ego-consciousness commands. After all, this self is the central symbol of the total personality, whose knowledge is more encompassing in all dimensions than that of the ego and the conscious mind. Initially it seems as though this knowledge were valid only for the individual and could only be seen as alive within the individual. But here, too, we encounter the paradox of the archetype and the need for views that complete the archetype's nature, as we until now have been accustomed to see it.

The collective unconscious is not merely a pantheon of forms possessing psychic significance. In reality all ar-

8. "Synchronicity," CW 8, par. 964.

chetypes are connected and fused with one another. They overlap in their effect as well as in their appearance, and only the total constellation of the individual person or the group permits them to appear as an image [*Bild*] under certain circumstances. Whether or not archetypes do appear or whether they are imperceptible, that is, latent images, their effect is continuous although it only partially enters the realm of our conscious experience. Therefore, we can only grasp partial aspects of their reality. Here the uncertainty-relation, which we mentioned before, is particularly valid. To the extent that the archetypal field is so constellated as to allow the archetype to achieve visual expression, the archetype is capable of becoming conscious and a series of elaborations begins. These lead from a deep emotional impact by the image and symbol to mythological conception and finally to creating consciousness and to assimilating image and symbol into the contents of the system of the conscious mind. At the same time a number of influences cease which, prior to this constellation, are characteristic for the transgressive effective field of the archetypal realm. Jung has defined the "transgressive character" of the archetype more narrowly for the synchronistic phenomena and their transcending of boundaries: "[they] are not found exclusively in the psychic sphere, but can occur just as much in circumstances that are not psychic."[9]

However, I do not consider this transgressiveness of the archetype an exception, even though each individual case, as an improbable borderline phenomenon, must

9. Ibid.

initially be appraised in this way by Western conscious minds. Rather, I recognize the transgressive unitary structure of the archetypal field as being the basis for an abundance of similar phenomena, in which the boundaries between inner and outer, psychic and physical realms melt away.

As a consequence I find myself compelled to regard the separation of inner and outer as principally invalid for the archetypal sphere and to replace it with the neutral concept of the extraneous. While the archetypal images emerge within the realm of the psychic personality, their corresponding reality is a field outside. This field is a metapsychic as well as a metaphysical structure; it is both formed and formless; it appears to us generally in either psychic or in physical effects; and in special cases—those that are synchronistic—it appears to be both psychic and physical. Moreover, it makes possible or real all those correlations which we describe as magical, telepathic, telesthetic, etc.—in other words, as T-phenomena.

I depict this layer of the archetypal field as something extrapersonal as well as something "beyond" the contrast between the psychic and the physical which the conscious mind posits. Accordingly, each archetype, or rather its underlying reality, would be able to appear in psychic as well as in physical terms, within as well as without.

It is true for archetypal symbolism that the outer always appears as an inner, and the inner as an outer. After all, the symbol *tree* is not a psychic copy of a tree in a meadow; rather, it corresponds to a reality present in the archetypal field, and which can be experienced as an inner image as well as an outer tree. Thus the outer world is experienced as an image, which is psychically given, just as the psychic image is the reactive impression of the psychic realm on something experienced as external. It just is not enough to regard the numinosity of a tree or, as in our earlier example, of a bird, as the projection of something psychic onto something physical. One would be equally justified in saying that this numinosity is the precipitate of the physical within the psychical—in reality, it is something central and something beyond. Numinosity is a characteristic of the archetypal field underlying all reality which appears in both psychic and physical form. So actually each manifestation of the archetype contains not only a psychic-inner but also always a component characteristic of the outer world. The experience of what we call archetype occurs within an extremely intense and consciousness-transcending context of human life.

When we say that the archetype always appears in projection, it means that it is manifested in a person-to-person or in a person-to-world context and is never merely a physically-outer or psychically-inner occurrence. One might, initially, want to argue with this latter statement if one thinks of the individuation process, for example, which appears to be an exclusively inner-psychic process. In reality however, an experience takes place—a process which here, as in alchemy, involves the world, human beings, nature, the elements, etc. That is to say, the whole framework that we call living in the world is always involved in even the apparently innermost events. What used to be referred to as "projection into matter" in alchemy appears in a new light as well, when seen from this point of view. The world as something-not-merely-psychic also plays a decisive part. You will see this more clearly if you recall the alchemy of transference which Jung described. Events are played out not only *in vitro*, but, in a certain sense, always simultaneously inside and outside. Thus, for example, the analyst is an inner as well as an outer, an archetypal and yet precisely a specifically individual and human reality. Complementing the polar experience of the *conscious* mind, reality always represents a paradoxical *coincidentia oppositorum* which at times expresses itself in the "true" identity of inner and outer, of psyche and world.

In the normal situation of the conscious mind, which our diagram attempts to sketch (a), it is the centering in ego-consciousness and the polarization into world and psyche which dominates, while the conscious mind is mainly trained on the world-field and the psyche remains unconscious to a large extent. In this constellation, the personality is at the furthest distance from the archetypal field. Both this archetypal field and the directing self-field lie in darkness if we disregard the archetypal images which appear as contents of the external world to this consciousness, as God, gods, daemon, etc. The ego recognizes no connection between the outer world and the underlying structure which lies outside the illuminated reaches of the conscious mind; or it may recognize it only to a minimal extent, and then only as a disturbance. The form-bearing component of the archetypal field appears outside. There is, for instance, no connection for the conscious mind between the Great Mother as an archetypal image within the darkness of the psyche and her worldly manifestation as a goddess or personal figure. Seen objectively, the world seems relatively completely split; its connection with or, indeed, its being directed by an underlying self-field is completely unconscious. (That this constellation is not subjectively experienced as a split is self-evident, since at this stage there is hardly any consciousness of the other side of the psyche, and what is present is only what appears to the ego as a unitary outer world.)

All those experiences which transcend the polarization into psyche and world, as for instance parapsychological, extraneous, and mystical experiences, are considered nonsensical, incomprehensible, paradoxical, and illusionary by this constellation of consciousness. All these phenomena remain outside the realm of possible explanation, since in this constellation, which is characteristic of the scientific viewpoint, it is impossible to recognize extraneous psychic knowledge.

The second constellation (diagram b) is fundamentally different. Here the personality is, as it were, "immersed in the archetypal field." This means that there is a reciprocal co-ordination between world and psyche when the personality is in this state, a co-ordination which is based on the archetypal structure which embraces both, or of which both are partial aspects. This coordination, characteristic of the state of *participation mystique* for modern and primitive human beings, leads to an emotionally toned unitary experience, but at the same time to the possibility of the emergence of phenomena in which the contrast between inner and outer is dissolved or at least partially inoperative.

The significance of the parapsychological as well as of the synchronistic phenomena characteristic of this constellation is quite considerable for many reasons. This is so despite the fact that within the Western world until recently they were regarded as negligible fringe phenomena, an attitude for which Judaeo-Christian theological prejudices as well as the opposing materialistic-scientific prejudices are much to blame. In India, for example, where the worldview is largely determined by extraneous experience, not by knowledge centered on ego-consciousness, the opposite is true.

When we trace the evolution of the vital process and the development within it leading from the formation of extrapersonal fields of knowledge—as is applicable for the instinctual—to the birth of ego-consciousness, it becomes obvious that in those periods, cultures, and constellations during which embeddedness in the archetypal field was axiomatic, such transgressive phenomena, now regarded as parapsychological, were more frequent than they are for us. They were reported in all places where the transgressive character of the archetypal field was dominant; for example, among primitive human beings who were therefore called magic (*homo divinans*) by T.-W. Danzel.[10] When Freud spoke of telepathy as a possible "archaic method of communication,"[11] he was referring to this same primary natural state which we have in mind and which is still traceable as part of the mantic reality of all early civilizations.

We need to emphasize particularly that it would be

10. Theodor-Wilhelm Danzel, *Kultur und Religion des primitiven Menschen* (Stuttgart, 1923).

11. Sigmund Freud, *New Introductory Lectures on Psycho-Analysis* (Standard Edition, tr. James Strachey, London; vol. XXII, 1964; orig. 1933), p. 55.

off the mark to speak of a "magic capacity of the soul."
The archetypal field which is the precondition for these
events is a reality which we have termed extraneous for
the very reason that, although it extends into the psychic
human realm, it appears also to have reality in the biological, extra-human, and extra-psychic realms, and
should by no means be considered a capacity peculiar to
the psyche.

Not only the phenomena of synchronicity, but all
phenomena hitherto characterized as magical, point to
the unitary archetypal field which is operative not only
between human beings, but also between human beings
and animals, human beings and things, and similarly between animals and their environment.

There remains more to be said about the relationship
of this phenomenon to the conscious mind and to the
shaping and unshaping of psychic images or forms. My
concern here is only to make a contribution to the understanding of the unitary nature and the connectedness
of these phenomena, the reality of such events being in-
disputable. It is a fact, even though proof is made difficult by the "uncertainty-relation" of the psychic realm.

Since my time is limited I have had to forgo a detailed
analysis of parapsychological examples. It is not my purpose to tell you "mystical tales," but I must quote a few
phenomena for exemplification and clarification.

It is well known that one can "happen" upon a constellated archetypal field, while the attitude of the conscious mind—in the sense of belief or disbelief—needs
to play no essential role. Some of you may remember
Goethe's report about his grandfather in *Dichtung und
Wahrheit*. The latter had the gift of prescience, "espe-

cially in matters that pertained to himself and his destiny." It came to him in dreams, and Goethe notes: "Perfectly prosaic, simple, and without a trace of the fantastic or miraculous, were the other dreams, of which we were informed." And he continues, and this is for us the most important part: "It is worthy of note ... that persons who showed no signs of prophetic insight at other times, acquired, for the moment, while in his presence, and that by means of some sensible evidence, presentiments of diseases or deaths which were then occurring in distant places."[12]

The physicist Jordan reports on information given him about experiments in Bali. While particularly sacred rituals were being filmed there, most extraordinary disturbances occurred. "In one case several different camera-people were surprised to find that the exposed films were somehow spoiled and showed nothing recognizable. In another case the European woman filming the events suddenly lost five unrelated but crucial screws from her camera, making it unusable at the decisive moment."[13]

These are disturbances which we consider field-effects, but which are not necessarily brought about by a "transmitter." "Happening" onto an archetypally constellated field can occasion—there are plenty of examples for this—phenomena which could be described as "contagion" or tele-induction, producing not only effects which might be explained as being psychic, but also those which we customarily describe as being physical.

12. *The Autobiography of ... Goethe (Dichtung und Wahrheit)*, tr. John Oxenford, ed. Gregor Sebba (New York, 1969), pp. 36-37.
13. Pascual Jordan, *Verdrängung und Komplementarität* (Hamburg, 1947), p. 140.

While in this case no image of a transmitting figure appeared in the conscious minds of the affected persons, this is not so in an example which I take from a book by Rhine. It concerns the "Chaffin Will case." "The first will, a duly witnessed document, had given all the family property to one of four sons. In a dream which one of the sons experienced, four years after the first will had been executed, the father told him to look in his (the father's) old overcoat pocket for his will. When the coat was found at the home of another brother a roll of paper was discovered stitched up in it, and on the paper was a reference to a page in the family Bible. This volume, when opened at the page designated, was found to contain a second will which the court verified as written in the father's script. This will, which left the property to the four children in equal shares, was accepted by the Court of Davie County, N.C., without contest."[14] Let us, with Rhine, leave aside the spiritualistic thesis, and let us assume that we are dealing with the spontaneous occurrence of the PSI function, in this case, clairvoyance, so successfully investigated in Rhine's experiments. The frequent appearance of this function in dreams was interpreted by Rhine, too, as being an instance of an unconscious function. The interesting point here is that this extraneous, non-ego-centered knowledge is personified, bound to a figure, in this case the father. The notion that an anonymous knowledge, under conditions to be discussed later, can shape itself into a figure within the human psyche brings us into the vicinity of phenomena which are familiar to us in depth psychology. The appearance of the father is only the configuring *embod-*

14. J. B. Rhine, *The Reach of the Mind* (New York, 1947), p. 184.

iment of the clairvoyance taking place in the dream, of the timeless anonymous knowledge which surveys the dreamer's particular environment in a detail unknown to his conscious mind.

As every student of depth psychology knows, the archetypal images which appear in dreams or in active imagination possess controlling power and have at their disposal a knowledge which goes far beyond the knowledge of the conscious mind. It is not enough to assume that the archetypal figures are bearers of "universal knowledge." Indeed, their compensatory significance often lies exactly in their grasp of fateful connections which their knowledge allows, but of which the conscious ego is unaware, and which apply to that individual only. When we say that the unconscious mind disposes of an immense number of subliminal perceptions, observations, etc., this easily obscures the fact that in the extraneous psychic realm we must assume the presence of one or several authorities which collect, arrange, and—at the right moment and in intelligible if archaic language—are able to transmit such materials to the conscious ego. The "editor of dreams" is one of these authorities. He assembles a meaningful (since it can be interpreted) structure out of the immense abundance of possibilities gleaned from the day's fragments, memories, associations, combinations, symbols, and archetypal images.[15] As you know, it is not an overstatement to claim for dreams a grandeur, meaningfulness, perfection of form, and emotional force that makes it impos-

15. Cf. Neumann, "Die mythische Welt und der Einzelne," *EJ 1949*, p. 231. [Cf. tr. Rebecca T. Jacobson, *Quadrant* (New York), Fall 1981.]

sible for us not to ascribe them to a creative inner authority which is meaningfully related to the individual ego on the one hand, and to the reality of life outside the individual on the other.

This merely points out briefly the important fact that dream-knowledge occasionally includes parapsychological occurrences and those which constitute "future" events from the ego's point of view.

Among the typical expressions of meaningful order provided by the formative powers of the extraneous psychic dimension we must include the creative process. No matter how great the contribution made by the intentional work of the conscious ego, it is always surpassed by this creative process. This marks the decisive difference between the creative process and the logical and methodical work of the conscious mind.

When we juxtapose all these phenomena, we see that numerous fields of knowledge are operative in the extraneous psychic realm, and that some of them, though by no means all, impress us as personal, that is to say, centered.

However, this is not to say that those figures which appear to us as personal are to be considered personal subjects—even though they have a directive disposition, possess knowledge and utilize it in a meaningful manner. To a naïve understanding this interpretation is irresistible, and even to one less naïve it appears eminently obvious. But in the same sense the archetypal image is also the figure of something extraneous which has become visible in the psyche, which we describe as formless or imageless archetype, and whose appearance as image represents just one of the dispositions of the archetypal field.

The propensity of the psyche to apprehend centered fields of knowledge preferentially as form appears to be a prejudice not only of human nature but, since it affords an adequate grasp of living reality, of the animal world as well (if not, indeed, in earlier life-forms).

In the second part of this paper it will be our task to come to terms with the form-characteristics of this living reality as well as with the connection between the ego and the self—the ego-self axis—the becoming conscious of which constitutes the prerequisite for a more refined means of grasping the underlying form of this reality. In this sense we must recognize that the development (for instance, of the instincts) from an extraneous field-knowledge to the ego-knowledge of consciousness, i.e., the living development culminating in the human being, is not an accidental happening, but the manifestation of an extraneous order which embraces both inner and outer and which ascendingly unfolds in the evolution of the living creation.

2

In the first part of this paper we set out from the various planes of knowledge found within and outside ourselves. And with the help of a model we attempted to explain our understanding of the archetypal field. When the personality "sinks" into this archetypal field (whether this is so because it has not yet developmentally freed itself from this field or whether it is because it returns from its existence in the conscious mind to the phase of embeddedness) we encounter a property of this field which we will describe as its "alternative character." At times this field appears as something without form, at others it appears as form, and paradoxically it seems to be both and neither at the same time. What Schrödinger has said of matter obviously applies here: "The point is not that particles generate power, or wave-fields, or are surrounded by them, but that they themselves can be regarded as wave-fields, that they are fields themselves."[16]

The dual aspect of reality, which as a unitary field represents both an energetic-dynamic field and a field of something perceptibly and recognizably formed, is mirrored in the human psyche, which itself evolved during the extensive dialogue and settlement of boundaries with this unitary reality. Jung formulates the following: "Man finds himself simultaneously driven to act and to reflect."[17] This human duality of orientation corresponds to a duality of reality itself. Drives and the subjection to the power of drives are part of the dynamic *numinosity* of that which is real. This numinosity possesses a causal and effective force; the living creation is gripped by this numinosity without initially being able to apprehend or comprehend it. Like earlier perceiving and reflecting stages of the living creation, human beings, in contrast, are as reflecting subjects related to

16. Erwin Schrödinger, "The Spirit of Science," *Spirit and Nature* (PEY 1, 1954), p. 334. [The translation of this passage is revised to accord with the context.]

17. Jung, "The Spirit of Psychology," p. 417. [Cf. "On the Nature of the Psyche," CW 8, par. 406.]

the *luminosity* of life, i.e., to the characteristics of that which is real in which the meaningfully knowable is closed and enclosed. Jung applied the term "luminosity" to particles of the unconscious mind which possess the power to illuminate, and which appear as sparks, fish's eyes, etc.[18] This luminosity, which we have also characterized as the "vector toward consciousness," is the unitary reality's immanent tendency to make itself known. This is to say, that content, meaning, luminosity, and "form" (as we must now add) are objective characteristics of reality and are not a product of the psyche in the sense of an interpretation. Like numinosity, luminosity is not a quality of the psyche which is projected into the world, but rather it is one of the realities to which the psyche is related. This already arises from the fact that luminosity as an anonymous field of knowledge, pertaining for instance to the instincts, antedates by far the evolution of consciousness as well. Conversely, it might appear rather as if the light-quality of the conscious mind were a "concentrate," so to speak, of the luminosity of reality; in a similar manner, for instance, gnostic mythology considers the collection and concentration of the dispersed light sparks of reality to be humanity's task.

Only in combination with each other do numinosity and luminosity constitute the paradoxical reality of the unitary field as a *coincidentia oppositorum*. An interpretation in terms of energy and dynamics therefore necessarily relates only to one aspect of the unitary field, i.e., to its living movement and ultimately to quantitative

18. Ibid., pp. 401, 407. [CW 8, pars. 388, 394.]

factors, even when these belong to different planes of reality, whether they be physical, chemical, biological or psychological. Yet it is impossible to grasp in this manner that component of the phenomena pertaining to form, spirit, and meaning, which can be experienced only in terms of quality. An orientation toward "luminosity" is therefore always concerned with content, and thus causes a quantitative and energetic view to fade into the background. Only a unity of these two mutually exclusive forms of observation can even approach doing justice to the complexity of the paradoxical reality to which it refers. It is a fundamental fact that the dynamic aspect and the aspect of form and meaning belong together. Life appears as an active force which is to be seen not only as free energy, but also as incorporated in forms and shapes that bind the energy into a body-like system. This occurs on all planes of reality—in the inorganic realm as ordered matter, in the organic realm as organized and centered being, and in the psychic realm as form that directs and confers meaning. On every plane the moving force appears as an unknown numinosum, which allows things to happen to the inorganic level, which is urge and drive on the organic level; and which allows things to happen and is the drive and that which takes action on the psychic level. Side by side with this dynamic-energetic aspect, which is in a certain sense the "wave-aspect" of life, there is the aspect of form, of being incorporated, which corresponds to the "corpuscular aspect" of life.

The energetic sequence of occurrence, urge, drive, and action represents the unreflected and unincorporated dynamism of life. Those branches of science which observe the dynamics of the process, rather than the form and transformations of form, are concerned with this aspect of reality. The consideration of that which we have called the alternative character of events thus attains decisive importance particularly for the field of psychology. The force and energy of dynamic depth psychology relates to this wave-aspect of events. It speaks of these groups of concepts: repression, suppression, displacement, and transformation of energies (not of contents); of fascination, attraction, repulsion, and deep emotion. It passes from the psychology of libido and drives to the psychology of volition. It deals with concepts like intention, concentration, etc. Wherever human beings appear as driven and acting, and not as reflecting, we are dealing with this dynamic aspect of the psychic realm.

The "heat-manifestation" of this psychic movement is the emotional element which occurs wherever free, unincorporated psychic energy occurs, as for example in processes of transformation in which nuclear structures (i.e., incorporated and systematized psychic formations) are completely or partially split, changed, or transformed. Observation of these energetic transformations is independent of the "content" and of the meaning of the occurrence. We thus speak of depression or elation, animation or torpidity, regardless of whether the manifestations are an expression of transition within a process of transformation, or whether they must be considered to be the result of the absorption of the energy of the conscious mind by an archetypal field with positive or negative content. This dynamic reality which mainly appears within emotion constitutes the numinous character of the world.

Without going into the multiplicity of analogies between psychology and physics, it makes sense for us to say that the archetypes are psychic nuclear structures which resemble the structures of atoms or the inherent organic structures known to us from genetics which determine species and their behavior. Also with respect to the archetype we are correspondingly dealing with fields of energy, charges, combinations, and attractions, with transformations of structure in the alchemical process, with the freeing and binding of psychic energy accompanying changes in the archetypal field, and with the bombardment of the conscious system, for instance by energies released in nuclear processes, etc. In alchemy, however, and in the process of change accompanying individuation which corresponds to alchemy, we see that the happening takes place in forms or, equally, in "corpuscles," or in incorporated energies, and that these forms, complexes, symbols, archetypes, etc., appear like psychic molecules or molecular combinations, whose psychical chemistry—that is, alchemy—must be known or learned if one wants to understand what happens in the process.

Probably every depth psychologist has suffered from the fact that we use concepts from chemistry and physics in our terminology even though their appropriateness seems doubtful, since they appear to be only "analogies." But the analogy obviously does not signify an unjustified transfer from one field to another field alien to it: it is, rather, an expression of the unity of the world-field and of the fact that the polarized structure of our conscious mind demands analogous concepts in all areas of application. Jung outlined the structural formula for the psychic process of transformation as an analogy to a chemical formula for the first time in *Aion*.[19] This is an expression of the fundamental recognition of the genuinely unitary nature of the world-field and of the analogy corresponding to it in concept formation, with which both the physical and the psychic realm must be comprehended.

Observation of the energetic-dynamic "wave-aspect" in the psychic realm stands side by side with the observation which focuses on the "corpuscular" aspect. In this aspect the form is understood as an incorporation of energy in which the incorporated energy becomes manifest. This observation of the unitary field and the archetypal field leads from the presentation of images, from conception and perception of corporeal as well as psychic forms, to the elaboration of their meaning, first through extraneous knowledge and finally through the conscious mind. The corpuscular or form aspect refers to the luminous character of reality as the basis of cognition. These two aspects, in which the unitary field is seen at times as a dynamic-energetic happening and at other times as a manifesting reality, are not merely aspects of the conscious mind, as mentioned before, but are also components of that reality whose existence caused the psyche and the conscious mind to form in the first place. For this reason there are psychic reactions whenever transitions between these two components of

19. [Jung, *Aion: Researches into the Phenomenology of the Self*, CW 9, ii; orig. 1951. Cf. par. 410.]

reality occur, i.e., when free energy becomes form and incorporates itself and, conversely, when incorporated form dissolves and becomes free energy.

The nature of creativity in the extra-human as well as in the human realm is always the incorporation, that is, the turning into form [*Gestaltwerdung*], of what until then had been just formless dynamic energy. The liberating element of creativity for the psyche consists in transforming unformed dynamic energies—which create unrest as drive, urge, or emotion—into that form which possesses a direction toward consciousness; for within this form a vector is urging the comprehension of its inherent luminosity and thus, finally, the increased comprehension of meaning.

Whenever formless forces thus become form, as they do for instance in the formulation of images from unconscious processes, the effect is liberating and, furthermore, transforming. This therapeutic effect, which constitutes one of the ritual foundations of all art, that is, art as the symbolic formation of archetypes, is familiar to us. We know it from the creative modelling of children and from the effects of phantasy and active imagination of healthy as well as sick people. We need only to hint at the freeing effects of the higher form of cognition in the processes of bringing to consciousness and realization unconscious contents—which include as well those contents which are effective though not recognized. The capacity of the conscious mind to construct syntheses, which is the shaping of a higher and more encompassing form, also represents form-giving incorporation. The world of our conscious mind is therefore a world of symbol and form; the abstracting thinking function is no exception in this, and even the world of science is a symbol and form-world of a higher order.

The effect of energies being freed as well as being bound reaches far beyond the psychic realm of the person affected (even if we disregard parapsychological effects). This is especially true when nuclear processes occurring in the archetypal field are concerned.

Every analyst knows the depressing and endangering as well as the freeing and redeeming effect of the archetypal within a group of persons who are closely related psychically. Jung pointed out a long time ago that raising one parent to consciousness can dissolve a child's neurosis and vice versa.[20] Changes within the partner and within the entire family situation as an unsought effect of an analytical process or a process of change in just *one* family member are strikingly frequent. This is also true for a more extensive group, for a nation, and so forth. The incorporation of free energies in transpersonal forms is the work of culture, which creates a form-world [*Gestaltwelt*] via religion, art, and cognition, and whose collapse then floods humanity with the most horrible consequences of formless energies, as is demonstrated in all periods when cultural forms are broken up. This is to say, according to the principle of incorporation, dynamic effects—and not only those restricted to the individual psychic realm—increase in direct ratio to the breaking up of forms and decrease as forms are shaped or reinforced.

I am purposely formulating the principle of formation and de-formation in such neutral terms because it

20. [Cf. Jung, *The Development of Personality*, CW 17, passim.]

seems possible that this principle is not at all limited to psychic forms. In the development of the conscious mind and in individuation we can trace a tendency toward increasingly distinct centering and form construction. Parallel to this we find a decrease of phenomena through which a free (i.e., in the highest sense, unbound) effective energy is expressed.[21] The world of our conscious mind is in this sense the highest form of incorporation. The closer a human being approaches the unconscious, the extraneous psychic realm, and beyond that, the archetypal field, the more striking becomes the effect of free energy or to express this more clearly—the effect of its nonincorporated excess. This phenomenon is related to the progressive de-formation of the form of the conscious mind [*Bewusstseins-Gestalt*] while approaching the archetypal field, which, however, does not at all mean that the archetypal field itself is unformed.

Regrettably, here again I can do no more than briefly outline; and in order to save time, I must pass over the consequences for the psyche (in terms of energy) of the processes of de-formation. I would like to point out, however, the connection between the processes of deformation of psychic forms and parapsychological phenomena. One of the conditions for the appearance of parapsychological phenomena seems to be the energic activation of the archetypal field through energy set free

21. Characteristically the free energy of the conscious system which is attached to the ego center in the form of energy of the will is neither emotionally accentuated nor disturbing—as free energy is, in a different context. Through its attachment to the center, this free energy is purely instrumental and therefore—its "freedom" notwithstanding—is a part of the formed system of consciousness.

during processes of de-formation, energy which shifts from being psychic to being physical in the transgressive field. Such processes of de-formation with corresponding parapsychological phenomena are typical, for instance, of primitive initiations, where the novice is drawn into the archetypal field and his conscious mind is intentionally dissolved. The unitary field embracing the group is thus activated, and the "spirits" appear as its incorporation [*Gestaltwerdung*].[22]

The assumption that "spook" or phantasmal phenomena can occur during the de-formation of psychic forms is confirmed by the reverse situation: "spook" phenomena or phantasms cease when the free psychic energy which causes them and works through them becomes embodied through the formative processes of the "corpuscular order," i.e., through image formation and through becoming conscious. There are for instance reports of cases in which the "spook" phenomena ceased because the "spook emitter" was in the process of becoming conscious.

We must pass over the relationship between the simultaneity of the archetypal field and the threefold time of the conscious mind which distinguishes between past, present, and future. This relationship is important for an understanding of the universal rather than the specific possibility of clairvoyance into the future. We encounter the problem of foreknowledge or prescience not

22. Cf. the literature on "spook" (*Spuk*) phenomena in initiation and in shamanism. [Cf. also Jung's foreword to Fanny Moser, *Spuk: Irrglaube oder Wahrglaube?* (Baden, 1950), in CW 18, pars. 754ff., accompanied by Jung's report of a case of "spook" phenomena that he experienced.]

only in some childhood dreams, in the initial dreams of analysis, and generally in prospective dreams, and in the *I Ching*, but especially also in the process of individuation, of which Jung writes: "Over the whole procedure there seems to reign a dim foreknowledge not only of the pattern, but of its meaning."[23] Jung also speaks of the archetype which determines the course of formation [*Gestaltung*] "with seeming foreknowledge, or as though it were already in possession of the goal to be circumscribed by the centering process."[24]

Beyond the normal threefold time of our conscious mind there seems to be a "time of fate," in which the personality is determined by archetypal structures of a general or individual nature. The events of this "time of fate," which for our ego is embedded in normal time, seem to be independent of the threefold time of the ego-world and its causality and run their course autonomously as is shown by research on the fate of identical twins, for instance.

We shall in this connection disregard the prognostications of astrology and its detailed and individual assertions about the archetypal field. We know that identical twins tend to become criminal at the same time in different countries independent of each other, or that they also tend to contract illnesses, such as tuberculosis, at about the same time and that their illnesses may run a very similar course. This means the hypothesis that during "time of fate" the archetypal field is active and prevailing beyond the split into psyche and world is more

23. Jung, "The Spirit of Psychology," p. 414 [CW 8, par. 402.]
24. Ibid., p. 419. [CW 8, par. 411.]

than just interpretation. The simultaneity of illness in identical twins speaks for the assumption that "time of fate" is not identical with the threefold time of ego-consciousness, to which the chains of causality are bound, but rather that it is the expression of an extraneous constellation with which the individual self is endowed and which therefore is very similar in identical twins. But if the self can determine the events of "time of fate," i.e., of life's decisive turning points, then the notion that those "times of fate" can be perceived beforehand is no longer so unlikely.

This brings us to the question: What is the relationship that exists between a general and uncentered field-knowledge, which we cannot connect with any cognizant subject (as for instance, the instinct-directedness of a beehive), and the self?

In the model we started with today a further field is assumed to exist below the archetypal field. I called this field the "self-field." We experience the self not only as the center of the psyche, but also as the transgressive totality of the personality which, during centroversion, directs the ego's development and individuation,[25] and in large measure fatefully guides the unified whole of the individual's life processes and of his or her way of coming to terms with the world.

The self is especially revealing in terms of the problems concerning us because it borders on the personal realm. It is the center of the individual, the specific, individual nucleus of the personality, that which is most specifically one's very own; but at the same time, it has

25. Cf. Neumann, *Origins and History*.

an archetypal character, i.e., it belongs to the extrapersonal reality and is, as the symbol of the godhead for instance, the symbol of the non-personal. Therefore the godhead is always both within and without, and the self as the center of the psyche is as godhead not just accidentally also the "creator of the world." Here psychology leads us to the same problems which have concerned the Indian Atman-philosophy.

As readers of Jung's *Synchronicity* know, even this antispeculative researcher had to conclude that he must speak of the existence of an "a priori and absolute knowledge." In this context he associated the "meaningful" or intelligent behavior of lower life forms, which possess no brain, with the "relative closeness to the formal factor" which, as he said, "has nothing to do with brain activity."[26]

We do not wish to burden Jung with our own train of thought; yet it seems to us that our concept of the self-field corresponds largely to that of the formally directing factor of absolute knowledge. Jung emphasized the "having been prescribed" and the "being there" qualities of absolute knowledge. In other works he emphasized its anonymity. This is precisely what we mean when we stress the field-character of the self, i.e., its being omnipresent and traceable in every physical, biological, and psychical structure as order, and as guided order. This self-field, however, is located "underneath" the archetypal field in our sketch. Consequently it corresponds to a deeper layer in terms of images. This implies that the omnipresent archetypal field, which con-

26. "Synchronicity," CW 8, par. 947.

tains in itself special types of order in the sense of individual plans and individual dispositions, is unified to a higher form of order through the self-field, and that it builds this order in ascending processes, as for instance in the so-called natural evolution of living creatures and in the evolution of the history of consciousness as well.

If, in positing a self-field—like Jung when he posits a pre-existing order—we feel cautious and not quite justified in assigning to absolute knowledge a single bearer or subject, then we have to acknowledge that our terminology, which combines the anonymous field-concept with the self, may be a conscious overstepping of our caution and in turn requires justification.

The extraneous structures of the archetypal field possess a guiding quality for the individual or for the group and direct them within the field; however, this field is restricted and rather rigid. We recognize this best in biology, where the species or group is determined by directing fields, which we call instincts. These fields are fields of extraneous knowledge within which the individual moves (for example, an individual animal). This knowledge determines the behavior of individuals in relation to each other, as well as that of individuals in relation to a certain segment of the world.

The fact that the instincts are relatively rigid means that the directing field is limited in itself and occupies only a certain segment of the archetypal unitary field. In this segment the contrast between inner and outer is cancelled or, rather, does not yet exist. If an order of a deeper layer were included, a change in the world-field could and ought to be answered with a corresponding change in the psychic-organic field.

In the deeper regulating or ordering field, which we call the self-field, a creative and spontaneous character of order is at work, in contrast to the fixed, rigid order represented by the archetypal structure as such. If we speak, for instance, of a compensation of the state of consciousness by the archetype in the psychic realm, we ought now to qualify that statement in this sense: the archetypal field is being directed because the archetype compensating the situation is activated by the self-field. This means the regulation does not originate in the archetype, which experience has shown to be intrinsically ambivalent—simultaneously meaningful and meaningless, destructive and constructive. Rather, this regulation emanates from the self, which as self-field consists of anonymously uncentered knowledge, and does not manifest itself as centered self with centered knowledge unless certain conditions prevail.

This self-field contains the knowledge of the archetypes, which by their very nature are transgressive. Indeed, the knowledge-field of the instincts is related environmentally to nature as well as biologically to the individual (or better yet, to the group) living within this nature, since it is apparently superior to both and is able to adapt both to each other. This is emphasized and seen more clearly in the freedom of the self-field, which is set above the archetypal field and which can assign the coordination of inner and outer more freely than can the restricted field of the intrinsically limited archetypal structure.

As we have suggested, every field of knowledge is specifically bound and restricted and exists between a living creature and a segment of the world which appears as its environment. The modern theory of evolution deduces natural evolution from a combination of chance and natural selection, and beyond that it has become almost entirely mechanistic. We cannot here give the reasons for this devaluation of creativity, which remains almost on principle ignored by the natural sciences, despite the fact that it is one of the fundamental phenomena of life.

It constitutes at any rate a fundamental oversight of three decisive factors of natural evolution. Natural evolution means, for one, that in the ascending series of organisms an increasingly large expanse of the world becomes open to experience. This is related to the second factor: that the anonymous field-knowledge of a group evolves to the centered ego-knowledge of an individual consciousness. This evolution leads, third, from a state of being almost rigidly bound, via relative spontaneity and freedom, onward to the essential expandability and changeability of human knowledge.

No theory of natural evolution should ignore this development of the "luminosity principle" in living creatures. In the human realm the possibility of expanding the area of world experience is so significant that groups and individuals even greatly differ among themselves because of their differences in this capacity. The difference between primitive and civilized societies, as well as between ordinary people and the "great individual," is characterized by precisely this differing capacity to experience a smaller or larger area of the world.

This capacity for change and expansion is closely related to the formation of ego-consciousness in human beings. For in spite of the fact that it is experience-restricting (a restriction which as juxtaposed to extraneous knowing is a prerequisite of consciousness), this adaptability to altered world-fields and the associated changeable and expandable world experience differentiates the human being specifically from other living creatures.

An essential condition of this consciousness, its centeredness in the ego-complex, is one of the human species' decisive developments. This development, directed by the totality with the help of centroversion, leads initially to the formation of the ego, then to the centering of the consciousness-system within the ego, and later to the overcoming and relativization of the ego in individuation. This psychic development of human beings constitutes a climax in the course of the evolution of life, but the creative freedom which distinguishes the totality of the human personality and of ego-consciousness no more begins only when human consciousness does than does luminosity. It is precisely the phenomenon of the individual's creative freedom that indicates anew an evolutionary direction, which becomes increasingly obvious in the ascending series of world domains, from the inorganic to the organic.

While it is true that there is a statistical probability that applies to mass-phenomena in the microphysical world, yet there is a kind of individual behavior that applies to the smallest unit—if I understand these matters correctly. A corresponding relation seems applicable to biology and, beyond that, to the psychic sphere. Occurrences in the archetypal field, which has also been called collective, are probably of a statistical order of magnitude large enough to encompass all humanity, or at least large groups. We are thinking now not only of the mass-occurrences of wars and religious movements, but also of the stages of the evolution of consciousness within humanity, and of phenomena like the *Zeitgeist* ("spirit of the epoch"), which sways simultaneously large numbers of creative people who are working independently of each other in entirely different areas of culture to work in a similar way. The simultaneous appearance of spiritual and religious developments in the most diverse spots of the world, as for instance, the simultaneous activity of the great founders of religions in China, India, Iran, Israel, etc., also suggests a collective psychic process directing large groups of people.

However, the individual, especially the creative individual, in whom the connection between ego and self is alive in a special way, appears subject to the law of relative autonomy, which also applies in physics to the individual behavior of the smallest unit. Some time ago Jordan pointed out that an ascending trend to freedom could be traced through all stages of nature. Biological experiments have shown that the body of the bacterium, for instance, which serves as an example for the structure of living creatures in general, contains, and I quote Jordan: "a very small group of special molecules which are distinguished by possessing a dictatorial authority over the total organism, that is, they form a steering, regulating center of the living cell. . . . Since it is the regulating organs, themselves of the minuteness of molecules and atoms and hence exhibiting in their reactions the unpredictability attending microphysical happenings, that govern the course of the living processes, they give the reaction of the whole organism a freedom of unforeseeable decisions which cannot be circumscribed by any future process in knowledge."[27]

27. Pascual Jordan, "Die Naturwissenschaft und das Problem der

The ego, for the conscious part of the personality, and the self on which the ego is based, for the whole personality, apparently correspond to that entity which in the living cell functions as a regulating center with its creative unpredictability of freedom. In the human psychic realm unpredictability appears as the individual's experience of creative freedom, in contrast to a determinateness in which the individual experiences him or herself as an object of inner or outer mass-occurrences.

The ego's freedom, however, which is valid for the narrower boundaries of our conscious life, is an outgrowth of the freedom of the self, which steers the individual's development in centroversion and in individuation. Thus the ego's freedom is embraced by the higher freedom of the self, which as psychic spontaneity, absorbed by the ego, determines an individual life's creative vitality.

Here the "concentration principle" of freedom applies as well, mandating that only the detachment from determinateness via statistic mass-occurrences allows an individual's creative aspect to emerge. It appears at first sight as if mass-occurrences possessed a determining force which restricts and annuls the individual's freedom. But the human situation and experience remain determined by the fact that the individual, as ego, experiences him or herself as free, and his or her creative vitality depends largely on the individual's continued sense of this freedom.

As we know, the creative development of the group depends on the creative "great individuals" within

Freiheit," in his *Die Physik und das Geheimnis des organischen Lebens* (Brunswick, 1941).

whom it takes place. This means that we seem to encounter, here too, a correspondence to what Jordan called the "augmentation principle of the organic."[28] This augmentation principle signifies that "microphysical free reactions of the steering regulation systems" are augmented "to large macro-effects." In the psychic realm the ego plays the part of the augmenter within the individual, and the "great individual" plays that part within his or her collective. In both cases we are dealing with "steering regulating centers," and in both cases these are distinguished by a creative freedom which, in contrast to determinateness, is characterized by unpredictability.

The transformation of the psyche manifests itself in the human being's changing relationship to the reality planes as they respectively become accessible to him or her, and the creative freedom of life as well as the extent and the luminosity of experience are directly dependent on the phase of transformation in which the personality of the human being happens to be.

In the first situation of our diagram (p. 19), representing the constellation of the conscious mind, the ego has a conscious relationship only to the world and, to a lesser degree, to the psyche. In the second constellation (b), on the other hand, during the embeddedness in the archetypal field, we noted a more encompassing relationship of the personality to world and to psyche.

Decreased consciousness with a dissolving ego, as seen in pathological cases, does not bring about an experience of the unitary world of the archetypal field, but rather

28. Ibid.

of its effective presence only, which also applies to the animal world. But wherever this ego, though changed (for instance, through deep emotions), is not dissolved, an experience of the unitary world takes place that is an expansion of world knowledge in which the conscious mind participates as well.

This experience of expanded knowledge, during which the personality is embedded in the archetypal field, is connected with the experience of the numinous, which—formless at first—appears to an increasing degree as formed numen. That is to say, in this constellation we also find a consciousness developing toward the self, which—in our diagram—I tried to indicate with the third arrow issuing from the ego. Having thus experienced the self and the original unitary world, no longer do world and psyche act as two worlds existing side by side and independently of each other, each possessing its own self-contained lawfulness. Both parts of the whole are related to each other in a complementary manner; they are not yet identical, but they form a connected, complementing unity. This is evidenced in numerous astrological, mystical, and alchemical statements where, as for instance in the *Tabula smaragdina*,[29] the unity and identity of above and below, inner and outer, is underlined. So, for instance, in astrology the outer starry firmament and its ordered course are identical with the constellations *within ourselves*, and it is impossible to decide which of the two skies, the outer or the inner, configures fate, since in reality they indicate a uni-

29. ["The Emerald Table of Hermes Trismegistus": see Jung, *Psychology and Alchemy*, CW 12, bibliography.]

tary "third" heaven. I have chosen the example of astrology because the experience of the unity of the world also is always connected with the experience of a meaningful fate, in contrast to the chance causalities in which the outer is not at all related to the inner. To the degree in which the centering process establishes itself within the human being, the experience of chance becomes a relative one while the experience of meaning and order becomes predominant, because centering of the personality and rapprochement of the personality to the directing self-field and its unitary knowledge belong together.

The centering process of establishing order and unity is, as the mandala shows, a process of higher formulation. Moreover, it now is clearly perceptible that the mandala must be taken literally. It is not only an image of the psyche, but—and it expresses this itself—it is also an image of the world, which is psyche as well. It is an image of the original and unitary world for which a division between psyche and world does not exist.

This centering of world and personality is essentially shown in our third diagram (c) in three instances. Firstly, in the changed position of the personality in relation to the archetypal field and the self-field; secondly, in the development of the ego-self axis; and third, in the attainment of the identity aspect of psyche and world.

The sphere of personality has now sunk into the self-field, which represents the higher order of the archetypal field. As you know, analytical psychology defines the self as the totality as well as the center of the personality. Yet only under certain conditions for which an integral transformation of the personality—described by

Jung as individuation—is a prerequisite, does the self also *appear* as the center to the ego.

This development is identical with the development of the ego-self axis, which seems to be the prerequisite for the formation of a centered unitary world and a centered experience of unity. We call the connection between the ego and the self an axis because the whole development and shaping of the personality circles around it. It is, as reality, inherent in the psyche from the beginning. The outgrowth of the ego from the self, as well as the effect of centroversion, are in themselves expressions of its existence. But as long as the self as center remains unconscious, the ego-self axis of the personality—which might therefore be termed self-ego axis in this phase—remains unconscious as well. This axis, however, is also the mainstay for the formation and development of the conscious mind.

The personality's formation into a unity, as well as its accompanying synthetic processing of reality which the personality initially encounters as an outer and an inner reality, depends on the functioning of the ego-self. All changes, expansions, and transformations of the personality, not merely the development of the ego and of the conscious mind, take place by way of this axis.

Unconscious, that is, extraneous self-regulation dominates all life, as long as it possesses no consciousness. But as soon as an ego-consciousness has arisen, as it has in human beings, this regulation is determined by the compensatory interplay between ego-consciousness and self. When, for instance, we refer to a constellation of the extraneous psychic realm by the consciousness-situation, then the importance of the ego-self axis is obvious. Yet while the effectiveness of the ego-self axis is independent of whether or not it has become conscious, it is only when it does so become conscious that a centering of the personality which includes the conscious mind will take place.

The ego-self axis makes the process of image-emergence possible, i.e., it makes possible the emerging visibility of the formed [gestalteten] field and thus the development of luminosity. Regulation and direction may occur on the purely effective plane of influence as they probably do in the animal world; but even when dealing with higher animals, we already find that the regulation of the field by extraneous systems of knowledge which are seated in the instincts becomes obvious as also a psychic image.

In human beings the ego-self axis brings about the conceiving of archetypal images and thus the beginning of the process-of-becoming-conscious itself. While the formation process [Gestaltwerdung] and the centering of the directing order depend on the self-field, its emerging visibility and luminosity are bound up with ego-consciousness and with its preliminary stages. In this sense, the ego-self axis is the prerequisite of cognitive processes which in their highest form lead to the centering process of the personality and to the emerging consciousness of the ego-self axis.

Where there is centering—as is indicated in our diagram by a prolongation of the ego-self axis—the self no longer appears as an anonymous self-field which is forming the unity of cosmic order in an area beyond world and psyche and which is directing the archetypal field and (along with it and its configurations) life itself.

Instead this anonymous entity now appears to the ego as form. It incorporates itself. And the self's form within the psyche and the self-field, which is incorporating itself as self-form, become indistinguishable.

At this point the inner-human and the outer-worldly self become one. The periphery, that is, the world-encompassing self-field, and the central point within the psyche become identical. And the central self-form, the godhead within us, appears the same as the godhead who is the creator of the world.

Now a quasi-conscious or super-conscious (at any rate a no longer unconscious) experience takes place, illuminating the fact that the world and the psyche, outer and inner, above and below, are only two aspects of the One, which are being parted by the conscious mind.

The ego's significance for this process is indicated in our diagram (c) by the extension of the ego-self axis into the self-field and by the ego-self axis constituting the central point of the self-form in this field. In this constellation the model is dissolved into a veritable paradox. Since the self as the personality's center is identical with the self-form within the self-field, personality and self can now experience their identity (as happens, for instance, in mysticism).

But, according to our model as well, the self-field is in fact infinitely more than the self-form of the self-field, as constellated by the ego-self axis. This preserves the distance between the human personality, the self-*form*, and the infinity of the self-*field*. Experiences of identity, dissolution, unification, adhesion, etc., are expressions of the various relations between the centered personality and the self-form.

In the presence of the unity of self-field, archetypal field, human personality, and ego-consciousness, the ego achieves, by way of its tripartite orientation toward world, psyche, and self, a fourth unitary orientation, which expresses the identity of that which was separated into world and psyche, self and ego. This unitary experience is in fact a highest form of "formedness" (or *Gestaltetheit*). In it an essential meaning of the outgrowth from self to ego[30] is being fulfilled, an outgrowth which is traceable throughout the entire evolutionary history and throughout the succeeding history of humanity.

Jung once said: "Image and meaning are identical; and as the first takes shape, so the latter becomes clear. Actually, the pattern needs no interpretation: it portrays its own meaning."[31] In the centering process the totality took form as image; it is its own interpretation and represents—as the highest self-revelation of the self—its own meaning.

When we speak of the self-field and its field-knowledge, we stress the imageless and formless superiority of that which surpasses our conscious knowledge as infinitely as does all extraneous field-knowledge. But since this field crystallizes around the ego-self axis, the anonymous appears as form.

The self as the center of the psyche does not only emerge in the symbolism of the human form. It also appears as plant, animal, or a star, as stone, or as a pure void. The embracing self-field as a unitary field is something beyond outer and inner. It is every single inner as

30. Neumann, *Origins and History.*
31. "The Spirit of Psychology," p. 414. [CW 8, par. 402.]

well as every single outer, and at the same time it is the unity of this polarity, its paradox and its annulment.

It seems to me that this unity which centered human beings' experience is most distinct—if one could indeed speak of distinctness in this context—in Zen and in the assertions of its masters or, better yet, in their non-assertions, in their acts and in their being, and in the unity of inner and outer, ego and self. Whether we consider the art of archery or painting, swordsmanship or flower-arranging, owing to the concentrated spontaneity of their action and their being (as far as we can grasp this situation at least approximately with our conscious concepts), an attainment of unity of psyche and world always ensues, resembling that of the original unitary field. Equally has the ego ceased to be the center of such action. Although the ego is not excluded, the activity of the ego-self axis is so great that it seems to lead onward to an ego-self identity. Zen's lack of images and its very conception, which appears atheistic to Westerners, are also connected with this experience. Just as the ego-self axis led to the constellation of a formed self-image within the formless self-field, so the meltdown of the ego-self axis—and the practice of Zen aims in this direction which appears paradoxical to the conscious mind— now appears to lead to the dissolution of the self's form and to the actualization of the anonymous self-field. As Tao, this anonymity is at once meaning and order, path and direction. Its realization is achieved through extraneous knowing, which is no longer identical with the system of ego-consciousness. It is not a regression in the sense of an *abaissement du niveau mental*, but rather a continuation in the direction which led from field-knowledge to consciousness-knowledge, and which now rises beyond this.[32]

For this reason the arrow in our diagram (c) which points to the unitary world is shown as an extension of the self-ego axis beyond the ego. In this centered situation the world is not only a unitary world of psyche and world, but also a totality in which luminosity and numinosity appear as one and the same. We find this world portrayed in the strange pictures of Zen masters in whose eyes a numinously frightening something is as much alive as is the highest enlightenment, and who in deepest concentration realize the central point of the world while their laughter brings reality to the void.

Still, we must not forget the following: though the Zen masters are no longer "normal" individuals with an ego-centered consciousness, though they no longer dwell as we do in a polarized world, but rather dwell in a unitary world which annuls all polarization, still, they too, as human beings, remain centered spontaneity; in them, too, meaning is incorporated not anonymously, but as individual form.

Thus the human being proves to be the highest and most important form of life, and the centered person appears as creative spontaneity which has attained form, as one numinously grasping and grasped, as well as one enlightened and knowing, in whom the world's luminosity apprehends itself, in the center of the world.

32. This concept is confirmed: according to Rhine, the Psi functions—like all higher mental functions—are depressed by fatigue, alcohol, etc., and elevated by caffeine, interest, and alertness.

II

THE EXPERIENCE OF
THE UNITARY REALITY

Again and again we find ourselves confronted by the question, "Is it really necessary to cross the boundaries of what is known as the practical work of analysis and to enter fields which are nowadays predictably dismissed with an unkind reference to 'speculation'?" In my view C. G. Jung himself fails to recognize his own significance as a theoretician in psychology when he maintains that he is an empiricist and that he has no desire to be regarded as anything else. Such a statement obviously invites the question, "Do we engage in the activity of theorizing simply because our temperament inclines us that way—which is perhaps sufficient justification in itself—or is the task of adumbrating the theory of a new *Weltanschauung* a real task for man today?"

I myself have made repeated attempts to sketch at

"Die Erfahrung der Einheitswirklichkeit," in *Der schöpferische Mensch* (Zurich, 1959); revised and expanded from "Die Erfahrung der Einheitswirklichkeit und die Sympathie der Dinge," *Eranos-Jahrbuch 1955,* on "Man and the Sympathy of All Things." Translated by Eugene Rolfe.

least the rudiments of such a theory, since I am convinced precisely in my capacity as an empiricist, whose work brings him into daily contact with the psychological bewilderment of modern man's situation—that in fact we have little choice in the matter. If we are not to lose our bearings in the inner world and fall victims to a dangerously chaotic situation, we shall simply have to fight our way through to some kind of coherent understanding of the reality that is pressing in on us from every side. Yet my own preference, in the interests of clarity, for a more or less systematic account of the position often obscures the actual state of affairs. The truth is that we are faced with the task of boiling down and extracting the essence of a reality which is overwhelmingly unsystematic, and that the infinite multiplicity and ambiguity of the concrete facts and individual experiences which confront us in our daily work with other people and with ourselves actually constitute the authentic substance and basis for exactly this kind of experiment in alchemical theory.

There is a striking contrast between the concept of the unitary reality and the familiar polarized reality of our ego-consciousness, which always operates in the split dimension between subject and object, man and nature, or man and the world. We now know that this polarized reality is related and specific to our ego-consciousness. And just as our conscious mind is only a part of the psyche and our ego only a partial instance among other instances in the psyche, so too the polarized world of our conscious mind is only a segment of the total reality of the world. The transformation of the planes of reality in their relationship to the psyche, which we have previously discussed in another paper,[1] must also be borne in mind in our present context. The emphasis, however, will now be laid not on man as the subject but on the world as the object of our experience. Yet these exclusive alternatives do not actually exist, since whenever we speak about the world, we always imply—consciously or unconsciously—some reference to a specific psychic constellation in man, and whenever we speak about man, the reality of a world which is co-ordinate with man's nature is implicitly assumed in everything we say.

The difficulty we have to overcome here arises from the fact that, to our conscious minds, the idea of the unitary reality represents a borderline concept. We are endowed with an ego and a conscious mind structured to think in terms of opposites and to inhabit a world split down the middle into an inner and an outer dimension; we then find ourselves constrained to make some kind of a statement about a reality that in fact transcends the sphere our conscious knowledge is structured to interpret. But this difficulty is not something we have invented or made up intentionally; it is a difficulty in which we find ourselves so soon as the conscious mind feels constrained to say something about the unconscious and the ego to say something about the non-ego.

Yet the unitary reality is by no means unknown to us—otherwise, how could we say anything about it? Nor is it one of those special experiences confined to creative artists and mystics. We find it as part of the typical experience characteristic of primitive man, and it is also one of the basic formative experiences of childhood: that

1. Essay I in the present volume.

is why every human being has an instinctive knowledge of what we call the unitary reality.

At the same time, this unitary reality which embraces both the world and the psyche extends, in our view, beyond the human sphere; its presence can be detected prior to and outside the human dimension and specifically in the organic kingdom—wherever, in fact, what we have described elsewhere as "extraneous knowledge" is prevalent.[2] The unitary archetypal field which we observed in that context is the same as the unitary reality which is our concern here, except that it was then approached from a different angle.

On the whole, the archetype has to a large extent been identified with the archetypal image; little attention has been paid to the "archetype *an sich*," which from the theoretical standpoint must be regarded as an entity independent of the archetypal image. On the one hand, the archetype has been regarded as the psychic precipitate of outer reality. A case in point is the myth of the Night Sea Journey, in which the hero's path through life is equated with the diurnal course of the sun. On the other hand, the archetype has been interpreted as the psychic category by means of which experience of outer reality is made possible in the first place, since it is clear that we experience reality only in terms of "psychic images."

Even what we perceive as outer reality is apprehended by us only with the aid of psychic images, and the nature of these images is really symbolic. For example, the outer sun is just as much an image as the inner

2. Ibid., p. 6.

sun, and natural science, which is also an attempt to apprehend the reality behind psychic images—e.g., color in terms of vibration, light in terms of waves and particles—remains, even then, to a large extent confined in psychic images.

However, in contradistinction to an idealist misinterpretation of these facts, it is necessary to emphasize what I describe as the *adequacy of these images to the world*. Life apprehends a reality which is itself unknown with the aid of images of prepsychic and psychic knowledge. By images of prepsychic knowledge we understand the world schemata in terms of which, for example, an unicellular organism orientates itself—or better, by means of which its behavior is directed. But this process of apprehension makes it possible for the organism not merely to fit in with reality but to adjust to it in a positive way, to develop within it and, as its development progresses, to achieve an increasingly comprehensive orientation towards it.[3]

This means that psychic images are "mundane" in character, and that they relate to the real world. Archetypes, for example, belong to "the world"; they do not

3. In the process of evolution which leads from the amoeba to man, an increasingly large segment of the world is experienced as the sensorium becomes more and more highly differentiated. It would appear, however, that the quality of the organism's apprehension of the world has nothing to do with its survival by adaptation in the struggle for existence, which has hitherto been regarded as its sole purpose. A species of snail which has survived for millions of years still retains its adaptation to its original minute segment of the world; yet the fact that its position in the evolution of living organisms is a low one implies inter alia that the segment of the world apprehended by it is small in comparison with the wider range achieved by a more highly differentiated form of life.

represent an "inner psychic" reality which can be isolated from the real world. Yet it is equally true to say that our images of the world are commensurate with the nature of the psyche—that is to say, the world can be captured by our images in such a way that, we can, e.g., in science, predict experimentally the form in which a particular "image" will present itself to us in the future. The two sides are tailored to each other and are interdependent, so that what our conscious minds describe as "world" and as "psyche" are not simply two aspects of the one reality but two manifestations of the same oneness which are interdependent. In the history of mankind, psyche and world have in fact developed together; for our human conscious minds they only exist together, they are always relative to each other, and in this sense it is true to say that there is no psyche without a world and no world without a psyche.

This is not the place to consider in detail the philosophical and epistemological problems that arise out of this formulation. However, the concept of the unitary reality seems to me to be a necessary consequence of the concept of the archetype, since the archetype is both a fact in the outside world and an image in the reality of the psyche; it is not simply a theoretical notion in our conscious minds.

To illustrate the impossibility of separating the inner and the outer dimensions of reality, I should like to quote an example from the organic kingdom which may also serve to clarify the concept of prepsychic knowledge:

In one group of slime molds (the *Acrasiaceae*) the individuals are single cells, each a very tiny and quite independent bit of protoplasm resembling a minute amoeba. These feed on certain types of bacteria found in decaying vegetable matter and can readily be grown in the laboratory. They multiply by simple fission and in great numbers. When this has gone on for some time a curious change comes over the members of this individualistic society. They cease to feed, divide, and grow, but now begin to mobilize from all directions toward a number of centers, streaming in to each, as one observer describes it, like people running to a fire. Each center exerts its attractive influence over a certain limited region, and to it come some thousands of cells which form a small elongated mass a millimeter or two in length. These simple cells do not fuse, but each keeps its individuality and freedom of movement. The whole mass now begins to creep over the surface with a kind of undulating motion, almost like a chubby worm, until it comes to a situation relatively dry and exposed and thus favorable for spore formation, where it settles down and pulls itself together into a roundish body. Now begins a most curious bit of activity. Certain cells fasten themselves securely to the surface and there form collectively a firm disc. Others in the central axis of the mass become thick-walled and form the base of a vertical stalk. Still others, clambering upwards over their comrades, dedicate themselves to the continued growth of the stalk. Up this stalk swarms the main mass of cells until they have risen several millimeters from the surface. These cells, a majority of the ones which formed the original aggregate, now mobilize themselves into a spherical mass terminating the tenuous stalk, which itself remains anchored to the surface by the basal disc. In this terminal mass every cell becomes converted into a rounded, thick-walled spore which, drying out and blown away by the wind, may start a new colony of separate amoeba-like cells. In other species the structure is even more complex, for the ascending mass of cells leaves behind it groups of individuals which in turn form rosettes of branches, each branch terminating in a spore mass. In this process of aggregation, a group of originally identic individuals is organized into a system wherein each has its particular function and undergoes a particular modification, some cells to form the disc, others the stalk, and others serving as reproductive bodies.[4]

It is beyond the scope of this paper to examine all the interconnections of the phenomena described here. The essential point in our context is simply that the unitary reality within which the directing agency operates embraces both the inner and the outer dimensions. We have to imagine that a host of independent unicellular individuals combine to carry out a single unitary plan, a plan moreover which results in the formation of a highly-differentiated structure in space, and that the execution of this structural scheme also involves a precisely co-ordinated sequence of events in time.[5] We should

4. Edmund W. Sinnott, *Cell and Psyche: The Biology of Purpose* (Chapel Hill, N.C., 1950), pp. 26-27.
5. It has been demonstrated that the cells excrete a substance

normally expect that plans and sequences of events which are co-ordinated in space and time in this way would be carried out by a single organism. In this case, however, we find the sort of arrangement which we should otherwise attribute to an instinct (to something psychic) not in a single organism at all but in a group of unicellular organisms, i.e., in an aggregate of individuals; and the directing centers around which these individuals group themselves—viewed from the standpoint of our conscious minds—are "outside" the individuals concerned.

Actually, this separation into an inner and an outer dimension is one of the necessary conditions of our ego-consciousness, and this very fact forbids us to derive either an inner from an outer or an outer from an inner dimension. But it is not until we have recognized and accepted this situation that we find ourselves confronted with the necessity of postulating a single transcendent "unitary reality" which exists beyond and before the primal split and out of which the polarized reality of our conscious minds developed in the first place.

So, too, in the case of our biological example, we shall make no progress towards understanding this phenomenon until we assume the existence of a field which embraces both the inner and the outer dimensions and which exerts an influence on the individual cells by means of central ordering arrangements that operate

---

known as "acrasin" and that as they move they seek out the places where the highest levels of concentration of acrasin are to be found. See C. H. Waddington, "The Origin of Biological Pattern," in *New Biology* 15 (Oct. 1953, Penguin Books), 118-20 [citing John T. Bonner, *Morphogenesis* (Princeton, 1952)].

both inside and outside them. It is not possible to account for the structure formed by these groups of individuals in terms either of a directing image in the psychic interior of the unicellular organism or simply of a directing factor in the world outside. Here, too, as in the case of the archetype, we catch a glimpse of a unitary field which embraces both the inner and the outer dimensions and is, in effect, a segment of the unitary reality. The "knowledge" revealed in the arrangement of the structure and the co-ordination of the time-sequences is an example of what we have described as "extraneous" knowledge. We cannot locate it "in" the unicellular organism, as our conscious minds, with their orientation towards an inner and an outer dimension, would like to do. It is a knowledge which is, as it were, suspended in the field,[6] an arrangement which brings the individuals together into a structure as the magnet attracts the metal filings, but which—contrary to the magnet—depends upon the co-ordinated action of countless individuals at prescribed intervals in time and space.

In the course of evolution, so far as we are able to trace the process, this extended diffusion of a unitary field embracing both the world and the psyche is increasingly replaced by a separating out of the elements now known to us as psyche and world. At the same time we encounter the phenomenon of a greater and greater centering and concentration of the psychic element in the units of life which we call individuals. Just as in the physical theory of Kant and Laplace the solid bodies which constitute our present world were formed out of

6. See the foregoing paper.

72

a nebular mass of matter which was originally distributed throughout space, so too in the psychic realm it is only at a relatively late period that we find closed units which are related to a counterpart in the world outside. Prior to this, existence in the unitary field is filled with something material and mundane and at the same time psychic; in this case no polarization into world and psyche has yet, in fact, taken place.

At first, this perhaps sounds simply fantastic; however, it becomes more intelligible and transparent when we remember that it is only after birth that the human child—and from now on we shall confine ourselves to the human realm—gradually enters the reality of space and time. From the beginning, this spatial-temporal reality is related to the body and to the body image. The following has been written about this body scheme or body image.

> The body scheme refers to that conscious or unconscious integrate of sensations, perceptions, conceptions, affects, memories and images of the body from its surface to its depths and from its surface to the limits of space and time. . . . In other words, part of the body scheme is a continually changing world scheme—the extended limits of which have to deal with what can only be called the limits of space and time.[7]

The less constant the ego is, the more indefinite is the body image and its demarcation and the more cosmic is

7. Clifford C. M. Scott, "Some Embryological, Neurological, Psychiatric and Psychoanalytic Implications of the Body Scheme," *International Journal of Psycho-Analysis* 19:3 (1948), 142-43.

the extension and diffusion of the body image in relation to the world. This basic fact can be confirmed from both the ontogenetic and the phylogenetic standpoints and holds good in both normal and pathological psychic life. The prenatal egoless totality is associated with an unconscious experience—which can, however, be recalled in later life as a dim memory—of an acosmic state of the world. In this totality there exists a prepsychic "nebular state" in which there is no opposition between the ego and the world, I and Thou or the ego and the self. This state of diffusion of the world-soul and the corresponding emptiness of the world is a borderline experience of the beginning of all things which corresponds to the mystic's experience of the universal diffusion of the unitary reality.[8] In the latter case, too, the dissolution and overcoming of the ego results in a borderline experience—the experience, that is, of the absolute knowledge of the pleromatic phase. C. G. Jung has convincingly demonstrated that this "absolute knowledge" is a central experience of the psyche.[9] A feature of this knowledge is a diffuse feeling of the world and a diffuse extension to the limits of the world of an existence no longer enclosed in the body and in the framework of time and space associated with the body.

The development of the body scheme is co-ordinated with the consolidation and differentiation of the ego. Concurrently with this process, the relationship to the reality which confronts the psyche in the form of the world develops, is differentiated, and establishes its

8. Neumann, "Mystical Man" (orig. 1948), in *The Mystic Vision* (PEY 5, 1954).

9. Jung, "On the Nature of the Psyche," CW 8.

boundaries. This means that the timeless and spaceless immensity of a diffuse world is gradually replaced by a configured world of precisely demarcated objects and periods. At the same time the originally indefinite, "uroboric" unity of the unconscious, which contained all the opposites within itself, is broken down and articulated. It is at this stage that we arrive at those processes of differentiation and representation in the experience of the unconscious by the ego and the conscious mind which we have exhibited in another context.[10] From the point of view of the ego, the acosmic emptiness or fullness of the world and the spaceless and timeless emptiness or fullness of the psychic dimension disappear at the same time. World and psyche combine at this point to form a single vis-à-vis.

It is then and only then, when we are entirely "incorporated" and identical with our egos, that we come to live at a fixed place and a clearly defined moment of time. Yet any process which alienates us wholly or partially from our bodies—whether it be intoxication, ecstasy, sickness, or exhaustion—removes us or kidnaps us, as it were, from the spatio-temporal definiteness of our existence.

It is not a matter of chance that one early representation of the uroboros depicts him as the Heavenly Serpent, in whom the day sky passes over into the night sky. For us, too, heaven comes up out of a hidden lower realm into which it sinks back again, and it is in the circling round of the original totality of Heaven, in the unity of upper and lower, day and night, that the first

10. Neumann, *Origins and History*.

pair of opposites, which is to a large extent symbolically identical with the contrast between waking and sleeping, conscious and unconscious, begins to assume a visible shape.

In mankind the earliest embodiment of that which we nowadays describe as "psychic" is to be found outside man's psyche, in the heavens. This was formerly misunderstood as a projection. In fact, the opposite interpretation would be equally justified—i.e., the psyche could be described as an introjection of the heavens—if we remember that the psyche itself apparently consists of introjections (i.e., of the "taking in") of something originally experienced as a world outside. In reality both these formulations are false. Man in the beginning lived to a large extent in a state of *participation mystique* with his social grouping and with the world outside and he did not experience himself, as we do, as a single, isolated being or "individual." The process of individualization is a historical happening which is co-ordinate with the development of human consciousness. The same process can be observed at work on the ontogenetic level; it is only gradually that the child "immigrates" into his own body, the symbol of that individuality of his which stands out in relief against the background of the world, and there, in the bodily self,[11] in the bodily totality, the earliest manifestation of a self which is experienced as his own, develops his orientation in both space and time.

It was only in the course of a long-drawn-out development, the origins of which are lost in obscurity, that

11. Ibid.

primitive man began to crystallize out from the undifferentiated unitary reality which embraces both the interior and the exterior dimensions and in which pre-ego,
unconscious life still presumably continues to exist. It is
not a matter of coincidence that the paradoxical unity of
inner and outer and the inadequacy of our conception of
opposing inner and outer worlds is brought home to us
most vividly by the way in which we experience our
own bodies. For example, we experience ourselves as an
ego contained, as it were, "in" our body, which therefore
represents something "outside," yet at the same time we
speak of an organ or of psychic processes as being "in"
ourselves, in a way which makes us identical with the
"outside" container. Again, we continue to experience
the "outside world" as a world which is related to us as
if we were identical with our bodies.

As is well known, Ernst Cassirer identified this process in primitive man by a detailed study of linguistics.[12]
It is not simply that—as might be expected—orientation
in space is dependent on the body; the human body also
supplies the axis of reference for the development of
man's conception of time, with its dimensions of "before" and "after."

But this experience of the unitary reality is not only
vivid and alive in the mythical early history of mankind:
it forms the starting-point for all the experience of the
individual, because it is the initial, crucial, formative experience of childhood which—though generally forgotten—continues to break through, again and again. In

12. Cassirer, *The Philosophy of Symbolic Forms*, tr. Ralph Manheim
(New Haven, 1953; orig. 1923).

proportion as the ego gains in strength and the body image begins to assume clear contours, the primary diffusion of the psyche progressively contracts. Instead of acosmic, it becomes cosmic, mundane, and terrestrial; a finite world dimension becomes co-ordinate with a delineated human realm.

In *The Origins and History of Consciousness* we have spoken of the prenatal state of the nuclear ego, which still predominates in the initial postnatal period. In this pleromatic phase, the child is still devoid of any process of ego-centering; it is contained in the mother, in the uroboros, in the circular serpent of the Round. This Round, too, still remains something entirely indefinite, which is simultaneously the One and the All. World and Psyche, self and body, I and Thou are undifferentiated from one another and merge into each other, without let or hindrance from an ego which marks out boundaries and separates and distinguishes between an upper and a lower dimension.

The relationship between the child and the mother, which we have described as the primal relationship, starts with the pre-ego, prenatal state of the child. Yet "pre-ego" by no means implies prepsychic, since the coming into being of the ego as the center of the conscious mind is preceded by a lengthy development of the nuclear ego, which is to a large extent directed by archetypes in accordance with the nature of the species. It is not until the postnatal years of early childhood that the ego and the individuality of the child gradually achieve their independence, and it is only by stages that they liberate themselves from their original state of identity with the maternal.

As early as 1912, Jung had drawn attention to the *participation mystique* or state of unconscious identity which exists between parents and their children.[13] For example, he describes a case in which it proved possible to carry out part of the analysis of a man through the dreams of his eight-year-old son, and explains how these dreams, in which the father's specific problems were reflected, disappeared during the course of the father's analysis.[14] If something of this kind can happen in an eight-year-old child, whose ego and conscious mind are already comparatively well developed, we can readily understand how far-reaching the identity between child and mother must be at the time of the original primal relationship, when there is nothing in the child's mind but an infantile, nuclear ego and some points of consciousness emerging like islands.

The American psychologist Harry Stack Sullivan speaks in this context of *empathy*—a process which may, for example, become apparent in the way in which "the tension of anxiety, when present in the mothering one, induces anxiety in the infant."[15] He emphasizes that this phenomenon cannot be derived from rational causes or external circumstances.

In the prenatal period and the first and second postnatal years, child and mother are so intimately connected that to the child the mother "is" both the world and the self. It is not simply that the mother represents

13. Jung, "The Theory of Psychoanalysis," CW 4.
14. Jung, "Child Development and Education" (orig. 1923), CW 17, par. 106.
15. Sullivan, *The Interpersonal Theory of Psychiatry* (New York, 1953).

these realities in terms of archetypal symbolism: she actually *means* them to the child. In the pre-ego acosmic phase in which everything is still acosmically unbounded, and in the cosmic early-ego phase of the child's development, in which the mother of the primal relationship guarantees a cosmos—a world ordered in her own image—matriarchy is the ruling principle.[16] For the child, the mother is something transpersonal and archetypal; she is simultaneously the world which determines the child's destiny from without and the self which regulates it "from within," as we may say. This finds expression in the fact that the existence of the child—its life or death—is dependent on the nourishing, protecting, warmth-giving, ordering, and balancing power of the mother. The child does not distinguish between its own body and its mother's body either in the pre-ego or in the early-ego stage of its development. Its self is located "outside" in the mother in a way which is analogous to the part played by the centers of arrangement among the slime-mold fungi. Just as the child's own body image is still undefined and lacking in distinct boundaries, so the child himself is not yet "incorporated": he is not at home either in his own body or in the ordered world of space and time.

At birth, man enters a new world, the world of spatio-temporal reality; at the same time, however, he also enters a new kind of knowledge and non-knowledge. The prenatal world is the world of "extraneous knowledge," which is the dominant form in prehuman and also in pre-ego life and the deepest level of which Jung

16. Neumann, *The Great Mother.*

has described as "absolute knowledge." In the same sense a Jewish midrash explains how the child in the mother's womb possesses this absolute knowledge: it can see from one end of the world to the other and it is not until birth that, by the intervention of an angel, it loses its original gift of vision.[17]

This phenomenon is the basis of the reverence which we find among so many peoples for the child as someone still inhabiting the Beyond, the embodiment of an ancestral spirit and therefore a being whose closeness to the unitary reality and its extraneous and absolute knowledge expresses itself in utterances whose wisdom does not seem to be derived from this world or the world of our ego-consciousness.

When we say that the unitary reality still exists for the child, this implies, inter alia, that the archetypes which direct its life are to be found just as much outside it as within it, that they are just as much a psychic image as part of the world. This brings us to a factor which is of great significance for a fuller understanding of the archetype: we find that the individual suprapersonal experience of the archetypal must always have a basis in our personal life. On the analogy of the modern theory of instinct in biology, we could also describe this as a phenomenon of "object-fixation" or "latching on." This would imply that what is psychic and what is extra-psychic are interdependent like the lock and the key, yet in such a way that each side is both lock and key in relation to the other. It is the unity of key and lock, or

17. August Wünsche, ed. and tr., *Aus Israels Lehrhallen (Kleine Midraschim)* (Leipzig, 1907-10), vol. 3, p. 216.

world factor and psychic factor, which is the only adequate expression of the reality of an archetype that embraces both the inner and the outer dimensions and is in fact a part of the unitary reality.

We are emphasizing this phenomenon here in connection with one of the great human archetypes, the archetype of the Mother, but it applies in precisely the same sense to the archetype of the Father, the archetype of the Wise Old Man, the animus, the anima, and so on. For the true evocation of an archetype, a concurrence between the tendency to form a psychic image of a certain kind and a factor in the world outside is indispensable in every case. But the factor in the world outside is not only a carrier of the image in the sense that an archetypal image is projected upon it; it has also to be seen as the mundane component of the archetype itself.

In human development there is a sequence of psychological stages which can be characterized as under the dominance of specific archetypes. For example, from both the phylogenetic and the ontogenetic standpoints the phase of the dominance of the father-archetype in human development is invariably based on an earlier, initial matriarchal epoch which is characterized by the dominance of the mother-archetype. Though what happens in these cases is the emergence of certain psychic potentialities which are performed by the nature of the species, these potentialities cannot, as it were, fulfill themselves in empty space. The phenomenon of the celebrated "wolf-children"—i.e., young human beings who grew up among wild animals from their earliest youth—proves that human nature cannot grow and develop in a characteristically human way simply by force of endopsychic spontaneity, but that its psychic maturation is in fact dependent on the personal relationships provided by a human community. Wolf-children who live outside a community of this kind are permanently deprived of essential human characteristics and may even be said to be incapable of development, though potentially, no doubt, they possess a collective unconscious and, within it, archetypal images.

We are familiar with the phenomenon, discovered and emphasized by Adolf Portmann, according to which the first year of a child's life, though postnatal, is in fact an embryonic year, and it is only after the conclusion of this period that the human child has reached the biological stage of maturation which in other mammals is already completed at birth.[18] This phenomenon makes man to a quite extraordinary degree a social animal, since it implies that, already as an embryo, he is not just physically enclosed within his mother, but that the vital final stages of his maturation are completed within his primal relationship to her, i.e., that he is enclosed within her psyche, as a part of its unconscious and conscious existence and as a part of the human community with which his mother is associated.

If we consider for a moment what is involved in this notion of a postnatal embryonic period, we shall find the archetypal power of the mother in the primal relationship and its overwhelming effect on the fate of the in-

18. Portmann, *Die Zoologie und das neue Bild vom Menschen* (Hamburg, 1956). [Adolf Portmann (1897-1982), zoologist, University of Basel, lectured annually at Eranos from 1946 until shortly before his death. After the decease of Olga Froebe-Kapteyn (1962) he was co-director of the Eranos Conferences, together with Rudolf Ritsema.]

dividual far more easily accessible to our understanding. And in this context we are not considering the positive and negative impact of the cultural canon and the values of the community, which may also have an effect, even in this early period.

In the course of a child's gradual development from a stage of life antecedent to the ego, we find that a being without psychic or physical boundaries between itself and a Thou or an outside world—a human creature at the level of early childhood who is still swimming in the Great Round of a prepersonal existence in a cosmic world—becomes an individual with clearly defined boundaries whom we are able to recognize as a human person; yet we must stress the fact that this whole development can only take place in the shadow of the sheltering mother-archetype—and that is what the personal mother *is* to the child.

The "latching on," i.e., the phenomenon that the personal evocation of the archetype in the psyche is dependent on the presence of a personal figure in the world outside and that it is only when both factors work together that the archetypal effect takes place, is an expression of the fact that the archetype is a part of the unitary reality which embraces both the inner and the outer dimensions.[19] It is the constellation of the mother-archetype in the child and the world factor emerging in the personal form of the mother which combine to trigger the reality of the archetype. This does not mean that the

19. Neumann, "The Significance of the Genetic Aspect for Analytical Psychology" (tr. R.F.C. Hull), in *Current Trends in Analytical Psychology* (New York, 1961). (Proceedings, First International Congress for Analytical Psychology, Zurich, 1958.)

archetypal image in the psyche and its characteristic effect can be derived from an external factor, but that it is invariably co-ordinate with a factor of this kind, and is, as it were, cut to fit its pattern as the key is cut to fit the lock. The paradoxical truth about the evocation of human archetypes consists in the fact that their activation is dependent from the outset on the dimension of social relationships between human beings.

It is necessary to stress this point in our present context, since the mother-archetype also contains an abundance of characteristics whose reference extends beyond the human realm to the world at large. For example, the sheltering symbolism of the maternal is also exemplified in the holes in the ground, nests, and caves in which animals find their shelter. These and many other natural symbols whose reference extends beyond the human realm are associated with the mother-archetype. The numinous appearance of the archetype invariably represents a union between mundane and psychic reality; yet the child—unlike our polarizing conscious minds—does not experience these manifestations as a duality, but as the indivisible unity of everything that is living.

When Portmann speaks of "appetitive behavior"[20] or of the inner search for a fulfillment based on a "co-ordinated entwinement between members of a species,"[21] this applies just as much to the mother-child relationship as it does to the sexual encounter. The position can now be formulated as follows: the appetitive behavior, which is also associated with "excitement" (i.e., the pre-

20. Portmann, *Das Tier als soziales Wesen* (Zurich, 1953), p. 160.
21. Ibid., p. 167.

dominance of the emotional component of the psyche), insists on the completion and fulfillment of the archetypal pattern which directs the inner experience and the outer behavior of two living creatures. The evocation of the archetype proceeds, by way of the psychic image or the appetition associated with a psychic image, to an action which is directed by a suprapersonal power that manifests itself as an archetypal field of the unitary reality both inside and outside the two living creatures and in a Beyond which transcends the dimensions of inner and outer.

It is now possible for us to understand why it is so essential to distinguish between the archetype and its representation in the archetypal image in the psyche. The difficulty here arises from the fact that our polarizing conscious egos find it simpler to grasp *either* the inner *or* the outer—*either* the conditioning of the inner by the outer *or* the projection of the inner upon the outer. If, on the other hand, we are expected to form an intellectual concept of the unitary reality, a deliberate effort is required of us—even though we may be fully capable of experiencing it in terms of feeling or intuition.

This situation can now be formulated as follows: wherever something archetypal appears, we shall find, beyond the archetypal image in the psyche, something mundane and external to the psyche which is also evoked and also intended and to which the original archetypal element points and belongs as the key belongs to the lock. This is a relationship of interdependence: neither element can be derived from the other, but both are polar manifestations of a single underlying unity which can only be realized by the meeting together and combination of both elements.

The symbol, too, which is always a part of a group of symbols that are co-ordinates of an archetype, points, in its turn, to the unitary reality. Even if it appears in the unconscious of a lonely anchorite, it invariably relates to something mundane, with which it is "co-ordinate." The nether world of our dreams and the heaven of our fantasies, the golden flower, the white light and the star of visionary experience—all these symbols point to a reality which exists in a Beyond that transcends the dimensions of inner and outer; they live as an image both in the psyche and in the outside world, but apart from all this there is an unknown third component in their midst which is also intended and included in their nature and of which the inner and the outer image are no more than different aspects.

Since they are images, symbols are of course inconceivable without the psyche, the producer of images; yet it is equally true that all symbols point beyond themselves to a reality outside the psyche. At the same time, however, we must realize that every symbol contains within itself a revelation of something which has an existence that is essentially independent of images. This applies just as much to the scarcely legible or even unintelligible symbol of a vision as it does to the psychic image of a stone. The only difference is that in the case of a stone it is self-evident to us that this object exists and that its existence is independent of our image of it and of our thinking about it.

If we ask whether statements about this reality, which borders on the psychic realm and manifests itself within it, do not lie beyond the scope of the legitimate research objectives of the psychologist, then we are posing the problem in the wrong terms. When we are confronted by this reality which is beyond the psychic realm and which in fact transcends the psyche, we cannot simply make a modest bow and withdraw from the encounter. In our living work with human beings we psychologists are not simply experts in a specialist field; each one of us embodies a human totality which in its encounter with another human being touches, and is touched by, his totality. Statements about this event can never be adequate if they make no attempt to understand the creative interaction which comes into play between the self of the one and the self of the other person in the full range of its significance, which embraces nothing less than the unitary reality.[22] It is true that we must always remain conscious of the relativity and incompleteness of our statements in any given case; yet the problems involved in our daily work with human beings challenge us to have the courage to venture out beyond the presumptive security of our psychological knowledge and to risk the encounter with the unknown.

Whenever a man is possessed by an archetypal symbol, something happens to that man.[23] In the experience of the numinous, something is, as it were, liberated and redeemed in the feeling realm; a man feels fulfilled—

22. Neumann, "Das Schöpferische als Zentralproblem der Psychotherapie" (lecture to the Fourth International Congress for Medical Psychotherapy, Barcelona, 1958; *Acta Psychotherapeutica*, 1960).

23. In our present context we will leave out of consideration all those negative phenomena—such as, for example, fear—which are triggered by this happening.

often in contrast to his general sense of dissatisfaction. This quality of fulfillment is by no means restricted to remarkable or exceptional events; it is in fact latent in all reality. A religious ritual can become part of an empty and banal everyday occurrence without the slightest trace of this quality of fulfillment, and an object of daily use can reveal itself as a miracle. But wherever the experience of fulfillment is found, it always creates the impression that something is being "unified," something previously split is coming together again, something is being redeemed which—in the language of Jewish mysticism—had previously been in exile or banishment.

In quite general terms, this experience of unification or fulfillment is characteristic of all human experience of archetypes and symbols. In every symbolic, archetypal experience—irrespective of content—this element of unification can be shown to exist. We are expressing the same truth in another way when we say that in every experience of this kind a content of the unconscious is being made conscious by our conscious minds. But in every case this process of becoming conscious corresponds to an encounter and a unification which is taking place between the I of the conscious mind and the Thou of the unconscious. The Platonic image of the reunion of the two halves of man, which originally formed a single whole but later became divided, belongs to the same context, and it is clear that the myth of the division of primordial man, who was round, and his reunion through Eros is one of the basic myths of our human existence. Yet the interpretation of this myth transcends the purely personal dimension—in fact it even transcends the transpersonal interpretation of Plato himself. The "man" who is referred to in this context is Adam Kadmon, the primordial man, who is man and world at the same time. This explains why his body is overlaid with the cosmic symbols of the Zodiac. But since Adam Kadmon is man and world at the same time, it follows that man must be the "little world" or microcosm and that, in terms of mythology, the origin, the fall, and the renewal of the world are identical with the origin, the Fall and the renewal of man.

The symbolic division of Adam Kadmon, the round primordial man, corresponds to the division of the World Parents,[24] who were originally united in the round calabash. Out of the dismemberment of their original unity arises the world of the opposites, both in the human and in the cosmic dimension, the separation of heaven and earth, upper and lower, male and female, conscious and unconscious. But since this primordial unity of Adam Kadmon is identical with the Great Round, the uroboros of the united primordial parents, its division and separation is also identical with the Fall of Adam Kadmon, the shattering of the Mexican Yucca-Tree of the primordial homeland, the cutting down of the plantation of Gan Eden in the cabala, and the loss of the primordial divine world as the unitary reality.

This image of the "Fall," of the destruction of the original unity, is in most world religions understood as a sinful Fall of Man and as a falling away or dereliction; in a certain sense it is true to say that it is misunderstood, if it is permissible to describe such a universal human

24. Neumann, *Origins and History.*

conception as a misunderstanding. The state of being or of existence in the world of the conscious mind, in the condition of "splitness" which prevails just as much within the psyche, between the conscious mind and the unconscious, as between man and nature, is invariably associated with a feeling of tragedy, of inadequacy, and, to put it tritely, of discomfort. This interpretation becomes more than plausible if we understand the heroic effort demanded of the ego and the conscious mind: they are required to break away from the primordial unity and to rely entirely on their own resources till they are capable of existing at a level of achievement which— because it is the product of division and polarization— is invariably exposed to the pain of tension. Yet that is not all, since at the same time the ego and the conscious mind are disquieted by their secret awareness of a complete and unitary state of existence—a state to which they themselves ultimately belong.

So long as the basic split within man and the world exists, the unbearable need for a release from this tension between the opposites will also exist. This will be accompanied by a suprapersonal "appetitive behavior" or tendency to reunite what has been separated and to restore what has been divided in the form of a new totality on a higher level. But this restoration must be of such a kind that it signifies a "redemption" both for man himself and for the world. It is at this point that a conflict arises that has preoccupied the human race from time immemorial. Can this dilemma only be overcome by the sacrifice of the conscious mind and the ego in a sort of regressive redemption? Or is there a possible form of realization which is capable of uniting the world and the psyche and which involves no surrender of that most precious achievement—treasured alike by nature and by man—the possession of the ego and the conscious mind?

The tendency of Adam Kadmon, the symbol of the vital principle in man, to move away from the incompleteness of his divided existence and towards the kind of reality we have—inadequately—named the unitary reality, is manifested par excellence in its "erotic" symbolism. It is for this reason that the supreme archetypes which bear witness to this meaning of the world are the archetypes of the "union" of Shiva and Shakti, God and man, man and nature, fallen world and redeemed world. The profound tension within the being of that which has been separated and is straining towards re-union finds expression in a secret sympathy between psyche and world, world and psyche, two dimensions of being which cannot let go of each other and are held captive in each other's arms in a kind of ceaseless mutual courtship. Independent of conflicts between contraries—between love and hate, separateness and disharmony—that determine the visible surface of our existence, another more mysterious yet always perceptible undercurrent strains to come to rest at a higher level at which the wholeness and fulfillment of man's nature is identical with the wholeness and fulfillment of the world, at least at certain supreme moments. This fulfillment takes place in a context of relatedness; it is a fulfillment in Eros. There is a living image of this fulfillment in every human being; the form in which it manifests itself can range from unconscious intimation to conscious yearning, from an experience which remains restricted from the personal dimension to a full mystical experience of reality.

The preliminary stage or image of this prototypical experience is already alive in our earliest childhood, in the primal relationship of the child to its mother. In this relationship the original unity of psyche and world is a matter of the most obvious and self-evident reality. Yet there is more to it than that, since the love which is revealed as the dominant characteristic of this relationship turns out to be the foundation of man's relationship to the world. In the prenatal period the mother represents the world to the child in the form of her own body; in the postnatal period she is still the representative of the world, but now it is in the form of her psychophysical totality. The result of this whole development is that the mutual love relationship with its sense of belonging together and of basic identity is one of the fundamental experiences of our early childhood. In this pre-ego and early-ego period, in which subject and object are not yet present, or at best their presence in only hinted at, the predominance of the Eros principle is the determining factor. To take one example, the child experiences his mother's breast simultaneously as part of his own body, as the world, and as nourishment, pleasure, and reassurance; this complex but simple relationship of identity with all that his mother means to him *is* the child's entire being-in-the-world at this stage. It follows that the mother, as the self of the child, becomes a symbol of the unitary reality, which is perhaps more clearly comprehensible in this context than anywhere else in our human existence. The progression from not-yet-being-in-the-world to becoming-an-ego and becoming-a-world is a constant feature in children's development, and in each new case we can see it happening afresh.

The primal relationship of the child to the mother is the essential foundation for every I-Thou relationship. The relationship of the ego to the self which is the ego-self axis of the psyche, is also based upon it. This establishes the central importance of the child's relationship of trust and love towards its mother for the ego's subsequent attitude of trust towards the self; in fact it provides the psychological basis for all faith and all security in the world.

We can also understand how the primal relationship determines man's relationship to the world in another connection. The experience of relationship, of Eros, is directly responsible for the fact that we experience the world as an interconnected totality in a context of meaningful interconnectedness. And it is no accident that this word "interconnectedness" once again contains a reference to the suprapersonal significance of Eros. It seems as if the deep and original experience of love which we come to know in the primal relationship is an essential precondition for our capacity to experience the world as something interconnected, a whole whose parts are bound together by a mutual sympathy, and to experience it moreover in such a way that all its constituent elements are interconnected as prior to, subsequent to, or contemporary with one another. Primitive man—and, like him, the child—experiences the world anthropocentrically, in relation to his body-image, and plants, animals, regions of the world, and colors produce and are produced by the human realm in the same unitary context of interconnectedness which is presupposed by sympathetic magic, with its abundance of analogies and correspondences, similarities and affinities.

In psychoses, too, where a failure in the primal relationship is a decisive causative factor, it is not only the unity of the psyche which breaks down but also the interconnectedness of the world itself. These psychoses are characterized by dreams, visions, and terrors relating to the end of the world. But there is also a more specific phenomenon. The fellowship and interrelatedness of things, their order, their functioning—their sympathetic conviviality, as it were—simply falls apart. The world collapses into an aggregate of dead and isolated fragments; even optical perspective—itself, of course, the expression of an ordered community of things in the world—simply dissolves.

On the other hand, the initial matriarchal phase of existence, dominated as it is by the mother-archetype, is characterized by that primary state of identity which is known to us as *participation mystique*. This is the real matrix of that interrelatedness out of which subject and object are gradually differentiated. These, too, are at first still bound together "magically" in an erotic relationship, but to early man and child alike magic is always the expression of an ego which is already increasing in strength, placing itself at a distance from the object and striving to achieve self-mastery.

The erotic symbolism of relationship, attachment, and harmonious matching belongs to the symbolism of nature, the Great Mother,[25] the great weaver, the matriarchal mistress of all the early ages of mankind. The

25. Neumann, *The Great Mother*.

interplay between harmony and opposition is the decisive factor in this context. The fabric that is woven is a unity of masculine and feminine, and weaving is a form of sexual connection; what is woven is a material that is generated in such a way that the movement of generation comes to rest as it were in a third thing, which is a unity that transcends sex. But it is not simply that weaving is generative and sexually connective. The inverse of the proposition is also true: what is alive and sexual is also something "woven"; the body itself is a "woven fabric." Fate, too, which binds and separates, brings to birth and destroys life, "weaves": the goddesses of fate are all "weavers." And for all their lack of precise definition, these most intimate associations of erotic symbolism are more eloquent witnesses and include within their grasp a larger measure of reality than the later Logos-principle with its causal chains.

Yet it is part of the very essence of human nature that it cannot remain permanently in this matriarchal phase. Man has to turn away from his mother and place himself under the ascendancy of the father-archetype, under whose dictatorship he will proceed to develop the Logos-principle and the discriminating conscious mind, with its principle of polarization.

Jung has pointed out that the solar plexus, that center, located in the upper abdomen, of what is appropriately called the "sympathetic" nervous system, often appears in the physical symbolism of the body as the seat of *participation mystique*. Telepathic perceptions, intuitions, unconscious developments, etc., are associated with the excitation of this center and are considered to be located in this part of the body. But this abdominal center is a "primitive" center in our sense of that term, and *homo divinans*, the intuitive, magical early man is obliged to give way to *homo faber*, the "modern" man, whose center is in the head and who is developing away from magic and towards technology. But if development means turning away from what is "early" and toward what is new, with all the one-sidedness and injustice this kind of alienation entails, then completeness and totality will involve an attempt to restore the lost unity of "early" and "late" and to embrace both these opposites in the universality and relativity necessary to each. For just as every archetype is something "eternal," a "being in itself," so every archetypal world is also something eternal and a being in itself; and in totality whatever is eternal must be preserved entire.

We have to learn that it is not permissible for us to remain permanently in any one stage of development and to develop the patriarchal principle without any restrictions at the expense of the matriarchal principle, although this inevitably happens at first both in phylogenetic and in ontogenetic development.

The world of our modern conscious minds is the world of rationality and of discrimination: its instrument is the separation of pairs of opposites. It is true that the knife of the intellect is not identical with the Logos-principle, which in its own way also arrives at a synthesis; however, the reality of our conscious minds and of our culture, conditioned as it is by the patriarchal outlook, is based on a principle of radical separation, carried through to the point of actual splitting, between the conscious mind and the unconscious, the psyche and the world, the ego and the self, reality and the unitary reality. The disintegration of the world into dead and un-related sections, which we observe in psychosis, is only a caricature of our own existence. The personal disturbance of the primal relationship in the individual patient is in fact no more than a clear illustration of the cultural disturbance of our own primal relationship, in which the mother has been murdered for the sake of the father's world and the Eros-principle has been dethroned in favor of the Logos-principle. The loneliness of modern man, who is identified with his ego and his ego-knowledge, the isolation of his terribly partial relationships, and the decay of meaningful relationship in his life and of whatever makes the world significant for him constitute a tormenting conflict which underlies a whole series of our contemporary problems. We have lost our sense of the unitary reality, our experience of identity and of the sympathy of all things, and as a result we have fallen into the solitude and isolation of a dead and empty cosmic space. If we try to find compensation and healing for this state by preaching sermons about some kind of love, our efforts will be fruitless, as history has convincingly shown; nor will better results be achieved by philosophical doctrines about existence which fail to take into consideration the capacity of the creative man, who is now emerging in the human psyche, to live a vital, independent life of his own.

Even in our own culture, however, the evocation of the unitary reality is by no means impossible, since the experience of the unitary reality is the foundation of our existence and in every period of the world's history and in the life and circumstance of every individual it remains, complete and intact, as an enduring presence.

2

The polar world of our conscious mind is connected not only with the deep layer of the psyche, but also, beyond it, with the reality which underlies it—the reality we have described as the unitary reality. Even if to all appearances our normal life exists exclusively within the world of the opposites, the world of subject and object, in fact this only happens when we are completely identified with the ego, the center of our conscious minds. The case is different, however, if we are living as "whole persons," beyond the range of the ego-centered existence.

We have perceived that the archetypes are elements of the unitary reality. But they are also invariably umbilical points of contact with it, as it were, since wherever the archetypal world forces its way into our life and exerts a determining influence upon it, we are— even if we do not know it—in touch with the unitary reality.

Since the archetypes, like the feeling-toned complexes of the personal unconscious with which they are associated, are also in fact disturbing elements, there is a tendency in our conscious minds, which is deeply rooted in man's psychological development, to emancipate ourselves from the deep layer of the psyche and to live in a relatively self-sufficient world of the conscious mind.

However, this attempt to live as nothing but an ego in a nothing but polar world of the conscious mind is rendered impossible by the psychological fact that for better or for worse we are expelled from this one-sidedness by our own totality and by the indwelling, dynamic process of centroversion which represents the tendency of this totality to realize itself. As a result, we are inevitably involved in the conflict which arises between the ego and the self, the one-sidedness of the conscious mind and the inherent tendency towards totality. This conflict finds expression not only in the suffering caused by the disunity of our human existence but also in our experience that our polar reality is "ultimately" not the true reality.

The archetypal image of the true reality, which is the unitary reality, appears in all the myths and religions of mankind as the divine primordial age and as paradise, as the age of peace at the beginning of time, as the "rightful" world of the great ancestors, as the age of the revelation of the bond of union between God, man, and the world—and in fact as the reality which lies "behind" all appearances. This is the world conjured up by ritual, religion, and art, and attachment to it invariably brings with it the renewal of polarized man through the profound emotion that sweeps his ego away from its fixed moorings in the conscious mind and the divided, "fallen," purely human world and regenerates it by contact with the great world of man's primordial origins.

In the process, the world of the unitary reality reveals itself as essentially superior to experience and experience-ability of any kind, and even when, as in mysticism, it carries with it the charisma of complete fulfillment, it always remains something infinitely overflowing, a sea, in which the experiencer—as it seems at first—drowns or is dissolved, because the nature of his comprehension is a finite vessel which is infinitely transcended by the object.

Yet though every normal person lives in the world of the ego and the conscious mind, there are differences—individual, typological or conditioned by age—in the relationship of different persons to the unitary reality.

We know that creative man is closer to the unconscious and to the world of the archetypes; we also know that he is closer to what we have described as the unitary reality. What distinguishes him is not so much a preponderance of the psychic dimension or of the unconscious as a greater proximity to the world of man's primordial origins. The salient characteristic of creative man is not one-sidedness but—in opposition to the necessary one-sidedness of our conscious development—it is precisely his openness to the original wholeness. If we are prepared to describe the unitary reality as *the* real, creative man is endowed by nature with a greater proximity to the wholeness of reality—though this may perfectly well go hand in hand with an inferior "sense of reality" in the meaning assigned to that term by our conscious minds, which so often identify reality with the outside world.

Creativity in man manifests itself in the most diverse ways, just as much in the personal relationships of everyday life as in religion, art, and science. All our scientific knowledge in fact originated in creative people. It is true that the knowledge of our conscious minds is knowledge of a partial reality; yet this in turn is derived from the unitary reality and is ultimately bound up with it. Even the initially unintegrated knowledge of our conscious minds, which only relates to sections of reality, may, in its sharpness and distinctness, ultimately yield points of light which illuminate the unitary reality; and every new and distinct piece of knowledge enriches the experience of totality which man needs to integrate. In every tendency of our conscious minds to seek a totality of experience, the deep connectedness which links our human existence to the totality of the world is a living element. Every child's natural curiosity and every scientist's thirst for knowledge contains a particle of yearning to obtain this, our deep and most ultimate relationship with the wholeness of reality.

Creative man is distinguished by a heightened tension between the conscious mind and the unconscious;[26] similarly, it can be said of the world as experienced by him, that it is characterized by the enhanced tension which exists between the polarized reality of his ego—consciousness and the experience of the unitary reality which he possesses as a total person. A child can tell us virtually nothing, and primitive man very little, about the experience of the unitary reality, but the work of creative man invariably reveals his genuine and enthusiastic concern not simply to grasp as a total person the experience he has had of the unitary reality, but to call upon the assistance of the conscious mind to fashion or to formulate the insight he has gained.

In very many creative people we find that the primal relationship is exceedingly vital and that the matriarchal stage has not been repressed by the patriarchal stage, but continues to exist quite distinctly beside it. This means that the emphasis is laid on experience of the unitary reality as revealed in the matriarchal world. Creative

26. Neumann, "Creative Man and Transformation," in *Art and the Creative Unconscious*.

man lives in a state of being not quite split off from the mother-archetype and its world, and this naturally expresses itself in the accentuation of the child-archetype in his psyche. This does not imply that creative man is childlike; he is that, too, and all that we have said in another context[27] about the child's symbolic world of totality is true for him, as well as—on a higher level—his awakeness, his symbolic experience of all that is living and his transcendence of the earthly world. But the fact that creative man can no longer identify with the world of the child that is so vital to him—for he also possesses, after all, an adult patriarchal ego and a modern conscious mind—is actually one of the crucial problems that cause tension in his daily life.

We cannot do more, at this stage, than to throw some light on certain facets of the creative process by using the world of art as an illustration and by trying to show what is meant by grasping and realizing the unitary reality in this context.

It is part of the paradox inherent in what we have described as the unitary reality that, although it manifests itself in and through creative man, it cannot actually be "known" by him. He does not grasp it, he is himself seized and possessed by it, and even when he helps to fashion and develop, with the full cooperation of his conscious mind, an experience which is intuitive or which gradually takes possession of him, the primary fact that he has been overwhelmed is always a significant element in the situation.

27. Neumann, "Die Bedeutung des Erdarchetyps für die Neuzeit," *EJ 1953*, pp. 54ff. [Cf. tr. Madeline Lockwood et al., *Harvest* 27 (London, 1981).]

What we are referring to here is not simply the relative autonomy of the creative process, which always partakes of the nature of grace and the origin of which, in the form of a "brain wave" or an insight that suddenly appears in consciousness or gradually gains acceptance, can never be manufactured or brought about by an arbitrary act of the ego. The fascination by which the ego is seized and possessed and by means of which the human personality becomes the instrument of the transpersonal is always identical with a state of being emotionally overwhelmed which is diametrically opposed to the normal situation of a conscious ego performing its regular function. It is precisely this state of being overwhelmed by emotion—even though, perhaps, only for a fleeting moment—which is the essential prerequisite for the process of unification and fulfillment that calls into being the totality of creative man and connects him with the unitary reality appearing within him.

This emotion belongs to Eros, the principle that seeks to reunite—and, at least in part, does reunite—the world of subject and object, inner and outer, which originally belonged to each other and were undivided. In this sense the Logos-principle of the artist, however strong it may be, is subordinate to the strength of his Eros-principle, which creates a third world in the form of art, whose essential nature it is to embody features of the unitary reality, to be a copy of that reality or to bear witness to it.

The world of art is neither psychic subjectivity, though it is most intimately connected with the artist as a subject, nor is it mundane objectivity. Even when—as happens rarely enough in the history of human art—it appears in a naturalistic and realistic form, it is always a transformed, always a symbolic world. The unitary reality expresses itself in symbols, it represents a dimension that is beyond the world of the opposites of inner and outer in terms of which our conscious mind experiences reality. A true symbol cannot be reduced to one of these two opposites; nor is it the sum of both. There is something more in it: there is an overflowing life by which the totality of man is embraced and possessed. It enables our total human nature to relate itself to a reality which intrinsically transcends all that the human conscious mind can grasp and formulate with the aid of its four functions. Admittedly, these four functions make it possible for us to orientate ourselves in the world and obtain a partial knowledge of it. What they never can give us, however, is a comprehension of the unitary reality in which and from which we live—the reality that, in spite of all the restrictions on the range of our experience, remains a central concern of us all and, as the experience of the human race demonstrates, never actually leaves us in peace. This symbolic experience, which is made possible for us by the nature of our psychic totality, comes home to us most vividly in our experience of art.

Every work of art, whether it is a piece of music or a painting, a sculpture or a poem, says something which in a certain sense is final and unique about the constitution of the world—about the whole world, that is, which embraces outer and inner, the world of objects and the human realm. In the uniqueness of every great work of art—not merely in the process of its creation, but also in the process of its genuine appreciation—the split in the reality of our conscious minds is overcome and abolished. In a true work of art we experience both the extension of the psyche to the limits of the world and the psychic aspect of everything mundane, which is, in fact, the world-soul. To regard this world-soul as a projection of the human realm is to do less than justice to the reality, since it was, of course, this world-soul aspect of the unitary reality that first caused the psyche to emerge from itself as something adequate to its own nature and was then subsequently experienced by the psyche as partaking of the nature of a soul!

Just as Goethe writes, "If the eye were not of sunlike nature, it could never see the sun,"[28] we too must say that if the psyche were not of world-like nature, it could never experience the world. Similarly, however, the world itself can only be described as "of psyche-like nature"; otherwise it could neither call the psyche into existence nor be experienced by the psyche. That is why we say that in the symbolic dimension of art the reality of the world is made more vivid and more human at the same time. In this context, the mundane enters into a relationship with the human by expressing itself and by addressing itself to us, and this relationship is derived from the unitary reality, which is the common home and place of origin both of the world and of ourselves.

Let us take a poem, for example. What is it talking about, what does it mean? Does what happens in it relate to the world or to the psyche? To whom are Goethe's lines actually addressed:

> Flooding with a brilliant mist
> Valley, bush and tree,

28. Tr. as in Gerhard Adler, *Studies in Analytical Psychology* (New York, 1967), p. 193. [From an undated epigram.]

> You release me. Oh, for once
> Heart and soul I'm free![29]

Is it part of the natural environment? Yes! It is the moon. But which moon—what is the moon? The "thing" called "the moon"? The luminous heavenly body known as the moon, the satellite of the earth, with its craters and coldness—how could it "release" one "heart and soul"? It must be something psychic then— a reflection of something within, so is it simply the psyche—in which case it would have no need of any moon to release it? Is the psyche mistaken and mixed up? How can it be mistaken? Every one of us knows and has had the experience: valley and bush, mist and moon—these are realities; the release they bring flows from our contact with them. Are they without or are they within? They are neither the one nor the other— something unitary which is beyond them both and contains them both becomes real and actual. The inner moon and the outer moon are one and the same—the same moon that rises above the horizon at the end of Mahler's *Song of the Earth*, a moon that is neither earthly nor psychic but corresponds to a living element in the unitary reality. And so it is with every poem, with all poetry, every image, every song. We can point out its indebtedness to influences of every kind, to form and style and the spirit of the age, to a particular nation and a particular epoch, to the creative artist and his individuality, to the phase and stage of his life at which he produced it, to the primordial images that were activated

29. From "To the Moon" (second version, 1789), tr. John Frederick Nims, in Goethe's *Selected Poems*, ed. Christopher Middleton (Boston, 1983), p. 63.

in his psyche—yet all this is inadequate, since the essential element that really touches us is to be found neither in the world outside nor in the inner world, but in a Beyond which emerges and speaks directly to our condition and, for blessed moments, actually redeems us.

In this experience we return to the unitary reality that we had lost, because it had become to us an object, a kind of vis-à-vis. In art, the sympathy of all things—the way they belong to us and we to them—is brought back to life and becomes vivid and clear to us, clearer, in fact, than generally happens in the relations between ourselves and what we call nature and the world. What coalesces in a painting and manifests itself as sympathy is not things or copies of things but symbols, which in their essential suchness and in their togetherness with one another bear witness to something other than their simple existence. What is the meaning of a painted bunch of flowers, when there is an infinity of flowers in the world that are lovelier and more living than anything that can be painted, if the work of art does not happily catch something that in spite of all its transitoriness is eternal and evokes a different dimension of reality? When things coalesce in a work of art through the instrument of the human psyche, without arbitrary intervention on the part of the ego, they reveal themselves as something "wholly other." In the unity, the totality, which is the distinguishing mark of every authentic work of art, something comes to rest and finds fulfillment which— even if it is a stream of colors and a shattering of forms—transcends both the purely psychic and the purely mundane dimensions of reality. This is true of all the arts, since they are all symbolic and in all of them a reunion takes place of those elements our ego is constrained to separate. The stone of the sculptor is body and soul, music is feeling, movement, law, and spirit, in the form of something not purely psychic but pointing beyond itself to something real—in fact, to what we, inadequately enough, have described as the unitary reality. A portrait, too, does not consist simply of a human being, or simply of his psyche, but, strangely enough, paint and canvas possess the power to be symbolic vehicles of something that extends beyond the human realm. Similarly, a chair by Van Gogh has "soul"—and at the same time it is ultimately something psychic and symbolic that exists outside the whole human dimension.

There are so many chairs—why then should we paint them? There are so many trees and mountains: how, then, are we to explain the fact that people whom we revere as creative artists spend their whole lives trying— and trying desperately—to paint them? It cannot simply be that they are all completely crazy, since in that case, all those of us who revere them (which is virtually the whole of mankind) would be as completely crazy as they are—and how would we explain that fact? Yet why is there this "reproduction" of nature in art?

Of course, as we all know, it is not "reproduction" at all. And yet—let us take a painting by Vermeer, for example. Isn't it "true to life"? Isn't it characteristic of him, as of so many other artists, that they do not in fact go beyond what we call "nature"? People, things, flowers. Just as they are. And they are not even illuminated for us in the way that, e.g., things are illuminated by Van Gogh, whose irises are flames, at once dark and luminous, that pierce through the world of every day.

But what happens in the case of Vermeer? It is beauty, we say, without knowing what that is and what we mean by it. There are so many opinions and so many theories about it, and yet there is actually nothing in these pictures which is not, or could not be, in reality. What, then, is the meaning of the reproduction, and why do we revere it so much? Is it simply because these paintings are the means by which we appreciate the beauty of the world and recall it to our minds? Simply because in these paintings the sympathy of all things and their human and superhuman beauty and vitality is brought home, once again, vividly to our eyes?

I do not fully understand it myself—but I stand by my feeling of reverence! However, I do not believe that it is simply a question of beauty and form and color and light, though these are undoubtedly essential and indispensable elements in the situation.

I think it is most likely a question of the process of restoration, which has taken place in the creative artist and which speaks directly to our condition in his work as something which has become eternal and which is beyond everything that is represented in the painting and beyond the way in which it is represented. The essential point is that the creative artist has become whole, and simply by virtue of this wholeness and in this unity of man and the world the unitary reality can appear and be reflected.

There is a Zen story[30] in which a master (Baso) shows his disciple some wild geese in flight and asks him,

30. D. T. Suzuki, *Essays in Zen Buddhism* (First Series; London, 1926), p. 238.

"What are these?" The disciple answers, "Wild geese, Master." The master then asks, "Where are they flying to?" The disciple answers, "They have flown away, Master." At this point, the master tweaks the disciple's nose and shouts at him, "You say they have flown away, yet they're here all the time and have been here from the beginning!" And the story goes on, "At this the disciple's back ran icy cold with sweat, and he experienced satori (enlightenment)."—I am not so presumptuous as to claim that I understand this story. Yet it seems to me that these wild geese which are there forever in a time which is standing still are representative of every true work of art.

After all, art is only an illumination of the world, and the world itself becomes almost indistinguishable from a work of art when it is irradiated by the lightning flash which shines from the unitary reality and lights up our reality of every day. Our reality then becomes as transparent as glass and a chair becomes interchangeable with the whole world which glows with the life within it, and the whole unitary reality contracts into the still moment in which the world ceases to be divided, time no longer flows and man and the chair no longer confront each other as alien entities. And at that moment, we may suppose, no wild geese are flying, either. Like ourselves, they have forgotten space and time.

Perhaps this is a fantasy; let us suppose that it is a fantasy. The fact remains that it serves to illuminate what might be meant by this concept of the "unitary reality," which perhaps does not exist at all—or rather, it does exist, of course, it is only that we forget it all the time and have to be reminded. But that is precisely the

THE PLACE OF CREATION

function of art, and that is what happens to the creative artist when the creative afflatus takes possession of him.

The distinction and elevation of art, which we describe as beautiful, always stresses and illuminates a genuine reality in the world that points to the experience of the unitary reality, which is more genuine and more real than the world that is normally accessible to our experience. We experience our world in a way that is coordinate with our spatial-temporal ego-consciousness, as something transitory, whereas in a true work of art the world proves its value as an enduring reality. In this world, the poet's cry, "O stay with us, thou art so fair!" becomes the foundation of our experience, and at that very moment we leave behind us the stream of our polarizing ego-consciousness. Inwardly, as it were, we stand quite still, and this is entirely irrespective of whether the work of art itself moves in a temporal sequence as in music or stands in an eternal space, as in sculpture.

It is no mere coincidence that we find in Zen a special emphasis laid on manifold forms of artistic expression, such as poetry, painting, and flower arrangement, and every artist who has read Herrigel's little book[31] will confirm how closely what he tells us about the art of archery corresponds to the nature of the creative process in general.

Rilke's formulation, "Beauty is only the beginning of horror,"[32] refers to something quite different from the

31. Eugen Herrigel, *Zen in the Art of Archery*, tr. R.F.C. Hull, with introduction by D. T. Suzuki (New York, 1960).
32. From the first of the *Duino Elegies*.

112

beautiful with which we are concerned in the context of our experience of the unitary reality—as Rilke himself was very much aware. It is not our concern here to clarify the meaning of the concept of the beautiful. The beautiful, in the sense we have in mind, and in the usage, too, which we encounter in Zen, is a happening, a "vital process," which can never be grasped by a logical formulation of the conscious mind. But there is always something in this beauty which has the unmistakable stamp of living truth; in some sense which is beyond all formulation it convinces us that it is right, it is one of those things of which we say, "That's it!" and by which, if we are open to it, we are overcome and possessed in a way that is simply indescribable. And this may happen to us just as much when we are in the presence of nature as when we are gazing at a primitive mask, an ancient Greek column, or a painting by Leonardo—or when we are listening to a toccata by Bach. In this happening of beauty man comes to himself just as much as he achieves communion with the world; it is at once a stage in the realization and integration of human totality and a stage in the integration of the unitary reality. Something in ourselves and something in the world appears as shaped, formed, centered, animated, and filled with meaning; both these things belong together and we find that they are grounded in a third thing, which is what we have called "the unitary reality."

When the numinous and overwhelmingly vital power of reality speaks to us in "great art," this always involves a change in ourselves and, simultaneously, a change in our world. Rilke writes in a similar vein about the torso of Apollo: "For there is no place that does not see you. You must change your life."[33]

Normally we live in a world which is equally characterized by effort and distraction. But when we are overcome by "great art" or by any form of creativity which really moves us, we pass into a zone of calm and arrive at a center that is not really of this world. This is not intended to imply anything mystical, though with mystics—those whose creativity operates in the purely religious dimension—we encounter the same phenomenon. Yet where mystics are carried away into the inscrutable dynamism at the heart of the world, the "divine Void that gives life to the world,"[34] artists—and we ourselves among them—experience the *visible* unitary reality (which lives in, from, and as this Void) as lovers.

Artists are not simply imprisoned in the invisible; rather, they are oriented toward that which is revealing itself and becoming visible. If they are great artists, the world and its visible manifestation, in whatever shape it may be formed, has become pervious to them and reveals the life-giving Void, which is also, invariably and simultaneously, an All. As they shape and fashion their material, they thrust their way through superficial elements in the foreground and seize hold of the background and the deeper layer of what they are fashioning. This can be done in many different ways and forms, and in terms of many different styles and techniques. The essential point remains that what they have fashioned is not an isolated reality of the foreground, but is

33. From "Archaische Torso Apollos," *Sämtliche Werke* (1955), vol. I.

34. Martin Buber, *Die chassidischen Bücher* (Hellerau, 1928).

embedded in a sustaining background, whether this background appears in their work in the form of light or color, of infinite space or eternal melody.

This experience of a self-revealing reality and of the indescribable mystery alive at the heart of it is an experience of Eros. In this sense artists are both lovers of God and lovers of the world, where to be lovers implies having the capacity to unite and not to remain isolated in one's own ego. Yet the union in Eros in which the unitary reality is revealed is no mystical disappearance of the human realm. On the contrary, it brings with it a reinforcement of man's existence. What is alive in this experience is an Eros of human wholeness, not of the ego; yet this ego is an offspring of the self and as such it is ideally adapted to render visible and creative the corresponding aspect of the self, the totality that stands behind it.

There is another very human way in which this Eros proves its power. Creative man is always typically distinguished by individuality, and in his approximation to the self he exemplifies the paradox that governs the whole of human existence, namely, that nothing exists except individualities and that in spite of this the self is an "everyman." Creative achievement is always at once individual and anonymous. Like every great individual artist, it is unique and not interchangeable—yet a great work of art could not move every one of us if an "everyman" was not at work within the individual artist. Here *too the* unifying power of creative Eros is clearly discernible. The individual achievement of the artist is invariably also representative. What it has won for itself it bestows generously on others and in its loving restoration of the unitary reality it makes restoration possible for us all. But the paradoxical nature of the self extends beyond the fact that this most individual of all things is also, always, an "everyman"; and this further dimension is already contained in the primal symbolism of the myth.

The symbol of the man-world equation at the beginning of time is Adam Kadmon, the primal man, and this Adam Kadmon is a symbol both of the world and of the self, the unity of mankind. But once we have grasped the fact that both the psyche and the world which is co-ordinate with it are only polarizations of our human consciousness, we are almost equipped to understand the paradox that the self is also a symbol of the unitary reality.

At the deepest level of all, we ourselves merge insensibly into the unitary reality. We are not only incorporated—i.e., real in our bodily selves—but we also constantly soar above this corporeal reality. It is as if the process of incorporation, which we described at the beginning as man's entry at birth into the world of time and the body, always remains incomplete, or at any rate, it is as if, in creative processes and in certain borderline conditions, it turns out to be incomplete, and in a certain sense unrealizable.

The mandala, which is ostensibly an image of the psyche, is always at the same time an image of the world. What is the meaning of the four elements, which so frequently appear in the mandala, and of the statement that we ourselves are formed out of them, and why are candidates in initiation rites required to pass through every one of these elements? We ought not to interpret the elements in purely "characterological" or "psychological" terms. On the contrary we must accept them in a most basic, earthly, and literal sense as the common ground between the world and ourselves. We and the world are made up of this common ground and the foundation for the sympathy of all things with ourselves is to be found in the fact that we are both made of the same matter or non-matter. We are the world on a small scale, just as the world as represented by Adam Kadmon is man on a grand scale. The symbolic image of the world as Adam Kadmon brings us closer to the religious interpretation of the unitary reality as a divine being and a being in the divine.

We understand what it means when we personalize and mythologize and say that the world and ourselves were "created." We encounter something here from which we originate, something beyond the world and the psyche which creates both the psyche and the world. But Adam Kadmon is a manlike figure as well as the world, a God-figure as well as the unitary reality, in a way that is closely analogous to something we have explained in another context, i.e., that the self is not only a center but a configuration of the self-field.[35]

We realize that it is simply not possible for us to arrive at anything approaching an adequate understanding of what Zen Buddhism means, or rather, is. How could it be otherwise, when the truth is that the decisive experience often only comes to the Zen Buddhist after years of intensive experience? Examples from Zen Buddhism should therefore be understood only as analogies,

35. See above, Essay I.

which to the Zen master may quite possibly be false. Yet it may still be permissible to make use of Zen in the way we have suggested, since otherwise there would be no point at all in any attempt to make Zen accessible to us. It is Zen teaching that every blade of grass, every leaf, every scent—in fact everything that exists, both great and small—"is" the Buddha and yet that this is not to be interpreted in any sense which corresponds to what we normally describe as pantheism.

This naturally raises a question in our minds. Is it not possible that the form of the numinous which emerges in every blade of grass and in everything "natural" is something impersonal and non-human and that this is in fact a lower form than the revelation familiar to Western man, in whose religion the numinous appears as something historical and—in contrast to nature—spiritual and human?

It seems probable that the contrast between the personal and the non-personal forms in which the numinous manifests itself simply reflects differences in the psychological constellation of the human beings to whom the numinous appears. Of course we must do our best to understand the different forms in which the numinous manifests itself and the historical and psychological correlations between these forms and the human groups in which they appear; at the same time, however, we must learn to refrain from passing moral judgments upon these differences. In this context it is a significant fact that the self-revelation of the numinous in history and the incarnation of the divine in a human person is not the only living religious experience known to Western man; the anonymous and imageless form of the numinous which appears in the experience of the unitary reality is also well attested in the West. The affirmation of the numinous in an imageless form enjoys equal rights, as it were, with the other tradition, in which the numinous, when it "speaks directly to" man, is experienced by man as a personal transpersonality." Since time immemorial the human race has experienced itself as standing in a particularly close relationship to the numinous, whether this takes the form of the myth that man is descended from the numinous, or, as it is formulated in the Old Testament, that man is created in the image of God. This association is so close that it has given rise to the belief that the existence of the world is actually dependent on man and his ritual behavior. It is easy to ridicule this anthropocentric attitude, especially if one takes the view that it is the result of a false self-assurance on the part of the human species. But it would be wiser to approach this attitude in a spirit of reverence, since it is based on the numinous significance of the emergence of consciousness in man, without which we should have no knowledge of the unitary reality at all. The truth is that this knowledge can only be born in us because we have grown up out of the unitary reality and into the world of our conscious minds. In spite of the modesty that we need so badly, we must still stand up for ourselves and for the human species to which we belong, at least to the extent of having the courage to believe that the song of thanksgiving on recovery from an illness in Beethoven's Opus 132[36] has a greater appeal

36. [Quartet in A-minor. See *Thayer's Life of Beethoven*, ed. Elliot Forbes (Princeton, revised ed., 1967), pp. 961f.]

and is far more eloquent than the thanksgiving of animals, though of whom the Psalmist says that they too praise the Lord.

The dilemma in which we modern men find ourselves arises from the fact that, as men of the West, we neither can nor ought to lose the anthropocentric emphasis. In the course of our recent history, however, we have arrived at such an exceedingly one-sided concentration on, and overvaluation of, the ego that there is a real danger our world may disintegrate. We have become entangled in an almost irreconcilable opposition between man and nature, ego and self, conscious mind and the unconscious, and today the counter-constellation of the unitary reality is emerging with a force that is all the more potent for this reason. Something is stirring in us and leading us away from the merely human, ego-centered realm and toward the great Anthropos, the Adam Kadmon, in whom the human and the cosmic have not yet parted company. Something is urging us toward an experience of wholeness and unitariness, and this drive is perhaps more insistent today than it used to be in earlier times. For us moderns, it is not just creative artists but children and "simple," unsophisticated people who are playing a part in the consciousness of our time which they have never played in any previous era. Their wholeness is undisturbed by our adult modern consciousness, and their experience of the unitary reality, though inarticulate, is very much alive; the sympathy of all things, animate and inanimate, is intact, alert, and radiant in them.

A woman patient once told me in a letter that she couldn't help feeling that God prefers to live with quite simple people and with children, since he can speak so much more plainly through their mouths. This again is a truth to which none of us can close our minds. But just as every human being is compelled by an inner law to leave childhood things behind him and to surrender the unitary reality as he had experienced it with his whole being when he was a child, so the yearning of modern man for his adult wholeness and for the experience of the unitary reality proves in turn to be an inner law of the natural process of the maturation of his psyche.

At this point a question arises which many of my readers may already have asked themselves long ago. We have been speaking about the unitary reality and about the relationship of the symbol Adam Kadmon to that reality, yet we have formulated the situation in such a way that it might appear that the experience of the unitary reality always appears in connection with nature and non-personal objects. With the single exception of the primal relationship, which is admittedly a crucial human experience, it would appear that we have omitted all reference to human beings and human encounters. We pointed out, it is true, that it is precisely when the "human" archetypes are constellated that the experience of the unitary reality arises. Yet the impression that in the experience of the unitary reality the cosmic dwarfs the human dimension is not without a basic element of justification. Even when the unitary reality manifests itself in an archetypally conditioned human encounter, a transpersonal element will intervene, spontaneously, as it were, and bring with it a symbolism that is universal and cosmic. We can see this very clearly in the language of love lyrics and of mysticism in every age.

If we wish to gain a fuller understanding of these relationships, we must remind ourselves that so far as the human realm is concerned it is the ego and the conscious mind which are the characteristic organs of the personality and that the all-too-human aspect of personal affairs also belongs to this part of the mind. However, when that deep level of the psyche which we have described as the self, begins to come into operation, interpersonal human encounters share in the radiance which shines out, not only from the human world of Adam Kadmon, but from the great world beyond and above the human world, for which Adam Kadmon is also a symbol. The encounter in love between two human beings reaches out beyond everything that is merely personal. Not only does it touch the presence of the divine, it is an event that encompasses the whole world, which is invoked as a matter of course by the poets, who include heaven and earth, flowers and rocks, and the rising and setting of the constellations in their hymns of praise to the beloved.

Does this mean that the one thing needful is loving and love, not the unique individual who is the actual lover? The solution to this apparent contradiction is to be found in the fact that the individual, as we have said, at the deepest level merges into the world of the unitary reality. The mark of the true individual is that he is constantly experiencing how the transpersonal manifests itself in his own individuality, which is unique in every single moment. At the precise point where the individual has left all purely personal considerations behind him, the cosmic aspect of the unitary reality will express itself in something most profoundly individual. The moment becomes eternity, and eternity becomes the moment.

The individuality of each particular person does not consist of originality or idiosyncrasy of any kind. That is something he shares with every stone on the beach and every cloud in the sky. It consists, rather, of the way in which he experiences and reflects the continually newborn uniqueness of life as an eternity which changes in every moment, and of the way in which he responds to the creative spontaneity of existence with a creative spontaneity of his own. It is works of art which provide us with the clearest and most vivid examples of this kind of more or less comprehensive but always deep and penetrating experience, in which the unitary reality shines out as equally unique and eternal.

Something similar occurs in the process of individuation which takes place in the second half of life. Here the integration of the personality and the shift in the center of gravity from the ego to the self is also identical with a change in reality. Now, on a higher level which embraces the conscious mind, a kind of reversal and return is experienced, in which the end once again links up with the beginning. Just as in the mandala the totality of man and the totality of the world are one, so, when the polarized world of the conscious mind has been overcome, the aspect of the unitary reality reappears on the scene. We can follow this phenomenon very clearly if we observe the process of individuation in modern man and study the creative productions, symbols, and sequences of active imagination that emerge as this process unfolds.

Here, once again, the creative artist is a living illustration of "everyman." The experience of the unitary reality has in fact never left him, and for this very reason the form assumed by this experience in the work of his old age, at the end of his voyage of individuation, often achieves a revelation as profound as anything man's nature is capable of receiving.

We have described this phenomenon elsewhere as "the process whereby reality becomes transparent."[37] This involves a reinforcement and clarification of reality based on the inner intensity of the creative artist. His awareness of the world does not grow weaker with age, but to the extent that he himself begins to become "transparent," the frontiers of the merely personal and ego-bound fade away and what we call the self and the unitary reality which is bound up with it begin to shine out with ever-growing radiance.

This process of becoming transparent can take possession of us on any ordinary working day, in the way we experience a tree or a cloud, a human being or an animal; it is not confined to the experience of "great art," but would appear to be one of the normal occurrences of the second half of life. It may perhaps have become clear by now that this experience has nothing to do with a state of rapture or convulsive ecstasy. Once again, the traditional wisdom is confirmed. God does not reveal himself in thunder and lightning but in the gentle murmuring of the wind.

We said at the beginning that the "incorporation" of the psyche should be understood in a figurative sense. It

---

37. Neumann, "Man and Time," in *Art and the Creative Unconscious.*

is as if the psyche gradually crystallizes out of a nebular state in which it is distributed over the world. It then assumes form, becomes concentrated and centers down as the self and the ego. Paradoxically, in the second half of life, though the process of crystallization is intensified, it is complemented, if we may continue the metaphor, by a kind of dissipation of the contoured form and a renewed extension of the range of the psyche till it again becomes co-terminous with the world and the unitary reality is restored.

Yet even this extension, this process of streaming out, as it were, from encapsulation and incorporation into an experience of breadth and distance, still remains ineradicably marked with the stamp of the uniqueness of the individuality of the subject. We can see this most vividly perhaps in a great creative artist as he approaches old age. If we interpret what the East calls "the Void" as imagelessness and as a condition prior to all imagery which is at the same time the All and the abundance of things, life and the movement of life, we shall perhaps come closest to understanding this process of enlargement, which coincides with the natural development of old age. This happening moves us most profoundly when—as in the late works of great creative artists—it does not remain mute, but even this ultimate transcendence still has the power to assume form, the imageless itself becomes an image.

There are many great works of art—of painting, of music, and of poetry—which can help to bring us closer to an appreciation of this phenomenon. If I now, greatly daring, risk the attempt to approach one of Goethe's late poems in this spirit, I do so in the hope that, after all the most unpoetical matter I have laid before you in this paper, an example such as this poem may perhaps speak more eloquently then any theoretical paraphrase.

> Twilight down from heaven wafted,
> What was near, now it is far;
> Gentle, though, and firstly lofted
> Lustre of the evening star.
> Off all things the contours shiver,
> Sliding mist, way up it goes;
> Mirrored deeps more black than ever
> Darken the lake in its repose.
>
> Now a hint of moon, I wonder,
> From the east, a silver glow,
> Boughs of hair the willow slender
> Dandles in the flood below.
> Through the sport of shadows gliding
> Luna's unsteady auras dart,
> Through the eye the coolness sliding
> Touches with a calm the heart.[38]

It is possible to do full justice to the beauty of this poem by reading it simply as a poem of nature, an evening song. If I speak of the symbolism of the poem, I do not mean to imply that Goethe has made conscious use of symbolism of a specific kind, though of course he did this often enough. What we have here is something far more simple and at the same time far more mysterious: it is the absolute identity of symbol and reality, the com-

38. Goethe, "The Chinese-German Book of Hours and Seasons," VIII, tr. Christopher Middleton, in Goethe's *Selected Poems*, ed. cit., p. 261. [For the original text, see below, p. 129.]

prehension and the expression in artistic form of a piece of the unitary reality.

It is at once a poem of evening and a poem of old age. The concreteness of the things which belong to daytime and to life is dissolved and a changing reality now appears which involves an enlargement both of the world and of the soul. "Twilight down from heaven wafted, / What was near, now it is far." Here the blurring and dissolution of contours is like a blurring of the waning daylight itself, and it is not without a certain element of disquiet. "Off all things the contours shiver, / Sliding mist, way up it goes." This could—in another context—indicate fear. As it is, there is not the slightest suspicion of anything of the kind. There is darkness, it is true, but this is nothing death-dealing or final, since the second half of the stanza shines out like a peaceful triumph or victory song: "Gentle, though, and firstly lofted / Lustre of the evening star." The glowing light of this star, which rises "first" in the midst of twilight, mists, and darkness, is a guarantee, a triumphant expression of a higher certainty.

Night now falls. The words "Mirrored deeps more black than ever / Darken the lake in its repose" bring us down to a realm of the uttermost blackness. Yet this utter blackness, is not an abyss. The mirroring calm of the lake—how familiar this is to us, as seen from the East!—includes and embraces everything in the silence of a world that is imperishable. But now, dissolving the darkness, a new and different light announces its approach in a verse which remains within the realm of our experience of the everyday beauty of reality and which is nevertheless the mystic center of the poem: "Now a

hint of moon, I wonder, / From the east, a silver glow."
In this context "divination" does not imply anything un-
certain or obscure; it is the foreknowledge of something
which is already there, but which is only gradually
emerging. The luminary of the night is ascending, and
with it rises the secret world which from time immemorial has linked the light of the moon with rebirth and
immortality.

Yet all this is only sketched in, as it were. The world
transformed and enchanted by night has nothing gran-
diose about it. It is eternal life, eternal movement, gaiety
and beauty. "Boughs of hair the willow slender / Dan-
dles in the flood below" and "Through the sport of
shadows gliding / Luna's unsteady auras dart." These
lines have the delicacy of filigree, but they also convey,
as an unspoken implication, the mysterious essence of
the mirroring, which in fact represents nothing less than
the inner life both of the moving branches and of the
shadow show.

Yet everything—the ascending moon and the mute
and delicate play of the moving forms—is immersed in
a living silence, in which even the dusk, which had so
recently enveloped the world, is completely dissolved.

But now, beyond all this, transcending it all and apparently coming from somewhere entirely different, are
the last two lines: "Through the eye the coolness sliding
/ Touches with a calm the heart." What a secret lives in
these simple words! What a splendid sigh of relief and
surrender in an old man at the end of a long life, and
what happiness at the approach of death is contained in
the single word "coolness"! How eloquently the suffering and the painful hot unease of the heart are expressed

and at the same time overcome by the little word "calm"! And now, perhaps the finest of all the miraculous things in this poem, comes the almost uncanny transformation of the world which is brought about through the imperceptible and paradoxical transition whereby coolness is shown entering the heart through the eyes. The symbol of the coolness of the night conveys the idea of the stillness and reassurance of the invisible presence which is stealing forward to encompass the world. The transcendence of everything that is visible is brought home to us vividly by the transformation of the eyes, which are no longer active like the sun or even receptive like the moon, but have become the gateway through which the invisible and imageless reality penetrates the real center of our humanity, the heart.

Imperceptibly, nature has disclosed her essence as a mystery of a higher order. Things move, they are inanimate, quickened and luminous with meaning, in a world which is a poem. Life, in a magical transformation of man and landscape, becomes transparent and manifest before our eyes; it is this world and the beyond at one and the same time.

*

Original of Goethe's
"Twilight down from heaven"

Dämmrung senkte sich von oben,
Schon ist alle Nähe fern;
Doch zuerst emporgehoben
Holden Lichts der Abendstern!
Alles schwankt ins Ungewisse,

Nebel schleichen in die Höh;
Schwarzvertiefte Finsternisse
Widerspiegelnd ruht der See.

Nun am östlichen Bereiche
Ahn ich Mondenglanz und -glut,
Schlanker Weiden Haargezweige
Scherzen auf der nächsten Flut.
Durch bewegter Schatten Spiele
Zittert Lunas Zauberschein,
Und durchs Auge schleicht die Kühle
Sänftigend ins Herz hinein.

III

CREATIVE MAN AND
THE "GREAT EXPERIENCE"

I

When we consider "nature" and the "evolution" of life
within nature, we are struck by certain lines of progress
and adaptation and by the growing richness of the world
of reality which is apprehended by living organisms. Yet
these lines of development are in fact no more than
paths which we trace out in the pathless jungle of life.
The characteristic abundance of varieties, the way in
which species and groups fan out from one another
within the framework of a reality in which we can never
distinguish between an outer and an inner dimension, is
a phenomenon which at every turn transcends our understanding. Adolf Portmann has repeatedly drawn our
attention to this typical abundance in the proliferation
of natural forms, which impresses us with the beauty
and overflowing richness of life, though we are unable
to comprehend it in terms of the categories of rationality

"Der schöpferische Mensch und die 'Grosse Erfahrung,'" in *Der
schöpferische Mensch* (Zurich, 1959); revised from the version in
Eranos-Jahrbuch 1956, on "Man and the Creative." Translated by Eugene Rolfe.

and utility imposed by our conscious minds. And when natural science teaches us—apparently in sober, realistic tones—that what we call chance, i.e., an undirected spontaneous happening, is in fact endlessly producing phenomena which we experience as, for instance, beautiful, then this chance, which is able to create beauty and to produce, out of its own nature, the colors and forms of inorganic and organic life, must be one of the essential properties of the vital process itself.

One of the most striking features of life in general is not simply the mobility and unpredictability that is almost synonymous with the meaning of the word "alive" but the characteristic superabundance of life, in the face of which our conscious minds, with their ordering, understanding, and thinking functions, invariably prove themselves inadequate. It is precisely this quality of superabundance and profusion, which is inherent in life as if it were something playing at random and which is in fact the creative foundation of reality, that is so essentially alien to our conscious minds, which mistakenly confuse profusion with superfluity. It is in the context of this typical profusion of life, which is still very much a factor to be reckoned with in the existence of early man and of the child, that the commercial and mercantile character of our rationality and of the categories of our conscious minds are revealed. Useful, reasonable, necessary, and purposeful: these are the epithets which the conscious mind employs when it wishes to pay a compliment to life. Accidental, futile, unreasonable, and purposeless are the negative attributes which it ascribes to everything that seems alien to its own nature. To comprehend, not to be comprehended, is the task of the conscious mind of the West, with which our own egos are so largely identified.

The puritanical impoverishment of our civilized existence is being constantly reinforced by our compulsive drive towards the excessive differentiation of productive efficiency and by the immeasurable complexity of the knowledge at our disposal. It is not simply that our conscious minds are attuned to a partial subdivision of the world, whether this takes the form of an inner, psychic world or of an outer, physical world; they are attuned to smaller and smaller segments of these partial worlds which are becoming more and more sharply defined, with the result that our total personalities are cut off from any access to a natural reality in which they can breathe.

In total contrast we find primitive, integrated man—including both early man and the child—who is still living in the "Great World" which is closest to what we have described as the unitary reality. Embedded in this world, which has not yet been torn asunder into a confrontation between subject and object, and in which the dimensions of inner and outer remain unseparated, man—the original, integrated man—lives in a state of constant interconnection and cooperation, action and reaction that relates him, in his whole being, with reality and reality with him. Since it is a fulfilled life, his life corresponds to the abundance that characterizes reality itself; the continuity of his existence has not yet been broken by the incisive activity of a reflecting and abstracting conscious mind. The performance of some "work," whether it is "useful" for life in our sense of the term or simply a "game," whether it is intended to be permanent or to last only for a moment, is so fulfilled by the intensity of the man who performs it that, like everything really essential, it remains in the realm of the timeless. Though the ritual objects prepared for a festival are produced over lengthy periods of time and fashioned with the total intensity of an unconscious drive to artistic creation, they are nevertheless often destroyed at the very festival for which they were created. The extravagant abundance of life itself is reflected in the abundance of creative man, who lives for a time that is fulfilled and within the framework of time which he himself has fulfilled, and for whom no time exists that is abstracted from the present.

This primordial self-evidence of a life which belongs completely to every moment, a life in which no distance separates man from himself, from his "You," from the world, from what he is doing and from what is happening to him, is only possible within the framework of an existence that has remained essentially unconscious. Here man is not yet identified with his ego and is still dominated by the non-ego, on which he is in fact as dependent as he is on the self and on the world. In spite of this, however, he often possesses a genuine sense of the meaningfulness of his own existence. The man who is integrated on a primitive level and is not constricted by the limitations of his ego experiences his actions as bound up with the destiny of the whole world with which he is connected. This character of centrality which embraces the whole of being and for which the whole of time is comprised in every moment as "present" time, and for which the entire cosmos is itself present in every part of the world, is also valid for man himself. His own integrated wholeness corresponds to the wholeness of the world which is experienced by him. Just as an animal lives in a world which is arranged in order around itself as its center, so early man—and, like him, the child—lives as the center of a reality which is shaped and structured in a creative fashion.

This fulfillment and wholeness of man's experience of reality is in no way dependent on the range of either his subjective consciousness or of his objective experience of the world. Both of these may be either small or great. By contrast, modern ego-centered man, in the partial reality that is shaped and structured solely by his conscious mind, never loses his feeling of "cutoffness" from reality and of the basic insignificance of his existence.

The wholeness of a man which is not centered in his own ego experiences the world itself as a whole. However, this world, with its lack of differentiation into an inner and an outer dimension, involves identifications, participations, and mergings of identity which make it a world deficient in the security of the firm outlines which are required by a discriminating conscious mind. If it was to exist at all, ego-consciousness was compelled to free itself to the greatest possible extent from its entanglement in this illimitable world. Its relative independence is in fact based on this painfully acquired disengagement, which is coincident with the polarization of our world and the reduction of man's original experience of wholeness to an experience of partial worlds, or segments of reality. Thus the normal development of Western man leads from a state of *participation mystique* to a state of clear and distinct consciousness, and from the feeling-toned experience of the unitary reality to a knowledge of partial worlds, of the world of objects and of the objective psyche.[1]

The light of man's primary experience of wholeness, which is unfocussed but illuminates a great world, becomes concentrated in the magnifying glass of ego-consciousness and contracts into a single distinct point of light capable of moving around in such a way that it can throw a sharp and isolating beam of illumination on a whole succession of the most diverse segments of reality. In the process, however, these parts of the whole become detached from their real context, and the unitary reality, which had been immediately accessible to the primary experience, disappears below the horizon of the conscious mind.

Basically, what we call the experience of wholeness transcends our ego-experience. The conscious mind has evolved as an organ of cognition in the course of the history of the human race, but today it is no longer an organ for the experience of wholeness. As the attitude of ego-consciousness becomes more extreme, it is protected by the erection of a cultural canon of acknowledged collective values and orientations and the "immediate" experience of wholeness is inevitably excluded as too dangerous. In this way the tendency of the cultural canon only to admit newly emerging contents of the unconscious insofar as they conform to the cultural canon is reinforced. The continuity of the cultural canon at any given time is regarded as more important than the "direct" experience of the individual. Furthermore, as civ-

1. Cf. Neumann, *Origins and History*.

ilization advances this process tends to become, if anything, still further exacerbated; it is by no means the case that this trend disappears with the growth of "partial" consciousness.

However, every human being is "by nature" creative. Yet it is only just beginning to dawn upon the West that one of the gravest and most menacing problems of our Western civilization arises from the fact that this civilization cuts man off from his natural creativity. Since it is obviously impossible to recapture the integration of man's primeval youth, our civilization cannot escape its responsibility for the simultaneous development of consciousness and creativity; it must not foster one quality at the expense of the other.

This simultaneity is by no means an utopian ideal; we find it in all the highest creative achievements of humanity, including those in the field of art. But creative experience is not confined to the "Great Individual." Closer contact with any human individual will reveal how much more experience is contained within him than his conscious mind possesses or his ego "knows." In fact, one of the essential aims of all psychotherapy is to make it possible for a man to become aware of his own real experience which is hidden from him at the outset by his identification with his ego.[2] Our task here is not simply to make conscious contents which have been repressed and have become unconscious for that reason: we have to try to learn how to lay aside the spectacles of ego-consciousness and to allow the reality of the

2. Neumann, "Das Schöpferische als Zentralproblem der Psychotherapie": see above, Essay II, n. 22.

world to stream in upon us as it does stream in unceasingly when man's instrument for receiving experience is not simply the rigid apparatus of his restricting and excluding conscious mind.

When we speak of the characteristic superabundance of reality, we are implying that even with our whole being we can only experience segments of reality, and that with our differentiated conscious mind we can only experience segments of polarized partial realities. This means that in every experience and in every reality that appeals to us an element of infinite superabundance has been excluded. And yet this element of superabundance colors and determines even our partial experience, so that every awareness of reality which we have experienced is bound up with an indefinite background of reality that is unexperienced and remains to be experienced. This superabundance that cannot be experienced finds expression in a numinous feeling of amazement in the face of something eternally enigmatic, which accompanies and relativizes our experience, but can also transform it and render it transparent.

The legitimate tendency of our conscious minds to stabilize and systematize what is given to us in experience and to develop it into a consistent and unitary experience corresponds to our compelling human need to erect a habitation within the flux of the infinite and to make this our dwelling place. But since this habitation can easily become a prison and consolidation can easily turn into rigidity, the creative nature of man impels him to disregard all settled boundaries, pierce through to the creative nature of reality, grasp its essence and shape it into artistic form. This explains why, in contrast to the normal course of psychic development, with its defense mechanisms and its techniques for the repression or belittlement of awkward realities, the psychic structure and development of creative man is characterized by a totally different set of attitudes, that is to say, by openness, emotionality, and spontaneity.

The openness of the creative personality finds expression in a heightened sensibility and in a capacity and willingness to be deeply moved and impressed. The creative personality is equally open to the psyche and to the world and is not so attuned as normal man to the exclusiveness of a partial world, whether this takes the form of a so-called inner, or of a so-called outer world. In the case of creative man, however, the capacity to be overwhelmed is combined with a higher degree of alertness. Thus the open willingness to live in a reality in which the non-ego, whether as psyche or as world, is the directing power to which the ego is subordinated, is not a matter of blind devotion; on the contrary, the characteristic profusion of reality which is experienced by creative man is matched by his alert capacity to be gripped by experience; this now in its turn begins to grip and give form to the profusion of the open world.

It is certainly true that the open ego of creative man is receptive. However—and this is one of the many paradoxes inherent in its psychic structure—it also possesses an activity peculiarly its own which makes it so elastic and so resilient that it can fairly be described as a "regenerative" ego. The normal ego is relatively rigid. Once it has adopted a given stance it defends it by excluding contrary viewpoints and contents, with the result that the conscious mind is systematized and consolidated. On the other hand, the open ego of creative man almost seems to drown in the abundance of the world that streams in upon it. Yet the peculiar virtue of its regenerative power is based on its willingness not to cling to itself but to allow itself to be shaped and formed by new experiences of the world, and then in turn to give shape and form to these experiences.

This unsystematized and open disposition of the regenerative ego makes it possible for creative man—for example, when he is an artist—to be a different personality in every work he creates; at the same time, in the changing phases of his development, he can allow ever new aspects of reality to assume artistic shape and form. Here the ego does not oppose the experience of being overwhelmed or catch the stream of inflowing impressions in a structure largely prefashioned by the conscious mind; creative man is himself the structure which is transformed by ever new influences.

This capacity for allowing oneself to be continually re-created in the process called by Goethe "Die and Become" is bound up with the fact that in creative man the relationship between the ego and the self is more strongly accentuated and has remained more alive than is the case in normal ego development. In normal development the personality identifies itself with the ego as the center of the conscious mind. Creative man, on the other hand, is not committed to the ego or to a habitual ego-attitude of any kind. His ego can withstand the experience of being overwhelmed by the non-ego because its attachment to the self makes it possible for it to grasp the nature of this self as both the innermost center of its own being and the essence of the non-ego at the same time, so that it experiences this "alien" element (for example in the world) as essentially "its own." It is only because the self and the world belong together in this fashion that the "alien" element can also find expression in the openness of creative formulation by the artist. The ability of creative man to suspend himself as an ego in a condition of openness is based on his experience that beyond the continual crises and transformations of his ego he is grounded in the self, a totality superior to the ego, which is the rootstock of all the fallings and risings of the transitory forms assumed by his ego. In his openness and alertness he is overwhelmed, he conceives, and he gives overwhelming form to his conceptions; yet in spite of this—and in fact precisely because of it—he remains unfixated and does not become identified either with what happens to him or with the creative form which he has fashioned out of his experience.

We do not identify Goethe—the supreme example of creative man—with the Goethe of *Werther* or of *Faust*, with "Wilhelm Meister" or with the *West-Eastern Divan*; nor is Shakespeare contained in any of his plays, though he is very much alive in every one of them. So also, creative man constantly experiences himself as the channel to himself and at the same time as the gateway between the inner and the outer worlds.

Klee once used the simile of a tree to illustrate the nature of the creative process. "The sense of direction in nature and life ... I shall compare with the root of the tree," he said. "From the root the sap flows to the artist. ..." The crown of the tree is the quite different dimension of the unfolding of the work. — The artist "stands as the trunk of the tree." He then goes on to say: "And yet, standing at his appointed place, the trunk of the tree, he does nothing other than gather and pass on what comes to him from the depths. He neither serves nor rules—he transmits."[3]

A number of objections may be raised to this metaphor, in which the artist's capacity to give form to his experience seems almost to have been forgotten. And yet in the most wonderful way it suggests to our minds the openness of the man who proves himself creative not as ego but as non-ego, though his ego does not disintegrate in the process, but actually realizes itself both within and outside the opposition between ego and non-ego.

This creative element presupposes an alert spontaneity, a more than eager readiness to respond to the continual collision between world and psyche. His openness to the never-failing possibility of new experience throws creative man into a state of animated disquiet, which, in contrast to the absentmindedness and distractability of the rigid normal ego, in no way excludes the quietness of a state of alert concentration. This elasticity, which combines rest and unrest, gives creative man a quality of aliveness that normal man generally lacks. The ego of normal man is rigid and repeats habitual, stereotyped reactions; in fact, it tires easily for this very reason and is subject to feelings of emptiness and boredom, which must be overcome by distraction, diversion, or the search for hobbies. Yet the spontaneous and concentrated receptivity of creative man should not be confused with the immediate reaction to an impression. An impression

3. Paul Klee, *On Modern Art*, with an introduction by Herbert Read; tr. Paul Findlay (orig. 1945; London, 1948), p. 13.

may be stored for a long period in all its original freshness without being incorporated into a context which already exists in the conscious mind, and it may then subsequently find expression in a new context which had possibly not been created at all at the time when the impression had originally been received.

A third factor in the openness and spontaneity of creative man is his enhanced emotionality. This is another trait which we can best understand in terms of its contrast with normal development, in which the dominant trend is to avoid emotionality, and to divest unconscious contents of their emotionality to the greatest possible extent.[4]

The formation of a stable ego within a relatively compact conscious mind serves the purpose—not only in the East but in our own civilization—of making it possible for the individual to function without undue emotion, or at any rate to possess and to display emotion only on those occasions which are prescribed by our cultural canon, and then only in a restrained manner. Equanimity, balance, self-control, coolness in reaction, etc., are among the unwritten requirements of normal education. Compensation for this régime of compulsory restrictions follows later in the form of uncontrolled emotional outbursts, those mass epidemics that counterbalance the deficiencies of our culture and force their way through, whether harmlessly as in sport or catastrophically as in wars, persecutions, etc.

The heightened emphasis on the conscious mind and the head in our culture, with its strict training of ani-

4. *Origins and History*, pp. 387-88.

mals, children, and the primitive within ourselves, points entirely in the same direction. And not only that; it is not simply the possession of "affects" that is dismissed as "uneducated" in our culture: even the possession of feelings, in the more human sense of the term, is regarded as little short of ridiculous and is at best tolerated among juveniles, who of course are not "mature." Patriarchal consciousness also allows woman to retain a certain residue of emotionality; it does so in the illusory superiority of its "knowledge" that the feminine is closer to the childlike than is man and that it cannot therefore be considered capable of attaining the full maturity of the masculine.

In sharp contrast to this, a heightened emotional reaction is one of the most marked characteristics of every creative man. Even a man who is creative in the sphere of natural science, a man whose attention is directed unambiguously and even one-sidedly to that single aspect of reality which is constituted by the world of inanimate objects, will be more profoundly gripped, disquieted, and impressed by that world than so-called normal man would be. It is only this quality of alert animation that makes it possible for him in the first place to notice what thousands before him have failed to notice, and leads him on to discover a problem there, i.e., something new, unknown, and not yet definitively classified.

It is not only the artist, then, who, like Stendhal's Henry Brulard,[5] possesses, in addition to his critical and overcritical intellect, a feeling capacity for living experience that for him (as for a young man) makes every ex-

5. [*La Vie de Henry Brulard*, 1835-36, publ. 1890.]

perience a novel and unique encounter: all creative men possess this gift of enhanced emotionality. Even an illness or a hardship, a fragment of nature like an animal or a plant, or a problem in mechanics or arithmetic, can become for him an exciting reality. And this excitement which grips him and which expresses itself in the form of interest and concentration or as a task by which he is possessed does not simply activate his creative temperament. Something else happens at the same time. The affective ignition between himself and the world points to a reality that is common to them both—to an "appetence" which is at work in nature as well as in man and which actually brings them together.

The typological structure of creative man is irrelevant in this context. He may be introverted or extraverted and his alert openness may express itself in terms of a heightened receptivity to sensation, an enhanced intuition, a profoundly stirred and dedicated feeling, or a penetrating intensity in the thinking function. Irrespective of the form of the vessels employed by the psyche that is apprehending reality, creativity partakes of the nature of a profusion whose intensity bursts through the stereotypes of the psychic instrument that contains it, but in so doing it at least partially transcends the sectional character of the reality which is being pressed into the shape of these stereotypes.

We have established that "matriarchal" consciousness is more dependent on what we call the unconscious,[6] and that the bisexual tendency in creative man is more

---

6. Neumann, "Ueber den Mond und das matriarchale Bewusstsein," in *Zur Psychologie des Weiblichen* (U. d. M. 2). [Cf. tr. Hildegard Nagel, "On the Moon and Matriarchal Consciousness," *Spring 1954.*]

pronounced than is acceptable to the cultural requirements of the West, and also that creative man's connection with the mother archetype and the anima is virtually a law governing the constellation of his psyche. Taken together, these facts form the structural basis for what, phenomenologically, we have tried to identify as the openness, the spontaneity and the unspoiled emotionality of creative man. The receptive-regenerative nature of the ego also finds its appropriate place in this context. At the same time creative man's enhanced susceptibility to transpersonal experience in no way detracts from the augmented inner and outer activity of his personality, which makes use of his ego and his ego-will for this purpose. It is essential, however, that this activity should be devoted to the serivce of the totality superior to the ego, the self, and that it should not be emancipated from the latter.

Creative man also suffers from complexes, those nodal points in the psychic structure whose significance is by no means confined to pathological cases. For a reductive interpretation it is always a simple matter to detect such sore spots in creative man; in fact, they are among the most striking features of his psychology. However, we shall never adequately understand normality, let alone creative man, if we persist in deriving the essential from the accidental and the transpersonal from the personal. A grotesque example of this approach is provided by Otto Rank, who derives Schiller's "Hymn to Eyesight" from the poet's habit of blinking, and supports his thesis by quoting the alleged fact that this complaint had earlier been responsible for the name

"Schiller," which had been given to an ancestor of the family who squinted! (German *Schieler* = "squinter.")[7]

We have learned from the law of "secondary personalization"[8] that in the normal course of development what was originally great and archetypal is subsequently experienced as small and purely personal and that the stability of ego-consciousness is supported by the most radical and thoroughgoing exclusion of all forms of "great experience." In the case of creative man, however, this process of restriction to purely personal ego experience is either incomplete or altogether lacking. For him the complex never entirely loses its original significance; it is never just a sore spot in his personal life but always at the same time a gateway into the world. Inasmuch as creative man suffers from a complex, it opens up for him the psychic background; but inasmuch as he overcomes this suffering and expresses it in an artistic form, the complex also provides him with a way into the world. The areas affected by the complex, and above all the cognate childhood experiences of being overwhelmed, are never entirely personalized by creative man, particularly if he happens to be an artist. In other words, childhood and the happenings of childhood always mean more to him than just "family history"; they always remain "experience of the world."

However, in the case of creative man this relative indissolubility of the complex is not due to any tendency on his part to cling to his complexes, but rather to the fact that his personal experience of and suffering from

7. Rank, *Das Inzest-Motiv in Dichtung und Sage* (Leipzig, 1912).
8. *Origins and History*, pp. xxiii–xxiv.

the complex is connected with something which we might describe as "archetypal resonance." Behind the personal level of the complex there is always, for creative man, a dimension of archetypal greatness which is meaningful and mundane at the same time. The archetype is in fact always the symbol of an eternal problem, which is in turn the gateway to the "great experience" that embraces and includes within itself all small and personal experience.

Just as in creative man the self, the reality in the background of his psychic totality, compels him repeatedly to thrust his way forwards through partial to total experience, through experience of segments of reality to the totality of the unitary reality, so too he always experiences the "little" happening that befalls his little ego as a symbol of something great which belongs to that undivided totality of the world which is the unitary reality. In this sense the thought expressed by William Blake in the following lines applies generically to creative man:

> To see a World in a Grain of Sand
> And a Heaven in a Wild Flower,
> Hold Infinity in the palm of your hand
> And Eternity in an hour.[9]

Blake also discovered that law of "reduction" which is related to the development of the conscious mind, when he says: "If the doors of perception were cleansed every thing would appear to man as it is, infinite. For man has closed himself up, till he sees all things thro' the narrow chinks of his cavern."[10]

9. "Auguries of Innocence."
10. [*The Marriage of Heaven and Hell*, pl. 14.]

This cleansing of the "doors of perception" is only connected with Huxley's confusion[11] insofar as this enhancement of experience can also be brought about with the aid of intoxicants, such as those used in many mysteries, both primitive and non-primitive, which are known to us from the history of civilization. But creative man attains this enhancement "by nature" and experiences in the intoxication of his suffering susceptibility to the transpersonal, the possibility of self-transformation and self-transcendence which is immanent in the reality of the world.

In this sense it is true to say that for creative man the upper is identical with the lower and the inner with the outer. At the same time everything great is small for him, since it is a transpersonal reality that speaks to him in personal terms. Yet it is equally true that everything small is great for him, since in everything personal and small like an object the great and transpersonal reality is contained.

For a normal man an experience such as this is altogether too paradoxical. He represses this basic fact of life because it is altogether too far beyond the comprehension of his ego-consciousness. He is aware, for example, in his conscious mind that the atom is infinite and cosmic, like a world, but this knowledge does not lead to vital experience, let alone to the transformation of the "grain of sand" into a world.

When Blake says "What is now proved was once only imagin'd,"[12] what he calls "imagination," i.e., the power

11. Aldous Huxley, *The Doors of Perception* (New York, 1954).
12. *The Marriage of Heaven and Hell*, pl. 8 ("Proverbs of Hell").

of the psyche to form pictures of things, is one of the most profound and accurate instruments for the perception of reality that man has at his disposal. This still contains in a living form that portion of "extraneous" knowledge[13] which man possesses beyond his conscious mind. It is the task of our conscious minds to extend this knowledge in such a way that we can make accessible to our experience the vision of the imagination of creative man and can extend the range of our consciousness and of ourselves by assimilating experience of this kind.

This creative imagination is very closely connected with the world of the complexes, whose archetypal resonance is stimulated by that region in the background of the psyche which belongs to the unitary reality. Wherever, as in creative man, this hurt area of the complex remains open, as an Amfortas wound of continual suffering and a spring of eternal richness, we find, too, that a living relationship with the reality behind the eternal problems that have always preoccupied the human race also remains very much alive. In fact, the phases and complexes of development through which every human being passes in childhood are indissolubly connected, not only with archetypal images and powers, but also, through them, with the eternal problems of the human race.

The archetypes of the collective unconscious are not only organs of the psyche and dominants of psychic development; they are at the same time "worlds" and "world enigmas." Whenever, by way of the wound of his complex, a creative man lights on the archetypal

13. See Essay 1 in this volume.

background that belongs to it, he becomes fascinated by the eternal problem that corresponds to this archetype and he will then in his own sphere make a new contribution to the treatment of this eternal human question, which is insoluble and at the same time cries out for a solution. The word "problem" in this context is no more intended to be understood in an intellectual sense than the word "treatment." The term "eternal problem" is no more than a kind of generic term to describe the enigmatic nature of a part of the reality of the world, and its treatment and processing through the work of creative man is a move forwards in the experience of this aspect of the world-reality and an attempt to decipher it, to formulate it, or to express it in artistic terms.

It is only when we have extended the complex to include the archetypal background connected with it and have amplified it by relating it to the corresponding world-reality that we shall be in a position to understand what it is that moves creative man so deeply and why his work is so full of meaning for us.

A few examples will suffice to illustrate these relationships. The world of "incest with the mother," which is a central complex in every psyche, is more than just a part of the so-called Oedipus complex, i.e., of the child's coming to terms with the personal parents, since the latter are always at the same time the carriers of the archetypal powers of the opposites in life, of which the prototypes are the sexual opposites. In the form of "uroboric incest,"[14] however, the child's incest with the mother goes even deeper; in fact it goes right back to the pre-

14. *Origins and History*, pp. 16-18, and passim.

patriarchal phase and to the child's earliest unconscious tendency to dissolve back again into the Great Round, which is what the mother means to him. Even psychoanalysis has related this tendency and its symptoms to the "eternal phenomenon" of man's reunion with the mother in birth and death,[15] and Jung has established its existence, as the archetype of "rebirth," in the psychic history of the human race.[16]

An interpretation that reduces this phenomenon to an "embryonic uterus-fantasy" makes the mistake of personalizing the phenomenon, of shifting the emphasis from the essential to the accidental, and fails to recognize its true nature. The important point is not that this interpretation is false—we cannot even say yet that it is false—but that in relation to the psyche and the phenomena and problems which appear in the psyche it is inadequate.

In connection with this mother-incest, i.e., the child's tendency to unite with the mother, let us consider the symbol of "penetration into" the mother, which is of course "later" and associated with a more advanced stage in ego development than the symbol of "self-dissolution" in her. If we reduce this personalistically to the infant's fantasy of incest, then it means the desire for genital union with the mother. Unquestionably, such a desire can emerge during a specific phase in the development of the male child. But it is almost always impossible to take the child's tendency to incest "literally," i.e., personally, since the personal aspect is invariably bound

15. Rank, op. cit.
16. Jung, *Symbols of Transformation*, CW 5, pars. 332ff.

up with the transpersonal, archetypal background. An archetypal interpretation is also suggested by the fact that the infant, with its still undeveloped ego, necessarily experiences the mother as something not yet personal and clearly defined, but rather as a transpersonal reality, i.e., as a Great Mother.

If, however, we see the incest problem in archetypal terms, then it is a case of union with the Great Mother, who is everything that is mundane, natural, sheltering, and unknown. Side by side with the tendency to seek protection in what provides shelter, which corresponds more nearly to the symbolism of hiding and dissolving oneself in it, we find the more active process of "penetrating into" it, which is the symbol of man's eternal tendency to experience something from within and to discover the secret of existence. It is as unquestionable that for the child the mother and in particular her womb is the symbolic carrier of this secret as it is that the womb of the feminine in its capacity as the place of birth symbolizes an eternal problem for human life in all its stages.

The tendency inherent in man's existence to experience and to penetrate into reality is in no way dependent on the infant's genital fixation on his personal mother, even though from the ontogenetic standpoint this eternal problem appears or may appear for the first time in conjunction with the personal carrier of the symbol, that is to say, with the child's personal mother.

When language creates and employs the symbol of "penetrating into," it is using it to grasp the tendency that presses and urges man to look within; it is the same tendency that impels primitive man to "penetrate into" the secret of the mountain,[17] the sculptor Henry Moore[18] to explore the figure of the Primordial Feminine and the secret of inner and outer forms, and the theologians and mystics to investigate the secret of the Godhead.[19] The fact that this transpersonal drive to penetrate into the nature of things is also experienced in personal terms in no way alters the given, primordial character of this symbol and of its significance, which includes the whole range of reality. Even when the incestuous wish really turns out to be an inner experience of the child or of the remembering adult and is actually associated with the personal mother, the insatiability of this longing does not depend on the unattainability of its fulfillment in concrete terms. On the contrary, it springs from an extraordinary compulsive drive to penetrate the secret of reality itself, and relates rather to the simple fact that it is impossible to return to the unitary reality which is symbolized by that Great Mother from whom—in both personal and transpersonal terms—the individual was born as an individual ego in the first place.

Behind the personal complex of the incest-wish, we have seen how the archetypal background and the eternal human problem that corresponds to it have become clearly visible; in the same way the archetypal reality of man's unsplit and unpolarized existence in the unitary reality lies behind the complex of "weaning," i.e., of the loss of the primal relationship with the mother. In ar-

17. Neumann, "Zur psychologischen Bedeutung des Ritus," *Kulturentwicklung und Religion* (U. d. M. 1).

18. Neumann, *The Archetypal World of Henry Moore* (New York, B.S. LXVIII, and London, 1959).

19. Neumann, "Mystical Man," in *The Mystic Vision* (PEY 6, 1968).

chetypal terms "weaning" represents the necessary loss of man's existence in the allconnectedness of *participation mystique*. That existence is in fact the opposite to the ego's isolated condition of "having-to-rely-on-itself" in the new "weaned" stage of existence which follows the phase of earliest childhood and dominates the scene more and more until final maturity is attained.

Similarly, we find an archetypal symbol as the background to the "primal scene," i.e., the child's assumed personal observation of his parents' coitus. We are confronted here by the primordial image of the First Parents united in a mutual embrace and the eternal problem of "Taigitu," the principle of the opposites bound together in unity, which plays such a decisive part in the interaction of Yang and Yin with and in one another in Chinese classical philosophy—and in fact wherever the underlying theme is the preconscious primordial unity of existence and the uniting of antithetical opposites to form a new and vitally integrated creation.

In every analysis that achieves any depth the same developmental sequence is observable: behind the childish conception of sadistic sexual intercourse in which the man represents the evil principle which inflicts suffering and the woman the good principle which endures suffering, the archetype of the invading dynamism of the numinous becomes visible. Here the feminine may actually be experienced as the overwhelming masculine power that we have described as the "patriarchal uroboros."[20] Once again a transpersonal reality is encountered in conjunction with the personal dimension and

20. Neumann, *Zur Psychologie des Weiblichen* (U. d. M. 2).

an eternal and insoluble human problem is bound up with the appearance of an archetype. It is in fact nothing less than the invasion of the overwhelming power of destiny and of the divine. This is the great destroyer and renewer which brings death to everything that is alive in order that new forms of life may be created—whether outside in the world or inside in the psyche, whether in the life experience of woman or of man.

So Picasso, for example, uses the figures of the bull and the horse, the mighty symbolic powers which, in animal form, dominate the traditional bullfights of Spain, to experience and express, over and over, this same clash between the opposites, with its motif of the overpowering of the (female) horse by the (male) bull. What an injustice is done to this creative process by an interpretation that seeks to reduce this archetypal experience and its artistic expression to Picasso's personal observation, as a child, of his parents' sexual intercourse! Yet how understandable the sequence of this creative development becomes if we watch it kindled into flame by the mighty symbols of man and woman, bull and horse, circling round them and experimenting with ever new forms of artistic expression, until finally, in *Guernica*, it produces one of the supreme masterpieces of our century, in which the heartrending cry of suffering feminine humanity, the mad onslaught of the destructive invader, and the light of a higher knowledge flooding all that happens with illumination achieve triumphant expression in a single moment!

If we continue to follow the sequence of archetypal phases whose nodal points are the complexes which bind the psyche of the individual, it becomes clear that, behind the "father" of the individual's father-complex, stands the father-archetype and the problem of the spiritual constitution of the world. Here again, we should note the characteristic way in which creative man responds to the complex-wound in his psyche and proves his creativity precisely by his unique response to his own woundedness. Let us take Franz Kafka as a case in point. There can be absolutely no doubt about Kafka's own personal father-complex—that is to say, about the complex involved in his relationship with "old man Kafka." If we require any further evidence, we already possess it in the form of the "Letter to His Father,"[21] that dreadful and desperate attempt to come to some kind of terms with his real father. And the powerful but totally uncomprehending form of the capable, psychically blind yet by no means inhuman father is convincing enough as a personal figure to enable us to understand the way the son's will was broken, over and over, the inadequacy of this son, and his hopeless attempts to offer resistance.

Already in Kafka's novella *The Judgment*, that nightmare of a son condemned to death by his father, the father expands beyond the figure of the personal father, and the might of the father-god Yahweh flashes out from him like lightning. Here the line that leads from Kafka to Kierkegaard, and to the sacrifice of Isaac and the father's willingness to sacrifice his son, is clearly revealed in all its monstrosity. It is intimately connected with the central mystery of Christianity, the sacrifice of

21. See *Dearest Father* (tr. Ernst Kaiser and Eithne Wilkins, New York, 1954).

the Son by God the Father and it brings us very near to the problem of Job and the protest of modern man in Jung's *Answer to Job*.[22]

Yet how close, too, in Kafka is the link between the background of his story and the tragedy of Jewish man and of his exposure to this hostile world, a world created and governed by the Father, as whose chosen Son and expiating sacrifice, both willing and unwilling, he experiences himself throughout a history that spans the millennia. Thus the world of *The Trial*[23] and "In the Penal Colony" grows out of Kafka's father-complex, as does his conception of the world as a place of inscrutably unjust justice. In this world, man exists in precisely the same condition of despair as Renée, Mme. Sèchehaye's schizophrenic woman patient, who believed she heard a madman crying, "I am in a hopeless situation. I am accused from all sides, and I am innocent—and yet guilty! My sufferings are beyond all measure. Why don't you help me? Brothers, I'm suffering! Brothers, I'm terrified! I'm an innocent criminal!"[24]

And then, of course, there is Kafka's *The Castle*—unattainable and remote in the unapproachability and invisibility of its imageless secret and in the hierarchy of its powers, which extend upwards into a void beyond all recourse or possibility of appeal. And yet we are told that, at the beginning, when K. is telephoning the Castle, "The receiver gave out a buzz of a kind that K. had

22. Orig. 1952; in CW 11.

23. See Neumann, "Kafka's 'The Trial': An Interpretation through Depth Psychology," in *Creative Man*.

24. M.-A. Sèchehaye, *Symbolische Wunscherfüllung* (Bern and Stuttgart, 1955), p. 145. [Orig. *La Réalisation symbolique* (Bern, 1947).]

never before heard on a telephone. It was like the hum of countless children's voices—but yet not a hum, the echo rather of voices singing at an infinite distance—blended by sheer impossibility into one high but resonant sound which vibrated on the ear as if it were trying to penetrate beyond mere hearing."[25]

In a conversation which concludes with the moving words "But this is only joking, so that you will not notice how badly things are going with me today," Kafka remarked, and with justice, "In fact, the poet is always much smaller and weaker than the social average. Therefore he feels the burden of earthly existence much more intensely and strongly than other men. For him personally his song is only a scream. Art for the artist is only suffering, through which he releases himself for further suffering."[26]

However, this emphasis on suffering and weakness does not alter the fact that creative man, and in particular the artist, copes with this suffering and liberates himself from it in an almost superhuman and inhuman fashion, and he does so by giving shape and visible form to something that belongs to the essential nature of reality. In a conversation with a young man about his poems Kafka told him that they were not yet art. He went on to say, "This description of feelings and impressions is most of all a hesitant groping for the world. The eyes are still heavy with dreams. But in time that will cease and then perhaps the outstretched groping will with-

25. *The Castle* (tr. Willa and Edwin Muir, New York, 2nd ed., 1941), pp. 26-27.
26. Gustav Janouch, *Conversations with Kafka* (tr. Goronwy Rees, New York, 2nd ed., 1971), pp. 16-17.

draw as if caught by the fire. Perhaps you will cry out, stammer incoherently, or grind your teeth together and open your eyes wide, very wide. But—these are only words. Art is always a matter of the entire personality. For that reason it is fundamentally tragic."[27]

Since an experience of this kind, which however is by no means always necessarily tragic, is an experience of the total personality, it also embraces the totality of the world. However different the experiences of artists may be, and in whatever different ways these experiences may appear to them and through them, their creativity always represents a breakthrough in which the dimension of the purely personal opens out into that realm of the intrinsic essence of things which constitutes the suprapersonal background of reality.

There is a volume of drawings by Picasso:[28] 180 large-size drawings which he dashed off in a period of slightly more than two months, between November 28, 1953, and February 3, 1954. We know the personal occasion for this outburst, or rather, to put it slightly more cautiously, we are aware of one intimate personal association with it. The septuagenarian artist had been deserted by the young woman with whom he had lived for many years and who had borne him two children.

The subject of these sketches in their endless variations and in the inexhaustible opulence of their beauty, wit, bitterness, grace, fantastic grotesquerie, and sheer magnificence, is almost always one single theme: the painter and his model. And with few exceptions this

27. Ibid., p. 46.
28. *A Suite of 180 Drawings by Picasso, 1953-1954* (*Verve*, 29/30), with preface by Tériade and contributions by Michel Leiris and Rebecca West (New York, 1954).

model is a woman—a naked, beautiful, young woman, whether mobile or at rest, in her infinite variety unerringly alive; and yet in all her aliveness, her beauty and her sometimes provocative sensual appeal, she remains unapproachable and incomprehensible. She is a goddess, although at the same time she is never anything other than a naked woman, beautiful or ugly, clever or foolish and—yes!—even young or old, as the case may be.

The painters, on the other hand, are without number. They include cripples and dwarfs, old and young, the handsome and the repulsive; some shortsightedly fumble at the easel or stare at a single detail of the body, while others are bold youngsters and masters of the art. Yet all of them—even the masculinized woman painter who poises her brush as if it was a spear—are exposed as human, all-too-human creatures when contrasted with the superior being of the naked, silent woman model. But the woman is always the miracle and the enchantress, even when she is only the female acrobat who transfixes the clown with delight and amazement or tempts with an apple the monkey who is clutching her—or even sits as a model for this monkey.

Here we see masks and masquerades, confusions of role and acts of seduction between the male and the female, but in the midst of them all there is the Old Man—the Old Man as painter, as cynic, as ludicrous, daubing graybeard, as a fool and as a cripple, but also as a man possessed and as a wise man.

The almost infinite abundance and the creative multiplicity of these 180 drawings is sufficient by itself to account for the change in the basic theme of what is represented. This transcends the personal suffering of Picasso, expands beyond the problem of painter and model or of man and old age and even beyond the magnificent archetypal pair of the Wise Old Man and the young beloved woman—till ultimately, behind a world which is vibrant with living forms we experience an eternal problem. In itself, each of these sketches is nothing more than a moment captured, an inspiration, a fragment of reality. And yet, together, they amount to something totally different from an aggregate of artistically formulated moments.

This is the abreaction of a trauma, the complex experienced as a wound, the personal element as the spark of ignition and the occasion for achievement—yet all this is fused together in Picasso's passionate concentration; and, though not one single page is formulated as a symbol, the opposition between painter and model becomes the opposition between man and woman, human consciousness and reality, art and life, and at the same time between the shaping, fashioning spirit of man and a nature that cannot be captured or grasped. In the process of artistic creation, however, all this and more is fused together to form a single, visible whole, and the higher unity of psyche and world, life and archetype, uniqueness and eternity, appears before our eyes in the form of an exceedingly earthly symbol: the painter and his model have become to us a symbol of a Great Experience of the totality of reality.

2

The development of ego-consciousness and its polarization into an inner and an outer world are necessarily bound up with the loss of man's primeval life in the unitary reality. It is only from the standpoint of our ego-consciousness that there exists an objective world at all which confronts us as subjects; the existence of a subjective realm of inner psychic processes is equally dependent on this ego-consciousness. However, we too, like the man who is integrated on the primitive level, may be totally present in any situation in which we lack the ego form of consciousness or are not completely identified with it. This can happen insofar as our totality is not disturbed by our existence at the level of ego-consciousness. But in our capacity as the self, as the center of our totality, we are always inhabitants of the unitary reality; and the gulf which has arisen in the development of modern man between life in the polarized world of ego-consciousness and life in the unitary reality is always identical with the gulf between the ego and the self.

The fact that existence in the unitary reality can also be represented by the symbolism of the uroboros, the serpent that bites its own tail, implies that in this reality a host of opposites that are mutually exclusive from the standpoint of ego-consciousness can live together in a state of unity. This is the realm of that unconscious knowledge which we have described as "extraneous"[29] knowledge and the realm, too, of receptive activity, i.e., of an activity which may even be *directed*, but which is at the same time a form of unconscious receptivity, an execution of pre-set directives. Like spontaneity within a framework of necessity, this receptive activity is most

29. See Essay I in this volume.

clearly revealed in the instinct-directed behavior of an animal which fulfills the law prescribed for it transpersonally by its species. But the absence of differentiation between inner and outer and the immediate connection between the individual and the group are no less characteristic of this level of reality where the opposites coexist.

It would be possible to discover a large number of other, analogous paradoxes of the opposites at what we call this "unconscious" phase of existence, which is represented mythologically by the uroboric state of the First Parents conjoined in the calabash.[30]

In the next phase, too, which is not dominated by the First Parents but by the mother-archetype, there is still no trace of an independent principle of consciousness; the father-archetype, which is inseparably connected with the dominance of the conscious mind, is still in the background at this stage. From the point of view of our modern conscious mind, which splits the unitary reality into the polarity of world and psyche, this means that existence in this phase is equally and alternately determined by, and dependent on, the world and the unconscious, though the ego is never conscious that the life of the personality is being determined in this way.

In this original experience of the unitary reality the mundane [welthaft] element is archetypal; this means that the world is experienced, as by a child, in terms of primordial images and not as an objectivized world of concrete entities. Equally, however, the psychic element is "mundane"; this means that everything which we

30. *Origins and History*, p. 9.

would describe as within the psyche is experienced in, and as, outside reality. But the mundane and the psychic are apprehended neither as elements nor as opposites but in a unitary experience. They are not differentiated until the ego and the conscious mind arise; then they become the two worlds, and the appropriate images are assigned to each. This process of splitting reality into partial worlds and the experience of these worlds impresses itself on the conscious mind and makes it appear that there is one image of, for example, the objective sun which is present in outer reality, and which corresponds to a simultaneously appearing symbol of the sun in the psyche. Yet both images are only interpretations of the total experience of the sun in the unitary reality; and this total experience is a third, quite different thing, in which the mundane and the psychic are contained at the same time.

In the course of the development of the ego and the conscious mind, the unitary reality (where it is not projected in mythological terms as a paradisiacal golden age at the dawn of human history) is identified psychologically with the world of the unconscious. From the standpoint of ego-consciousness, existence in the unitary reality is a preconscious and unconscious state of being and the ego and the conscious mind actually experience themselves as having been born out of this unconscious world. Thus the state of being in the unconscious is not, as the polarizing conscious mind supposes, a psychic but a unitary reality, which is just as much outside as inside, just as much psyche as world. When we experience the self or any other archetype in the depths of the unconscious, we always pass from the "purely psychic" realm into a mundane dimension. This is in fact one of the basic phenomena of existence which persuaded us to formulate the concept of the unitary reality: as soon as we leave the narrow circle thrown by the concentrated light of the conscious mind, everything psychic seems to want to link up with something mundane and everything mundane with something psychic, so that something different, a third dimension, seems to be formed.

When ego-consciousness develops away from the unitary reality and the unconscious and at the same time from the dominance of the mother-archetype, it defends itself by erecting a barrier between the ego and the self and by replacing the unconscious total experience of the unitary reality by the conscious ego-experience of the partial worlds, which encompasses the modern individual in the form of the "outside world" and the "psyche." In the normal course of development the conscious mind directs its attention to one or other of these partial worlds; its experience of the world is based on the psychological fact that the original unity of reality has been replaced by a state of separation.

The psychic constellation of creative man differs from that of normal man, and if we fail to understand this, we shall never be able to enter into his psychology, his experience of the world, and his achievement, which are in fact of an essentially different kind. He is actually in a state of heightened inner-psychic tension. On the one hand, he passes through the normal cultural development of the conscious mind; in fact his conscious mind is often—though not always—very strongly developed. On the other hand, however, the relationship between the ego and the self, i.e., the ego-self axis, remains at the very center of his existence, and the separation between the ego and the self has not, as in the case of the average development, resulted in a far-reaching repression of the self. For him, ego-experience does not exclude experience of totality; openness to the partial worlds and perviousness to the unitary reality which underlies them, patient acceptance of the experience of being overwhelmed, and active artistic forming and shaping—these are the tensions between the opposites which are the stuff of life to creative man; his very existence and his productive work depend on the fertile interaction between them. In contrast to the normal course of development, neither the self nor the mother-archetype are repressed in creative man; even the image of the First Parents united in fruitful congress, which is the symbolic representation of the unitary reality, remains very much alive in his psychology.

By calling into being a new "third world" between the partial worlds of inner and outer, art is expressing its determination to create an analogy to the unitary reality or to summon up, at the highest level, an authentic symbol of it. That is exactly what compels the artist, with the aid of color and form, movement and sound, word and stone, to make the inner world into something "outer" that is a new creation, in which outer and inner form a unity. And the same process is at work when, overwhelmed by the shock of some impact from the outside, he responds to this call with the total psychic spontaneity of his personality, allows it to permeate his inner being and to find expression in the form of a third thing which is new and transmuted by his inward experience.

The more one-sided a work of art is, the more it will

partake of the nature of a copy. This means that the more it expresses a partial aspect of the world, whether this is only objective or only subjective, the more imperfect it will remain. Portrayals in naturalistic or in purely psychological terms will be equally photographic and will suffer from the same kind of flatness and artistic inadequacy.

The unitary tendency which is inherent in art always strives to transmute the outside world in the light of the artist's inward experience and by so doing to make it more psychic and more spiritual. And contrariwise, the character of the inner world of the psyche, as revealed, for example, in a vision of hell, will require an infusion of elements from the objective world, with its wealth of plastic colors and forms, before it can be embodied in a new reality. The transformation of a landscape by Rembrandt involves the rendering into artistic form of that living dimension of the unitary reality which spans the gulf between man's soul and nature; while the exteriorization of a tract of the inner world in the paintings of Bosch, El Greco, or Goya and the transformation of a "thing" or object from the so-called objective world into an animated being with a living soul in the work of Van Gogh or Cézanne both result in a new synthesis of reality. Most frequently this conquest of the polarization of the conscious mind and the tendency to reunite the opposites are revealed in the most natural way in that function of art which unites the elements, contents, and tendencies of the conscious mind with those of the unconscious.

The unitary world of the First Parents and the unity between the opposites represented by the father and the mother archetypes which is the dominant influence in that world are succeeded in the course of the development of the ego and the conscious mind by a constellation which—to put it simply—takes the form of a tension between the opposite poles of the Heavenly Father and the Earth Mother; this in turn corresponds to the opposition between spirit and nature, and also to that between the subjective inner world of the psyche and the objective outside world.[31] However, whereas Western man, insofar as he is conscious, lives in this state of polar tension, the activity of art as an expression of the creative principle in man is continually finding new ways of bridging this gulf between the opposites.

At this point we can distinguish two differently accentuated creative and formative artistic processes, depending on whether the main emphasis lies with the archetype of the mother or of the father. We shall try to throw some light on these opposite forms of the creative principle, though in modern times we shall encounter mainly mixed forms and in fact even in the development of a single artist we can identify periods in which first the one and then the other principle is the dominant influence.

The fact that in creative man the dominant influence is matriarchal implies that not only the content of his art but also the nature of the creative and of the formative principle in his work is determined by the predominance of the mother-archetype. In matriarchal consciousness,[32] fantasy, inspiration, and "sudden ideas" are

31. Ibid., passim.
32. "Ueber den Mond" (see above, n. 6).

the dominant influence, with the result that there is a spontaneous productivity in the unconscious, while the manner in which this is treated and developed by the artist is a process that happens essentially "of itself" in the form of an inner growth, a pregnancy and a birth, or even as a breakthrough or an inundation in which the unconscious takes over the leading role. Possession, mediumship, and passivity are the outstanding characteristics, of a personality of this type, in which the ego is comparatively weakly developed and tends to play the part of an accompanist or of a midwife rather than that of an active shaper and molder of the material.

All primary art is matriarchal. This applies not only to mantic and prophetic poetry, but also, for example, to those forms of art which are bound up with ritual.

Primary art is dictated to the ego by archetypal powers. Yet matriarchal art is by no means confined to the early history of the human species. All forms of romantic, intuitive, and visionary art and almost all lyrical poetry belong to the sphere of the matriarchal. Wherever the expressive element is dominant and the formal element is in the background, the world that is accentuated by the maternal principle is the controlling power.

Yet it is not only the content of art and the type of creative work involved, but also the formal principle itself that is determined by the dominance of the archetype. Under the governance of the matriarchal power, the formal principle corresponds to the creative unconscious itself, which is only received and to some extent reproduced by the personality of the artist. In this case the primal form acts as an autonomous power that dictates to the ego, and the formative artist resembles a tool as he "obeys" and "serves" a form already pre-existent in nature that imposes itself and is neither made nor invented by ego-consciousness. The Great Mother[33] is also the bearer of the world of spirit, light, and form, and as such she is the mistress of the matriarchal world of the creative. However, in spite of the dominance of the matriarchal principle, patriarchal traits are also to be found in this type of creativity. Here too the ego and the conscious mind already intervene; they play a part in, and carry further, the process of formation. Contents of the conscious mind are now fitted into the material received from the unconscious; they transcend this material, and as development progresses, patriarchal consciousness begins to assert itself with ever-increasing power and to process, interpret, and formulate what is happening from its own point of view.

The dominance of the father-archetype, in complete contrast to that of the mother, invariably entails an accentuation of all those aspects of the material that are bound up with the affirmation and development of the conscious mind. In this sense patriarchal art is a celebration of the principle of light and of the hero; its real concern is the victory of goodness and of the conscious mind and the glorification of the highest values of the cultural canon—modified according to the requirements of the age and culture concerned. In the process, however, the scope of the father-archetype is reduced in a way characteristic of patriarchal art. The original ambivalent numinosity of the father-archetype, which contains both good and evil, is broken down, the unfath-

33. Cf. Neumann, *The Great Mother.*

omable nature of the *deus absconditus* (the "hidden god")
is repressed and split off in the form of the devil, and
the father-archetype becomes identified with its exclusively good and just side.

However, more is involved in patriarchal dominance
than a specific formal principle that is opposed to the
corresponding matriarchal principle: a reinforcement
and over-accentuation of the formal principle in general
is also entailed. Here "formal principle" denotes a "will
to form." In contrast to the process of being led by the
unconscious this conscious formal principle imposes its
will by working on the formal aspect of artistic creation
and by striving, over and over again, to "work up" what
has already been formed in the interests of a higher order which is known, seen, and willed and to which ego-
consciousness now conforms.

For the patriarchal type of creativity, beauty is not
something pre-existent in nature that man is bound to
obey. The endless abundance of beauty poured out by
the unconsciously formative reality of nature is not recognized by the patriarchal artist as something "given,"
while from the *matriarchal* point of view the "Right
Form" only requires, as it were, to be extricated from
the slag in which it is embedded, and its character as
something previously given and already existent in nature will be recognized by creative man. (In Dürer's
phrase, "Art is hidden in nature.") From the *patriarchal*
viewpoint, on the other hand, the process of formation
is seen as the imprinting of a higher stamp on a passive,
lower material that is, in itself, chaotic. And the stamp
is in this case co-ordinate with the form of the patriarchal spiritual world of heaven, whereas matter is co-or-

dinate with the formless *mater materia*, and the connection between the form-giving and the form-bearing principle of the mother-archetype remains unknown. Here forms and the conscious mind appear together in the guise of a principle of strife, which subordinates, dominates, and compels; and beauty, in the words of Herbert Read,[34] is "set up in opposition to the chaos that surrounds us on every side."

Strict form, considered in its tendency to abstraction as essentially a triumph over matter, is therefore invariably patriarchal; and this tendency ranges from the geometrizing principle of primitive man to the loftiest examples of hieratic art, and from stylization as a means of transforming the "merely natural" to the supreme formal austerity of Bach's music. The patriarchal trend reaches its most radical extreme in the principle of hostility to images as such which distinguishes the religions of Judaism and Islam. Here the only imagery that survives is the pure form of symbolism represented by written characters, and this in fact excludes everything matriarchal and is the most abstract affirmation of the father-archetype that exists.

If the great danger of the matriarchal principle is to be found in quivering chaos, the great danger of the patriarchal principle, bound up as it is by its very nature with the ethos and will of the conscious mind and with law, order, and strict form, is to be found in rigidity, as we know very well from the decay of all art that is academic, tradition-bound, and only "conscious"—from

34. [The critic and poet Read (1893-1968) shared the Eranos platform with Neumann at this and several other Eranos conferences. This quotation could not be traced.]

captious criticism of the Beckmesser[35] school to solemn moralistic didactic poetry.

The content and form of "great art" is almost invariably a combination of matriarchal and patriarchal elements, and the creative process involved in such art also consists of a synthesis of both types of creation. The youthful work of so-called classical poets is in general typically matriarchal, while their maturity is characterized by a reinforcement of the patriarchal emphasis. From Schiller's *Die Räuber* to his *Wallenstein*, from Goethe's *Götz von Berlichingen* to his *Torquato Tasso*, from prose to verse, from free rhythm to metrical form, the trend towards synthesis is always the same. Yet even a radically patriarchal principle cannot exist without the matriarchal world.[36]

This dependence on the matriarchal principle has perhaps never been so distinctly and unequivocally expressed by any other poet as it has been by Hebbel. His formulation is all the more remarkable since the conscious, thinking side of his nature is in general almost too strongly emphasized. He expresses his surprise that "even men of insight never cease to quarrel with the poet about what they call his choice of material. By so doing they reveal that when they are thinking about ar-

35. [A commonplace pedant in Wagner's *Die Meistersinger von Nürnberg*.]

36. Only a detailed individual analysis can reveal the nature of the archetype that dominates the process of artistic production in any given case. For example, in addition to the primary expressionism of the unconscious in modern art, there is an expressionism of the conscious mind, and in surrealism we have a quasi-matriarchal dominance of the creative process which is nevertheless demanded by the arbitrary preference of a patriarchal principle in the conscious mind.

tistic creation, whose first stage, the stage of receiving and conceiving, is to be found, after all, deep down below the level of the conscious mind and sometimes in the darkest remoteness of childhood, they invariably picture it, albeit glorified, as a kind of 'making' and project into the psychic process of giving birth an arbitrariness of selection which they would certainly never attribute to the corresponding physical process, whose inseparable connection with nature admittedly springs far more clearly to the naked eye."[37]

This cooperation and interaction between the matriarchal and patriarchal principles, between inspired idea and conscious elaboration, between what is given and received and what has to be shaped and realized, can be shown to exist in all creative processes, but particularly in all forms of art; the work of synthesizing inner and outer as well as subjective and objective components is an essential part of all types of artistic production and can be found in painting and sculpture as well as in music and poetry.

On this question of the concerted unison between matriarchal and patriarchal elements which characterizes the work of every great artist, Dostoevski expressed his opinion in the following simple words, which are taken from his letter to his brother: "It is only now and again that sudden inspiration is vouchsafed; everything else means painful toil. . . . It is clear that you are confusing, as often happens, inspiration, that is, first momentary creation of the picture, or the stirring of the soul, with work. Thus, for instance, I make note at once of a scene

37. Friedrich Hebbel, foreword to *Maria Magdalene* [1844].

just as it appeared to me, and I am delighted: then, for months, for a year even, I work at it ... and believe me, the finished article is much superior. Provided, of course, that the inspiration is vouchsafed! Naturally without inspiration nothing can be accomplished."[38]

Jung connects the "transcendent function" of the pysche, which arises out of the tension between the opposites of the conscious mind and the unconscious in the form of a third thing which creatively overcomes this tension—with the symbol, considered as a content of the psyche.[39] As we have hitherto understood it, this uniting function comes into play on the inner side of the psyche, between ego-consciousness and the unconscious. On the other hand, if we approach the subject from the point of view of the unitary reality, which underlies both the world and the psyche, it becomes apparent that the symbolism of the transcendent function is also more than simply psychic. Although it approaches us by way of what we call the unconscious, it invariably contains within itself a mundane element. Whether it contains the solution of an inner or an outer problem, the transcendent function always includes within itself a "way," a transformation, something which has to be done; it never remains, in its essential nature, a "vision," but is always a guiding principle whose demands have to be fulfilled in life.

This special emphasis on the unitary element in the archetypal, the theoretical implications of which for our

38. Quoted in André Gide, *Dostoevsky*, tr. anon. (London, 1925), p. 16. [Letter to brother Michael, March 24, 1845.]

39. Jung, *Psychological Types*, CW 6, par. 828. [Cf. also "The Transcendent Function" (1916/1957; CW 8), pars. 131ff.]

conception of the unconscious cannot concern us here, does at least make it possible for us to understand one absolutely essential factor in the psychology of creative man. We can now grasp the nature of the compulsive drive of the so-called "inner" contents and tendencies to "realize" themselves, the trend that leads them, in co-operation with, or even against the will of, creative man to force their way through and "to come into the world." The inner contents yearn to break out from their purely psychic habitation, and like the shades in Homer's underworld they thirst for the blood that will make it possible for them to realize themselves. This compulsive drive to realization, which is a living factor in everything creative, belongs to the essential nature of the unitary reality, which manifests itself alike in the creativity of nature and in that of the psyche, and urges man on to unite them both.

Not only is creative man constrained to endure the tension between the opposites of world and psyche; he must also obey the trend to realization of the unitary reality itself, which impinges upon him from within and without. This forces him to "transcend"—i.e., to break through the partial worlds—and by so doing to achieve the "Great Experience." In fact, creative man must be actively and regeneratively engaged in an open relationship, not only with the unconscious and the world, but also with the self; as a personality he is at once imperilled and inspired by his position as the center of an existence which embraces him, as it embraces every man, in the form of the creative unconscious and the creative world, but which at the same time continually appeals to him and challenges him in the name of the creative self.

In its highest manifestation the task of the artist would appear to be the opposite of the deed of the mythical hero of consciousness, who separates the World Parents from one another and splits the world itself into a system of polarities.[40] The artist's task is the reverse of the hero's, inasmuch as his work requires him to reunite the split world through the formative power of his creative Eros, and in this way to restore a fragment of the unitary reality.[41]

Whereas in normal development, when the primal constellation of the earliest period (i.e., the unitary reality or, in mythological terms, the unity of the combined Paternal and Maternal principles) has been repressed, something more than a simple archetypal memory is retained in the open structure of creative man. Precisely because, in his heightened state of total tension, he experiences the "dismemberment" of the world and the corresponding dismemberment of his own psyche in an acuter and more disquieting form than normal man, the imperative need to counterbalance this tension is one of the fundamental constellations of his creative existence. In fact, it is only by restoring his connection with the unitary reality that he can achieve the restoration of his own personality, on which in turn the fashioning of his work is based.

It is one of the prerequisites for the creation of a "great work of art" that the total personality of the artist

40. *Origins and History*, p. 9.
41. See above, Essay II.

should be committed to the task. If no more than his conscious mind—his will, his knowledge or his organizing ability—are actively engaged, or if only parts of the unconscious, such as his personal complexes, enter in, he will undertake his work as only a partial personality. This implies, however, that the world which encounters the artist and enters into the fashioning of his work will be as narrowly personal and partial as the layers of his personality that are committed to the task. And when we distinguish—however problematical that may be—between a work of art and a great work of art, this distinction is actually based on the fact that the extent to which the creative personality is integrated in his involvement corresponds to the extent to which reality is apprehended in his work. It is only when the personality has been mobilized in this way that the tension between the opposite poles, represented by the personality and the objective psyche on the one hand and the personality and the world on the other, can be transcended, and a new constellation emerges, in which the personality and the world experienced by it can be seen to be a part of the unitary reality. This unique condition of creative man, which is at the same time collected and ecstatic, since it is not exclusively centered in the ego, imparts to the work its transcendent appeal and that unmistakable stamp of revelation which makes it independent of style, time, and the individuality of the artist and guarantees its status as a "great work of art." In the unity and totality of such a "great work," we are in fact experiencing something more than the corresponding qualities in the creative man who produced it. It is only when, through a great work of art, we have been able to experience the unity and wholeness of reality itself that our experience becomes the "Great Experience."

Whether we look at it from the phylogenetic or the ontogenetic standpoint, the original *participation mystique* of the child is prior to ego-consciousness. On the other hand, the more recently attained form of *participation mystique* which comes into play between creative man and reality is accompanied by a very high degree of concentration and development in the conscious mind. This constellation of wholeness and unity into which creative man and his old reality have become absorbed is the indispensable prerequisite for that general "loosening-up" of existence from which the great work can crystallize out as a symbol of the unitary reality. We shall find it scarcely possible to formulate this constellation in rational terms; however, if we apply the categories of our conscious minds, we can say of it that it involves a total extension of the psyche over the world, so that it would appear to us as if reality had been "psychized" or animated by a soul. At the same time, however, we should also be obliged to formulate the situation from the opposite point of view. The world would then appear to have absorbed everything psychic and it would only be through this absorption of the psychic dimension that the world could realize itself as a cosmos of wholeness, in which everything is at the same time living and mundane, and even the contents of what used to be called "psyche" would assume a mundane character. It is difficult indeed to formulate this borderline experience and constellation in such a way that it does not appear to be "mystical." Yet what we are concerned with in this context is in fact an exceedingly everyday phenomenon. We must never forget that it is only in our ego-consciousness that we live in the partial worlds: in our relationship with the self and with wholeness we always live our lives in the unitary reality. And if we look closer, we shall find that every "Great Experience" and the experience of every "great work of art" always transports us into this state of deep involvement, quasi-mystical because it transcends the conscious mind in which the unitary reality can truly speak to us.

In the case of one artist——Leonardo da Vinci, for example——the intensity of this all-embracing experience leads onwards, through a long process of maturation, to a final stage in which a reality becomes transparent whose spiritual beauty can be experienced as the personal presence of the World Soul.[42] In contrast to this, the work of another artist—Picasso for instance—is invariably the spontaneous response to a single "impression." Art as a type of continuing work is replaced in Picasso by the rendering into artistic form of what Braque has called "the everlasting present."[43] Yet this total response presupposes nothing less than Picasso's total commitment. It has been said of him that "he is so completely dominated by this total response that the most competent observer could only describe his mental condition at such moments as a trance. The doors of the unconscious then open before him and new visions flood his imagination and enrich his memories of the visible

42. Neumann, "Leonardo and the Mother Archetype," in *Art and the Creative Unconscious*.

43. "Vivre et faire vivre le perpétuel présent," in *Eight European Artists*, ed. and photographed Felix H. Man (London, Melbourne, and New York, 1954), opening page (unfoliated).

world with memories of other, invisible worlds. 'If you want to draw, you must shut your eyes and sing,' says Picasso. And this same Picasso, who sometimes practiced drawing in the dark, often said that painting is an occupation for a blind man."[44] This basic attitude of Picasso's, which insists that only the fulfilled creative moment can comprehend the world, is in complete accord with Blake's aphorism, "Exuberance is Beauty,"[45] and the same attitude again finds expression in words of Blake, when, with specific reference to works of art, he tells us, "To finish a thing is to kill it, to destroy its soul."[46]

The differences in temperament, style, and method or type of creation which distinguish different artists correspond, in each case, to a different facet or aspect of the many-sided radiance that streams out from the unitary reality. But wherever, shining through the partial reality, this wholeness of reality finds it possible to manifest itself in a work of art, we may be sure that we are in the presence of a precipitate of a "Great Experience." The breakthrough to the "Great Experience" which is characteristic of creative man always involves a conquest of fear and of constricting narrowness. Life in the conscious mind and in the nothing-but-partial worlds is invariably subject to a feeling of dissatisfaction and deficiency, since there is something within us all the time that is aware of another and greater reality, in the presence of which our life might be lived. This basic feeling

44. Wilhelm Boeck and Jaime Sabartés, *Picasso* (Stuttgart, 1955), p. 60.
45. "Proverbs of Hell," *The Marriage of Heaven and Hell*, pl. 10.
46. [Untraced in the published writings.]

of deprivation, which is a living element in all religions of redemption, is caused by the inescapable contrast between the experience of the ego and the experience of the self. As Kafka put it, "There exist in the same human being varying perceptions of one and the same object which differ so completely from each other that one can only deduce the existence of different subjects in the same human being."[47]

When normal man, in the course of his development, achieves identification with ego-consciousness, he automatically falls into the world of polarization, which is a narrowed and, in religious terms, a "fallen" world. He has been driven out of the paradise of the unitary reality; with the loss of the attachment of the ego to the self he has also lost his life in the world of man's primordial origins. The religions of redemption represent an attempt to regain this world in the future, or, alternatively, to abolish the world by means of a mystical breakthrough of the individual ego to the self. "Great art," on the other hand, derives its life from the "unlost" present of this primordial world itself; it represents a continual effort to attain and to depict this world by means of a breakthrough to the "Great Experience." And whereas in the conceptual language of religion the unitary reality appears as the beginning of the world (in paradise) and as the end of the world (in the final redemption), for "great art" and for creative man it is the real world of the enduring present.

The narrowing down of conscious existence, which

47. Kafka, "Reflections," no. 68, in *The Great Wall of China: Stories and Reflections*, tr. Willa and Edmund Muir (New York, 1946), p. 295. [In Neumann's original text, Betrachtung no. 72.]

excludes our own unconscious experience of wholeness, is felt inwardly by us as imprisonment in a conditioned existence, an unfree state in which we have been squeezed into the experience of the polarizing ego. Though we fit into the partial worlds in an apparently sensible manner, we still remain in this condition of imprisonment. When Dostoevski warns us, "No high aim is worth a life wrecked,"[48] what he has in mind is this same self-imprisonment, which in the shape of goal and task, work and the finished product of work, threatens creative man more, perhaps, than it threatens anyone else, since it stands in the way of the real meaning of existence—that is to say, of life in freedom and abundance.

This state of being shut into the world, into the body, into a situation, a milieu, a task, a belief, a condition, is always a state of being buried alive. To be bound down in this way, and not to be in one's real place, is a form of suffering and is invariably accompanied by a feeling of anxiety. Just because "great art" is a breakthrough from this state of constriction, this is one of its basic themes. Whether it takes the form of a medieval representation of hell, of a naturalistic milieu painting of a slum, of man's fallen state as a result of sin or of political imprisonment, of a Kafkaesque condition of being fettered by the authorities,[49] or of the apathy and torpor of Van Gogh's potato-eaters—in every case, since it is ar-

---

48. Gide, *Dostoevsky*, p. 36.

49. [Cf. Neumann, "Kafka's 'The Trial,'" *Creative Man*, p. 12: "It is significant that there is a passage in *The Castle* which informs us that accidents are always on the side of the authorities."—Tr.]

chetypal, it is a basic problem of creative man, and of man and existence in the world as such.

When, however, we are gripped and deeply moved by "great art," we are liberated from our "shut-in" state and transported into the restored, total reality, and this happens irrespective of whether the experience that makes us whole is the effect of light in a Rembrandt, a melody by Mozart, or the experience of the wholeness of a fully realized creative structure, when we are carried away by the unitary reality that speaks to us from out of the unity of the work. The redeeming power that grips us and moves us so deeply, however widely we may differ in period and nationality, in individuality and age, in mood and levels of development, is always an expression of the "Great Experience" and without exception represents a liberation of our personality. At the same time, however, it also clarifies our vision of the world. For example, even when the power that overwhelms us appears in the guise of the symbolic world of narrowness—the image, that is, of our own imprisonment—we are liberated by the distance imparted to our experience by the artistic mastery of the creative man, who is only able to give form to this constriction because his own roots lie outside that experience, so that he is in a position to direct our attention to another, quite different world of freedom.

Since we ourselves are the mass men of the great cities, the sinners in hell, and the prisoners in the dungeon, the darkness of art is always speaking to us out of ourselves. But the state of redemption as it is depicted in art also grips us and moves us in a multiplicity of different levels and forms. We are the liberated captives in Bee-thoven's *Fidelio* and in Wagner's *Liebestod*; as we absorb the streaming torrent of associations in Joyce's *Ulysses* we also leave behind us the fetters of our constricting narrowness, and whether in the tranquillity and open-ness of a Chinese landscape or when a great poem comes surging through our being, we are liberated from that state of imprisonment which is actually ourselves.

The representation in artistic form of the archetypes that are living forces in the human race has from time immemorial been one of the quintessential contents of all art, and of religious art in particular. However, this process of rendering visible the transpersonal has always in practice been committed to the service of the cultural canon of a given epoch, whether the subjects prescribed were gods and saviors or narratives depicting the origin of the world and of man. As we know, the treasure house of the art of humanity is replete with the inex-haustible multiplicity of the images that speak to us of the "great" experience which transcends the ego. But what we would assert concerning the "Great Experi-ence" of art is a different matter.

When that which is religious in an archetypal sense is built into the canon of a specific culture, the archetype, in that very process, inevitably loses part of its numinous content; the archetypal figure is, to a certain extent, "grasped," and often enough, in its treatment as part of an established world-picture, it becomes a representa-tion of something "known." As a result, the nature of the holy, as it is canonized in this sense, is something essentially different from the experience of the unitary reality. For religion, that which is represented in this way is no more than a memorial of the archetypal event, irrespective of its artistic value or valuelessness. It is questionable whether, for the believers in any particular form of religion, the greatness of a work of art has any significance at all—questionable, for example, whether Grünewald's *Crucifixion* must necessarily mean more to the man who is contained within the religious canon than a cheap oleograph of the same "happening." Yet a "thing" which is shaped and given form by an artist—a chair, for example, or a vessel of some kind—can be an expression of the "Great Experience," whereas a primordial image, given shape and form as part of a religious canon, does not need to be anything more than a pointer and a channel of information.

On the other hand, the relativity of human experience is shown by the fact that the inspirational moment of a person's religious experience can be precipitated by the most abysmally sentimental kitsch, if that is how the primordial image is actually encountered by him or her, whereas a work of genius by an inspired artist may prove incapable of penetrating the barrier set up by the conscious mind of that particular person.

However, for a period such as our own, which is no longer contained within any cultural canon, art and its "Great Experience" mean something more vital and essential than ever before. For us, the experience of the transpersonal is no longer bound up with specific contents prescribed by our culture, in which "true" life is concentrated; and yet, in an inner compensation for this deficiency, the whole of reality has come to be, for us, pregnant with the possibility of the numinous. We may encounter the "Great Experience" as a possibility in the "great art" of the entire world, and, equally well, in every part of a reality that has become transparent to us. That is why we can have a living encounter with the "Great Experience" in the images created by both religious and profane art, in the total artistic output of creative man, and, just as effectively, in a fulfilled moment in the life of an anonymous individual.

In every case, this experience involves a breakthrough to the greater reality which embraces, completes, and crowns our partial realities; yet at the same time it always involves a dawning of transparency, in which the super-real, whether it appears in the guise of the terrible, of grace, of destructibility or of the indestructible, becomes visible to our sight as the authentic reality.

The forms assumed by the transition from the partial world to the unitary reality are manifold; yet in every case the experience includes a process of being gripped and stirred to the depths by archetypal atmospheres or "moods," which throb through the world of archetypal contents; or alternatively, the experience can take the form of a mood which is felt as such, in its own right. The indestructible or the terrible can present themselves in an endless variety of archetypal symbols: the former as a mandala, a diamond, and a blossom, and the latter as a devouring mouth, hell, or an abyss; but it can also appear as the atmosphere or mood (of a landscape, for example), which penetrates, like a kind of invisible essence, the visible atmosphere that we see.

The experience of the archaic is one of the forms that can be assumed by this openness in the face of a specific mood or atmosphere of the unitary reality. The world of the childlike dawn of mankind can appear in the guise of the magnificence of Giotto or as "primitiveness" in the paintings of "Le Douanier" Rousseau; alternatively, it can become visible to us in the abstraction of lines and forms and in their reduction to cubes and cylinders. It can emerge when the simplification of the human figure, a presence without perspective before the golden background of the world, a hierarchical stance viewed in profile, or the tightly dovetailed fuguelike structure of a choral work provides us with a living illustration of the eternity of a world that is everlastingly present; yet in every case, we find ourselves confronted with the ineffable magnificence of something which can never be grasped, but which animates everything that is real as a crowning, super-real essence.

However, the world of the sublime and the ideal, of the exemplary or of the primordially symbolic, can appear just as well in the human figure; it is possible, for example, that in the closed completeness of an ancient Egyptian statue of a king, in the ideal humanity of a classical Greek torso, or in the superhuman grandeur of a Michelangelo prophet, the "Great Experience" of art can lift us beyond the limitations of our egos into that freedom of the self which belongs, as it were, to the "Great Man" and which can be our own in every moment that is fully grasped and realized. For the freedom of the greater reality is a human possibility that is open to every one of us; like the world itself, it is ready for us at any time, and this in no way excludes its super-real dimension. Franz Kafka's testimony about the world of the Trial, which is valid for every "Great Experience," is no less applicable to this super-reality: "It receives you when you come and it relinquishes you when you go."[50]

50. Ibid., p. 108.

Yet side by side with this world of magnificence there also exists a dimension of uncanniness and sheer horror which treads the world beneath its feet with the deadly momentum of the dancing Shiva. The realm of the daemonic, of malicious sorcery and enchantment, of the morbidly grotesque, the perverse and the bizarre, lives out its spectral life cheek by jowl with the windows and gates of the dwelling place of our consciousness; it is the primordial serpent at the bottom of the sea that girdles our world, creeps up the sky as the dark moon, and brings with it unrest and despair, torment and hopelessness, mental aberration and madness.

In the musical hell of Hieronymus Bosch, the instruments that in Paradise resounded with songs of praise are transformed, by a frightful inversion, into instruments of torment. Today, infected as we are by the daemonic side of existence, we ourselves are living in the uncanny world of a hell created by modern physics; the mandala-like cosmos of a universe consisting of world-systems and atoms revolving around one another in orderly measure has started to jump about like quanta and to radiate its energy outwards into nothingness—only to emerge out of it again, from somewhere or other, in such a way that this same so-called nothingness that is beyond the range of our experience has itself become one of the "Great Experiences" of our time.

Human reason struggles to eliminate this world of creative and at the same time deadly explosions, which threaten us with annihilation, by enlisting the aid of the order of our conscious minds and the magnificent logical consistency of our intellect. But Blake's aphorism, "Improvement makes strait roads; but the crooked roads without Improvement are roads of Genius," is all the truer in that it originates among the "Proverbs of Hell."[51] Creative genius is never possible without the proximity of the devil, who, in his capacity as God's shadow, is apparently unable to discriminate between destroying and creating. The crooked ways—or what seem to our conscious minds the crooked ways—of our unconscious: these are the ways, so disconcerting to ego-consciousness, of the serpent, the representative of a greater and more uncanny reality than we are able to bear. As Blake, once again, puts it: "The roaring of lions, the howling of wolves, the raging of the stormy sea and the destructive sword, are portions of eternity, too great for the eye of man."[52] This uncanny world is alive in Dostoevski's characters and in man's power to conceive of an existence such as hell; it is alive, too, in the daemonic power of mental illness and in the vitality of evil in the world. It is alive in that aspect of nature which seems to us to be destructive—in the meaningful way in which snakes are guided as they pursue their prey and the no less masterly fashion in which the rabies virus is directed as it destroys human life.[53] When we are confronted by this uncannily destructive force, the "Great Experience" grips and fascinates us in the form of what appears to us as the ambiguous aspect of the Godhead, which holds the world and ourselves as help-less objects in its mighty hand, and in face of which the

51. *The Marriage of Heaven and Hell*, pl. 10.
52. Ibid., pl. 8.
53. Adolf Portmann, "Das Lebendige als vorbereitete Beziehung," *EJ 1955*; idem, "Die Bedeutung der Bilder in der lebendigen Ener-giewandlung," in *Biologie und Geist* (Zurich, 2nd ed., 1959).

logical consistency of our conscious minds and the efforts we make to plumb the unplumbable are turned into a laughingstock by this terrible daemonic power.

Yet the indestructible, which seems to find no place in the narrow world of our factual actuality, is just as capable of providing the content for a "Great Experience" as the destructive aspect. This indestructible element is always something formless which is given artistic form; its true location is to be found neither in the "reality" of the world nor in the human soul when it is removed from the world, but in the unitary reality which is apprehended and given form by great art.

The indestructible can manifest itself alike in the sustained treble of a string quartet, and in the fleeting, elusive shimmer of colors in an impressionist landscape, which can often tell us more about the enduring beauty of everything transitory than a philosophy that proclaims the reality of the enduring. The indestructible is equally alive in the smile of a portrait by Leonardo, in the attitude of a Gothic statue of a saint, in a poem by Li Tai Po, in a Greek torso, or in one of Hokusai's woodcuts of Fujiyama. For the simple reason that Hokusai does not portray Fujiyama as a holy mountain with the sacral solemnity of a religious painting, but shows it embedded in the everyday reality of an earthly existence, the eternally real world of the indestructible achieves authentic artistic expression in his work. From time immemorial, Fujiyama has been, for Japan, the holy mountain, a holy place, a symbol of eternity, a revered and acknowledged concept. But what does a holy mountain mean to us—whether it is called Sinai, Olympus, or Fujiyama? Ashamed and almost literally embarrassed, we let our eyes slip away from these mountains, which are living examples of symbolic reality, but to ourselves represent simply rocks to be climbed, and as such rather sobering portions of our outside reality— even before the holy place has become the destination, first of a procession and then, later, of an excursion for tourists.

But Hokusai's Fujiyama is eternal. Whether it rises above a landscape animated by people wandering at its base, or almost disappears, as a strange and disconcerting presence, among the umbrellas of an umbrella-maker; whether it shrouds itself behind veils of rain or rests, calm in its unchanging majesty, above the thunderstorm that threatens the little village far below, or stands, remote on the horizon, as if on the margin of the world, above the peaceful bay on which people are sailing in little boats, or looks down, in falling snow, on people laboriously picking their way—Hokusai's Fujiyama remains eternal. As the Fujiyama of the animals it is always the One, always the same, always consistent with its own being—and yet, at the same time, it is always alive, though in a dimension that is wholly other than anything connected with "here!" or "there!" The stag breathes in the air that is dominated by this Fujiyama, and by night the wild dog howls before its black silhouette, the wild geese fly above its reflection in the water, and in a world of meaningful interconnections the white heron stands in the white snow by the white mountain. But again, behind the young bamboos as they thrust their way up towards the light in the dense abundance of their clustering leaves, its shielding eternity rises still; and it stands, too, unshakably there, behind the gigantic parabola of the crashing wave.

The eternal dimension of the "Great Experience" does not in any way depend upon whether it takes the form of mountain or flower, animal or man; in every case it is something transcendent which leaves mere reality behind it. Whether this transcendent dimension appears as something unreal or super-real, beautiful or ugly, as primordial form or as sheer superabundance, as the ideally perfect or the grotesquely horrible, it is always something more, something different, a "not-only-this," where "this" takes the form of a partial reality in the experience of our conscious minds. It speaks to us in the purity of abstract form and in the riotous sculptural overgrowth of an Indian temple, in the archaic simplicity of early Greek plastic art and in the uncanny musical graphics of Klee, in the turgid grandiloquence of Wagner and in the formal virtuosity of Bach's *Art of the Fugue*; we meet it again in the wild forest notes of a woman singer from the jungle of Peru and in the homely simplicity of a European folksong, and in every case it speaks to us about the "Great Experience" of the unitary reality, which is alive in us and around us and constitutes a unique dimension of creative existence that can never be grasped by our conscious minds.

Yet this unitary reality is capable of being experienced by every human being, and creative man the world over has the power to be gripped by it and in turn to fashion it and express it in artistic form. In man, too, the profusion of reality bubbles over in the abundance of the material that is struggling to express itself and in the forms assumed by the expression of this abundance itself. In fact, everything speaks to us of this abundance—from the miniature paintings illuminating the pages of an early medieval sacred text to Ice Age Man's cave paintings and the pyramids of Mexico. We find it alike in the biblical story of man's salvation and in the bringers of salvation among the primitives, in the enlightenment of the Buddha, and in the death of the saints. But the same abundance can also appear in the great tide of human existence portrayed for us in the novels of Balzac or Zola. It can shine in the flowering of an individual, whose reality may be concentrated in a single day of his life, as in Joyce's *Ulysses*, or in the day of his death, as in Hermann Broch's *Death of Vergil*, which reaches out from the age of Augustus to the background of eternity.

Yet even "great art" can still be a negative influence that clings to tradition, if it fails to provide the people who experience it with a "turning" point, a streaming moment, as flowing and ungraspable as the vitality of life itself.[54] For the infinite abundance of the art of humanity presupposes a corresponding abundance of human responses. Creative man, the world that appeals to him, and the fruit it bears in his own work are in fact only one side of the "Great Experience." Human openness and readiness to receive "great art" or alternatively to remain closed and unmoved by it form the other side of this living happening. Like the world in its entirety, art itself is a world of the Holy Spirit that bloweth where it listeth, and we too are in this sense continually climbing and falling, open and closed at the same time.

54. See Neumann, "Creative Man and Transformation," in *Art and the Creative Unconscious*.

In our closed-ness we share in the world of anxiety and narrowness, in our openness we share in the world of the unitary reality and of fulfillment.

The tendency to pass beyond the boundaries of partial reality in the "Great Experience" is so deeply grounded in man's innermost being that in the most extraordinary way it makes no difference to our state of being gripped and profoundly moved if, for example, a human figure that makes it possible for us to attain this experience is derived from the reality of art or from the reality of life itself. It does not matter whether this super-real reality grips and moves us in the form of Don Quixote, Don Juan, and Faust, or as Alexander the Great and Julius Caesar, Goethe and Nietzsche. The great figures in human history stand cheek by jowl with the figures of great poetry as the bearers and realizers of "Great Experience." In every case it is the overflowing abundance of the myth within ourselves that is renewed and confirmed by its echo in the world outside. And whether at one time it is an individual and at another a whole nation that is lifted up by this abundance, whether it is human figures from the inner or the outer world, whether styles and *Weltanschauungen*, philosophies and sciences, rise or fall, it seems that mankind is not so greatly concerned about a truth that only come to life in the changing forms in which it is manifested, but rather that its attention is held by an eternal dimension which illuminates all these changing forms.

For creative man himself, the "Great Experience" and its fashioning into artistic form constitute the reality of his existence; however, in a wider context it is a vital necessity of life for every man, since without the "Great

Experience" either direct or mediated, man atrophies and pines away. It is not simply that its fashioning into artistic form has a therapeutic effect on creative man: its experience has a therapeutic effect on everybody. Since the creative work of art is only made possible by the artist's connection with the self and the restoration of the wholeness of life, the man who encounters the "Great Experience" indirectly as an experience of art is also enabled to transcend the restrictedness of his own conscious mind and his ego. And by experiencing the process of becoming whole in himself, he also—without knowing it—experiences the split world as restored and made whole.[55]

However, there is something of even greater and more central significance than the "Great Experience" of art (which in a sense is still always a product of culture), and that is the individual's direct experience of the unitary reality, which remains unexpressed—apart from the fact that it transforms him. The effect of this experience appears to be invisible; but while "great art," for whoever experiences it, represents a new opportunity for the subject, at least temporarily, to overcome his own narrowness, the anonymous "Great Experience" of the moment that is lived, the moment whose true life is only to be found in the innermost being of the subject, is nothing less than the living core of the vital principle itself. In every moment, every thing, every plant, every animal—in all of them, as individual beings, there lives

55. Cf. the religious and cosmological significance of the concept of Tikkun in the cabala, as in Gershom Scholem, "Tradition und Neuschöpfung im Ritus der Kabbbalisten," *EJ 1950.*

the possibility of wholeness. It is possible to experience the abundance of reality in and as each one of them. It is not for nothing that anything or everything can occupy the center of the mandala—the timeless symbol of the unitary reality. Every moment carries within it the creative potentiality to transform the world and ourselves with it into the dimension of greatness, so that we are standing in the abundance of a whole and streamingly alive world. The transfiguration of reality and the process whereby it becomes transparent in the "Great Experience" is contained as a creative happening within the capacity of every living human being; the creative indeterminability of life includes within itself, for every man and in every moment, the possibility of a breakthrough to a world beyond the narrowness of our purely and exclusively conscious existence. This lies concealed in everything, and it can grip us and move us when we look at an unfolding bud or equally when we savor the taste of a piece of bread or a sip of water. We only need to keep ourselves open and not to exclude the abundance of reality. The fact (known to our conscious minds but not realized in our living) that every single fragment of the world contains an infinite abundance of worlds and powers is no more than a symbol for the truth that in every single fragment of the world the whole unrealizable abundance of the unitary reality lies hidden—and waits upon our readiness. Once again, our imperative human need to face life, not that we may cling to it and possess it, but that we may merge ourselves in the flowing of the stream, has received what is perhaps its most beautiful expression in the verse of William Blake:

He who bends to himself a joy
Does the winged life destroy.
But he who kisses the joy as it flies
Lives in eternity's sun rise.[56]

It is simply not true that the eternal appears exclusively in the form of a fixed and indestructible element in the diamond nucleus of the mandala. On the contrary, in its highest and most creative form reality reveals itself as something infinitely mobile and indeterminable. Everything that has been or can be expressed in artistic form is in danger of becoming something consciously known and believed, in which the original "Great Experience" is consolidated and consequently falls into decay. The greatness of "great art" is derived from the fact that the creative power incarnate in it does not speak to us about creative man and his attitude and beliefs, but that through this art reality is telling us directly about itself. The relationship between creative man and the unitary reality that animates everything does not appear in the guise of conscious knowledge or belief in a specific cultural canon; it is alive in the form of the hidden life which is to be found at the heart of the "Great Experience."

The secrets of creation are the secrets of the creative power which constitutes the authentic background of the world. In the great and binding attraction of Eros, which draws creative man onwards to the unitary experience of reality, the divine reality also appears as a state of being in Eros. The Jewish midrash, which is not alone in this insight, recognizes that creation, when it

56. "Eternity," in "Poems from the Note-Book 1793."

produced duality and the Two, in fact gave birth to the primal disaster and the downfall of the original unity, which stepped outside itself and became divided into the Two and polarized; on the other hand, it is precisely the unity of this twoness on a higher level that constitutes the creative life of the vital principle itself.

It is not surprising, then, that in the symbolism of mankind the creative principle should often appear in the form of the love play of a supreme divine couple, who enact the mysterious life of the unitary reality. Behind the World Parents, from whose loving procreative embrace, in the figures of Shiva and Shakti or Kether and Shekhinah, the world of opposites is derived, the supreme creative reality of love appears finally as a divine couple in the perfect fulfillment of eternal youth and loving unity in duality. Here we meet a counterpart, on a higher level, of the intimate entanglement of Eros and Psyche[57] (which is closer to the human realm); we find the youthful pair who represent the Indian conception of the love of God and of mystical union: Krishna and Radha, intertwined with one another in Līlā, the supreme manifestation of divine Love.

So we read that "When the Krishna of innermost Līlā, the Krishna who plays the flute, looks inwards upon his own infinity, he sees before him as his true Self Radha. And when He, 'for whom there is no inner or outer,' looks outwards, he again, sees Radha before him. He sees her, and seeks her, everywhere."[58] This Radha, the loving power of the living God and of the vital prin-

57. Neumann, *Amor and Psyche*.
58. Walther Eidlitz, *Die indische Gottesliebe* (Olten, 1955), p. 267.

ciple in creation, is the chosen bride of his profoundest inner aloneness; at the same time, however, she is also the object of his passionate creative love for everything that is living in the world outside. And so, in a supreme mystical inversion of the doctrine of the dancing Maya, Radha becomes the initiator and dancing mistress of the supreme God Himself. As we read in that dialogue between Radha and her woman friend which is so profoundly disturbing to the religious sensibility of the Westerner, "Radha asks, 'From what part of the Kunda forest do you come?' Her friend replies, 'From the feet of Krishna.' 'Where is He?' 'He is taking a dancing lesson.' 'Who is his guru?' 'You are; he sees your image and figure in every tree, in every climbing plant, and in every quarter of the universe. It is your form, dancing in golden light, which moves in front of him and is his dancing master; and everywhere you go he must dance behind you.' "

The loving union of the Supreme God with the living image of his beloved both outside and within, is the source of the creative mystery of reality, which comes into being as the fruit of this union, and is at once its essence and its inner life.

The dance of the loving maidens around Krishna, the loving core of creation, is itself a mandala of love in vital movement, and as such a supreme symbol of the creative principle, but the center of this movement is the even higher vital mobility of the Two-in-One, symbolized for us in Krishna's dance with Radha—the dance of the central, innermost happening of life. This is the dance of which we are told: "Now Radha's color glows with the splendor of molten gold. But when Radha and

Krishna dance in ecstasy together and Krishna surrenders to the supreme love of God and clasps Radha to his breast, it may so happen that Krishna's deep, unearthly blue is at times altogether enshrouded and eclipsed by the radiant, luminous golden glow of Radha's ineffable love for him. And then Radha alone shines revealed, and the power of her splendor is so overwhelming that when she reveals herself fully in Līlā, Krishna disappears and only Radha remains. And then again, it may so happen that Radha at times completely disappears when Krishna in turn reveals himself fully in the love play of Līlā."

This dance of the Godhead, of the youthful divine pair, can now be seen as a central symbol of that unitary reality which transcends us, but which discloses itself to man in the "Great Experience." The creative principle in mankind, which in loving devotion fuses into a new unity a world that has fallen asunder, is part of the creative love of the Godhead; and the dance of the divine lovers, from whose mysterious unity the overflowing abundance of life is fed, now reveals itself as the vitally moving center of existence.

IV

MAN AND MEANING

I

Meaninglessness, suffering, anxiety, guilt, despair—the very things that call the so-called patient into question, that bring him to me in the expectation that I can help him—these same things always call me into question as well, because I suffer from the same or similar problems, or have suffered from them in the past, and I have no more found the answer than he has. For what is at issue here is not finding *an* answer but finding *the* answer. Mental illness, indeed, merely presents in sharper focus the problem of human existence itself, and in being problematic to himself the patient calls into question the existence of man in our time and therefore also my own existence, at once appealing to me and challenging me to find the answer.

Yet on the other hand the questions my existence poses, as well as the ways these questions call me into question, do not and cannot resemble those of any other person; therefore what provides an answer for me can-

---

"Mensch und Sinn," in *Der schöpferische Mensch* (Zurich, 1959); revised from "Die Sinnfrage und das Individuum," *Eranos-Jahrbuch 1957*, on "Man and Meaning." Translated by Krishna Winston.

not provide the answer for someone else. My experience of being ill and of finding health, of losing my meaning and of discovering my meaning, is unrepeatable and wholly individual.

And the fact that I respond on the basis of my own experience can certainly create the risk that I may wound the other person with my otherness and in turn be wounded by his. The touchy aspects of our being do, after all, result largely from the clash between our individual differentnesses, and only when we are united in a common basic configuration does our vulnerability to others end. Thus what I have to say may strike one person as absurd and mystical, another as heretical and godless, one as too detached, the other as too involved—and all this is probably at once correct and incorrect. I shall simply have to accept it, as my opposite must accept it, for just as the Thou of my opposite constitutes a question and an answer for me, so I constitute a question and an answer for him. In therapy that which we call the transference and counter-transference establishes the basic mutuality out of which the answer to questions may emerge, if, indeed, it emerges; so, too, there exists between the speaker and the listener or reader the same sort of mutuality in which each reaches out to and accepts the other, and this is the prerequisite for creation of that overflow which we experience as delivering meaning.

The process of transference and counter-transference is an occurrence grounded in the fact that all humans share a common structure, that they are bound up with one another in the world- and life-situation of Adam Kadmon, the original human being, who is unfolding

within each of us, for we are all he, and we all participate in him through our existence. But this Adam Kadmon is the self that resides in us as our core, that lives
around us as the totality of the world, and that determines our unfolding in time as fate. That means: our
fundamental human kinship is the bringing together of
self and self which also occurs beyond the ego in the
guise of oppositeness and fellowship.

Fellowship in work with the psyche depends on
whether our being as a whole can endure seeing the very
existence of its opposite called into question and allowing an answer to be arrived at. In this process, accepting
the Other means accepting oneself. To the extent that I
can tolerate and accept myself, with my doubt and my
despair, my dubiousness and my not-being-called-into-
question, I shall also be able to help this other person
(who embodies a task assigned to me) find his way to
himself.

The salient experience of modern man is meaninglessness. In the neurosis and psychosis manifested by the
individual and in the mass epidemics afflicting entire
peoples, this experience represents the central problem
of contemporary reality: the dissolution of all bonds that
confer meaning. The atomization of the individual who
unconsciously and defenselessly is abandoned to events,
or who consciously experiences himself as being so abandoned, is the symptom of an external and internal process of collectivization which has attained only its most
striking visibility in the political terror of our times. The
actual experience of modern man—with the exception
of those few who still live within the old system of order—is one of meaninglessness and despair, of anxiety

and loneliness and a feeling of personal annihilation in the sense that everything essential is reduced to nought.

The transpersonal as something that confers meaning has more and more disappeared. The religions no longer have any hold, the *Gemeinschaft* as a natural unit of people and nation lies in disarray. The symptoms of this oft-described process manifest themselves in the existentialist sense of the world, as well as in rootlessness of the individual. It has become problematic even to raise the issue of meaning, for the absurdity of human existence seems so obvious that merely enduring and accepting this absurdity is now considered man's highest and ultimate challenge.

This loss of meaning is not the sickness of our generation but a process that has extended over generations in the Western world and has not yet reached an end. Nietzsche's "God is dead!" announces the end of the patriarchal image of God, whose roots have begun to die in Western man. Modern man experiences much personal suffering, has seen too much suffering; his eyes are filled with horror. The death of masses of human beings, the torturing to death of millions, has broken his psychic endurance.

It is understandable and obvious that belief in a just and loving God may fail a person who has witnessed how—among other unspeakable events—one million Jewish children could be slaughtered with no great impact on mankind—not on psychologists, theologians, believers or unbelievers, from the Pope to the Communists. Belief in the immortal soul is not strengthened by such occurrences.

Even for the religious Westerner, the remoteness of

God seems ever more clearly to have become the fundamental experience. Even a person who cannot accept the mythological image of a Divinity that turns its back on man will understand that man's turning his back on the Divinity and the Divinity's turning his back on man are one and the same thing. In this case the apparent godless nothingness of human despair becomes the underlying basis of existence.

The Western religions literally no longer "measure up to" modern man in his despair. They no longer take his measure, are not suitable to him anymore, because the old image of God—and let us not forget that we are speaking of *images* of God, images of the divine in man—has not kept changing along with the development of Western man, his consciousness, his experience of the world and his experience of man, that is, of himself. All these sacred images—and they remain sacred even when they have lost their effectiveness for modern man—correspond to eternal truths, but these truths no longer have the capacity to shelter existence as man must experience it today.

Yet the images of the Deity are what guarantee the meaning of human life; with them stands or falls the possibility for the individual and the group to experience in life the shelter of a transpersonal element, or at least to experience ties with such an element, without which human existence is apparently unable to bear life. The great peaks of intellectual and spiritual orientation are sinking. Christianity, Buddhism, Islam, Judaism—all seem to be dissolving, and desperate clinging to these sinking systems only drags one deeper into destruction.

The ego in its isolation is floundering in despair. It is

overwhelmed by the process of collectivization which fragments the individual into collectively serviceable but otherwise irrelevant segments; and when, in the knowledge of his own impotence, the individual silently accepts this violence, he becomes a victim of terror, not only in Russia or Nazi Germany, but everywhere. Everywhere Western Reason has triumphed, and as it continues on its triumphal march, a consciousness shaped in its image effects the transformation and domination of the world; these changes bring with them industrialization and collectivization, which atomize and rape the individual.

The atomized ego is an ego in isolation, and, unable to withstand the pressure, it has been hurled into the abyss of meaninglessness. In the West the dignity of the human ego was always something sacred, and this sacredness was intimately bound up with that patriarchal image of God central to the canon of Western culture; the dissolution of the God-image and the catastrophic threat to the ego of Western man are one.

The fatal split in Western man, the gaping abyss into which we have fallen, did not come about, as is often claimed, because of Descartes and his *cogito, ergo sum*, nor because the rational self achieved autonomy, which so greatly intensified the splintering of the world into internal and external, subject and object. In actuality this split is much older, for it arose during the West's ill-fated attempt to radicalize the development of the rational ego, while at the same time retaining religious experience, which stood in direct contradiction to Reason, and in addition pinning the creative numinosity of the divine to historical revelation.

The rupture in the psyche of Western man stems from the development of a false humanism characteristic of him, a humanism that grew out of the ultimately unsuccessful attempt to combine Judaeo-Christian articles of faith with Greek philosophy. No matter how magnificently Western civilization has developed as a result of this effort—the magnificence was purchased at the price of a crucial sacrifice, namely the schism that occurred in the soul of Western man, which failed to unite Greek Reason, extraversion, and aesthetic harmony with the Judaeo-Christian religious experience.

Western humanism is based on two mutually exclusive images of man: the Greek image, according to which man as a rational being is the measure of all things, and the Judaeo-Christian image, according to which the dignity of the human ego depends on its filial relationship to God the Father. According to the Judaeo-Christian view, the human ego can assume its proper autonomy and freedom only by virtue of its son-hood vis-à-vis the father archetype. But this son-hood is a sacred bond,[1] just as the release of human ego-consciousness from the overwhelming influence of the unconscious and of nature is a sacred event.

Thus two basic aspects of Western man are constellated: one is the ego as a moral ego, as the carrier of responsibility in God's image, according to the saying, "Sacred shall ye be, for I am sacred, the Eternal, your God"; the other is man as an individual soul. But this "soul," too, was understood as the image of a divine ideal—an ideal, to be sure, about which the documents

1. See Neumann, *Origins and History*, passim.

of the Judaeo-Christian tradition contain not a word. According to this dangerous and downright inflationistic view, "original" man would have had to be more angelic than the angels and more good than any knowable goodness. This mistaken view was certainly more than compensated for by the doctrine of "real" man's fallen state and the corresponding fallen state of the world, but there remained the demand upon man to be that which he cannot be. The fact that he was created just as he is was obfuscated with talk of "Original Sin," according to which he had allegedly broken a highly dubious commandment of Paradise and was thus "evil from his youth" (Genesis 8:21). In this way Western man's experience of himself was catastrophically undermined by a sense of guilt occasioned by the supposed fall of man.

Since the development of consciousness forms an essential part of the development of the human race, the loss of Paradise, the loss of the child's primary experience of reality as an unbroken unity, becomes inevitable. Theological and moralistic manipulation of this misunderstood fundamental human law proved the curse of Western man. In the instructive confrontation between Western and, for instance, Asian man, this historical premise, the profound guilt of the Westerner, who sees himself as a fallen person living in a cursed world, becomes strikingly clear. But this basic situation connects to another constellation that remains alive with danger up to this day, that is, Western man's readiness to live provisionally.

As an ego each one of us is part of whatever collective he must grow into; we are part of suprapersonal groups and participate in religion and civilization, as well as in those suprapersonal events that will be recorded in the history books. As an ego-person each one of us is a useful or a useless member of society and receives from this suprapersonal construct a purpose and a meaning which fade like the suprapersonal construct itself, of which we, as ego, form a part. Part of a people, part of an epoch—who could deny or be allowed to overlook this way in which we are interwoven with the horizontal dimension of time's passage? Yet the Western individual has made it almost impossible to solve the problem of his meaning, placing himself as an ego too much in the midst of the abstractness of historical processes for which he is used as a tool. He has surrendered his stake in himself in return for a temporary condition in which he, as an ego, outruns himself in pursuit of future goals which he in his finitude cannot fulfill; he fails to notice that he loses track of himself along the way.

Living in anticipation of the "end of time," of the Messianic epoch as the Beyond or a future condition that mankind will attain, lends Western man the possibility and the strength to leap over himself, his individuality and his own life, and to sacrifice himself heroically for the transpersonal future of that future group. According to this belief, the present and present-day man are in a state of "fallenness," of provisional existence, of "inauthenticity"—in the religious, ethical, psychological, sociological, political sense—and with that leap into anticipation of the end, man leaps over his own inauthenticity.

Such a system of meaning, which bypasses man, the present, and reality in the name of something yet to come, is abysmally dangerous both in its religious and in its secularized form, even where it enables man to "overcome himself." Heroic and martyr-like self-conquest does, to be sure, correspond to a fundamental archetypal potential within man; it is worthy of reverence; yet this posture, like all postures, must first prove its significance within the new nexuses necessary for the solution of the problem of our being.

We shall have to learn that even something that in itself is "worthy of reverence" represents a great danger if it does not follow the path of Abraham, along which man must sacrifice all gods, i.e., that which is always worthy of reverence, in order to reach the land of which is written, "that I will show [it] thee" (Genesis 2:1). But this divine principle that forever points the way is by no means identical with the old Western patriarchal image of God.

Understandably enough, the Greek heritage was adopted with such fervor by the West precisely because it was expected to provide an antidote to the sickness visited upon Western man by the Judaeo-Christian peril. In fact, this antidote only exacerbated the split in man already implicit in the Judaeo-Christian world view. That from this aspect man is the measure of all things implies that the rational mind of self-aware man is the measure of all things; and over time this humanism centered on the rational ego repeatedly received new impetus from the extraordinarily influential philosophy of the Greeks. But the world of this supposedly supremely humane man is the "mere-world" of externals, which in the course of Western history produced what was doubtless the very opposite of Plato's brilliant vision: the victory of Reason, of abstraction and of scientific thinking.

One result of this rationalizing process was that even the father-archetype was reduced to the Western patriarchal image of God. The Godhead's numinous-irrational and ambivalent-terrible aspects which pervaded the reality of the Old Testament, as well as of the New Testament sacrifice of the Son, faded more and more in the course of Western development; and once stripped of its original numinosity the Godhead became merely the creator of the best and most reasonable of worlds. In order to demonstrate that he was made in God's image, man had only to grasp by means of his reason the rational laws of nature, the product of a rational Creator, and adhere to the laws of morality implanted by the Creator in his conscience in the form of the super-ego.

The attempt to unite the scientific-philosophical heritage of Greek antiquity with the religious and moral heritage of the Judaeo-Christian tradition ended with the catastrophic triumph of Greek science in Western man's consciousness, and the equally catastrophic triumph of the Judaeo-Christian moral and religious values in his unconscious. As the conscious mind more and more identified the Divinity as the carrier of the highest purely rational and moral values, the numinous aspect of the God-Father archetype was relegated at first to the devil, then completely repressed.

The ego of modern Western man, isolated and reduced to mere rational consciousness, knows nothing of God, the devil, or the fallen human soul; but in his unconscious, Western man is dominated by a truly bottomless sense of guilt. Within him the image of the old demanding Divinity still holds sway, whispering that the once-perfect creation suffered the Fall as a result of man's sinning. The very unconscious nature of this guilt makes it archaic and cruel, and the ego, in its isolation and rootlessness, gives way under the strain of this nagging unconscious guilt which demands punishment. What makes the situation especially acute is that the ego's individual existence is also buffeted from without by modern collective society.

The symptom of this collapse can be found not only in the contemporary philosophy of despair but also in the universally discernible rebellion against any sense of guilt.

I have often enough emphasized the significance for humanity of the "great individual"[2] and the "creative man." But in the context of modern man's lack of a sense of meaning and his despair over himself and humanity, something else must be stressed, something that is indeed almost the opposite. Certainly humanity without the "great individual" is unthinkable, for it is he who leads mankind and he to whom civilization owes almost all its landmark accomplishments, and a mankind without religion, without literature, without art, without philosophy, would not be mankind. But the "great individual" merely exemplifies the possibilities inherent in each and every human being. Mankind has never existed without religion, literature, art, and philosophy, even in times when the individual still formed part of a group and the group had not yet thrust him out into a position of his own; even if the group someday

2. [Cf. ibid.]

once again integrates the individual more fully, nothing will change in this regard, for man is not only *Homo sapiens*, he is also *Homo creator*. By its very nature his existence is creative, like existence itself.

To suggest that man is finished, merely because the Western concept of man has been pushed *ad absurdum* and we are all trapped in the fatal consistency of this error, reveals a ludicrous lack of faith. Hölderlin's notion that "where peril is greatest, salvation is nearest" expresses not merely optimistic wishful thinking but a truly profound understanding of reality. To be sure, that which perceives this reality is not the rational ego, the mere-ego [*Nur-Ich*],[3] and the conscious mind, but the whole person, who has knowledge of the wholeness of the person and the wholeness of life, the life of the creative divine element present in every person.

The philosophy of rootlessness so characteristic of our times is the philosophy of a deracinated ego which also suffers from megalomania. It is rootless because it speaks as a "mere-ego" only for itself and knows nothing of its connection with the self on which it rests, from which it springs, out of which it lives, and which remains indestructibly present in its own numinous core. But when the "mere-ego" is confined to its own superficial zones, it loses the breath breathed into the ego as a living soul, and therefore necessarily experiences a sense of limitation and anxiety, of abandonment and despair. Yet precisely this ego thinks that by standing on its head it can "pro-ject" [*entwerfen*] itself and the world. It forgets that it itself is only a projection, and it experiences

3. [In another translation, *Nur-Ich* is rendered as "exclusive ego."]

itself as absurd, because it absurdly forgets the paradox-
icality within which it exists creatively.

Out of sheer care, this ego forgets that something exists within man that takes care of him and that the ego's
forethoughtfulness is only an afterthought, that his foresight is only anxiety. Precisely because of this excessive
care, a heritage of the misguided Western conscience,
the ego so often collapses when some dictatorial other
ego appears willing to assume this foresight for it.

How suspect are all these forethoughtful egos, stran-
gers to that freedom from care that can let one walk
straight into danger, knowing that everything has been
taken care of because one has an indestructible core
which need have no care! The rootless ego in its care
and sorrow sees only death, not life, for it knows nothing of the death-encompassing nature of the self.

I hope I shall not be misunderstood. Who would want
to contest modern man's right to feel care, who would
question the significance of death; but it seems to me
that modern man's care focuses on the wrong thing, that
he has a mistaken notion of death, which he fears.
Both—this misplaced care as well as this mistaken notion of death—are such common, regular symptoms of
the mental illnesses which we are called upon to treat
that it seems justified to identify them as expressions of
a personality disorder characteristic of modern Western
man.

For the sake of contrast, one should think of the figure and teachings of Lao-tse, whose freedom from care
means being free of an ego that clings to care and sorrow; it means open, carefree, spontaneity in harmony
with the Tao. But even though we have chosen the for-

mulation that something within us takes care of us, that is actually not quite correct, for what goes on "within us" is not taking-care-of in the sense of human caring-for, but care-free caring. This care-free caring is the creative spontaneity that guides us. We are certainly wrong if we confound it with that which we call "care." For when we have cares, when I have cares—and unfortunately I am care-ridden all too often—I am always in the wrong. In the Western sense I am ethically certainly "good," for under the best circumstances I care about something which it is necessary and rewarding to care about. But this care does so little good; it is one of the narrow paths of my being mere-ego, which does not coincide with the infinite paths of the living. But when I—as happens all too seldom—am free of care, things flow by themselves: problems get solved, tasks are attended to, help comes. It seems as though the gates to the living only begin to open when I have drawn back the bolt of my care. Far be it from me to pretend or want to pretend that I possess this carefreeness, for by nature or in my unnaturalness I tend on the contrary to be excessively careworn; but I am aware of this unnaturalness and therefore also of my, and our, misplaced care. It seems permissible, even desirable, for me to speak of myself, precisely because I and we are one in this respect, for good and especially for ill.

The danger to the ego lies in the fact that by virtue of its origin it develops within an environment into which it must also grow as the world of objects and objective conditions. The ego is formed by this world and, in spite of its innate creativity, is shaped so extensively by the cultural canon that it becomes obscure and opaque to itself, wavering in its self-sufficiency and in its bond with its self. In the process, it loses its creativity, and only when it recalls or re-experiences the fact that it is a "king's son" and stems from the self does it surmount the alienation by which it is overwhelmed in the abandoned state of the mere-ego. Not until the ego escapes from the enslaved condition of the mere-ego in a mereworld does it recover its ego-self-integrity [*Ich-Selbst-Sein*]. And that signifies not retreat and isolation, but a breakthrough to the god-likeness of the ego-self and discovery of the unitary reality in which the contrast between the worldly and the divine no longer exists.

There is nothing finite in the world which does not contain a spark of creative infinitude; for that very reason the world does not really display the character of a prison. Outward freedom can contain elements of confinement, just as outward confinement can contain elements of creative freedom. That does not mean that the struggle for creative freedom will not need to be waged externally as well as internally, but it does mean that from the outset, or in the last analysis (which amount to the same thing), this struggle is decided in favor of creative freedom.

Man is always more than an atomized ego, and industrial development and specialization cannot rob him of his innate creativity. Even in the state of stultification and numbness imposed upon him, yes, even when his personality is apparently obliterated, the personality simply withdraws into a secret core of which it itself may be unaware. In the secrecy of the unconscious, future liberation is prepared. Yet even during this waiting period man's awareness of and insight into his true being and the true being of the world persist; they remain a possibility to be experienced in the presentness of the fulfilled moment.

Without a doubt the individual is a part of his group and his culture and is partially shaped by the cultural canon, whose positive and negative values he eventually takes for granted; they become second nature to him. But the pessimistic diagnosis of our times always uses as a reference point those values that have prevailed in the Western world up to now, and sees any upheaval in those values as signalling the downfall of man and of human civilization. Yet this Western civilization, which considers itself the only valid one, is nothing but the culture of a small portion of humanity, and actually it does not even extend to the entire population of the West. The superficial unity of Western multiplicity is presently being replaced by an as yet invisible unity: the expression of the infinitely greater multiplicity of all the peoples of mankind entering the realm of civilization.

Anyone familiar with man's creative genius, which, developing out of the earliest primitive beginnings, eventually produced human beings like the Buddha and Jesus, Rembrandt and Bach, and anyone familiar with the genius of Western, Asian, African man cannot seriously believe that man will be at a loss in the face of problems yet to come or that man as the carrier of the human spirit and human values will perish.

Yet how great the fear on this score must have become if a man like Erich Kahler can say, in his book on the transformation of the individual: "The gain in expansion of the genus and the loss in selfness of the individual appears to be one and the same process."[4] The series of negative factors that have led to the crisis of modern man paradoxically terminates for Kahler in "the expansion of man's introspective experience," which allegedly has led to the "split within," for which he cites psychoanalysis and the existentialist experience as star witnesses. But it is fundamentally mistaken to think and to cause others to think that modern psychology caused or deepened the inner split in man. It is true that it stumbled upon the psychic split when it undertook to examine modern man's illness, but it also discovered the compensating, healing, integrating powers of the psyche; and depth psychology, with its links to biology, animal psychology, instinct psychology, and even physics, is discovering more and more evidence that the creative side of man and the creative powers characteristic of life as a whole are the decisive phenomena that set off being from non-being.

The way in which consciousness and the ego have developed in the West, in isolation from the unconscious and from nature, can certainly be blamed for the fragmentation of modern man, but such isolation is by no means a necessary outcome of the basic structure of the human psyche, nor is it the only conceivable mode in which human consciousness can develop. On the contrary: the collective unconscious, i.e., the archetypal dimension of the psyche, is by its very nature the distillate of the human race's assimilation of the world, an experience which has guided mankind as a whole and in all

4. Kahler, *The Tower and the Abyss: An Inquiry into the Transformation of Man* (New York, 1957), p. 233.

its multiplicity through the interminable crises of its existence, conferring meaning along the way. But that suggests that precisely the creative link between consciousness and the unconscious is an integral part of man's nature.

In the course of its development, this guiding psychic element has spawned not only consciousness but also the ego and the individual. From the outset, the individual as a creative person, in his function as an instrument of the collectivity, has not only been the one who makes "expansion of the genus" possible in the first place, but in the course of the expansion he has increasingly attained his "selfness." For although from the beginning the relationship of individual and community may be rich in conflict and often tragic, it is always inherently creative. Man is an individual not as a rational "mere-ego," but in the wholeness of his psyche, and he carries all of mankind within him in the form of the collective unconscious. This means that the unity of mankind and the link of every individual with humanity extends beyond the merely human aspect of consciousness and into the unitary reality where the creative psyche becomes reality beyond consciousness.

The archetypal, as that mold which molds us, is itself a formless form, and when in our need it shows us the way, the creative transformation we undergo always transcends that which would have been predicted for us as mere-ego. For the self, as a divine element at work in every psyche, employs primeval images in the creative psychic process, without being restricted to them alone. For if the self were restricted, the psyche could be surveyed, its laws determined, and neither the psyche nor the self would be creative.

But precisely because the divine resides in every individual, the unpredictable miracle of creativity is everywhere possible. The diagnoses arrived at by the rational conscious, whose Cassandra-like cries echo through our times, striking terror into our hearts, are the product of the mere-ego, which thinks linearly, i.e., allegedly in a logical fashion—and therefore never perceives the infinite paths of reality. For miraculous though the laws of reality may be, even more miraculous is its unpredictability, for good as well as for ill, and any genuine knowledge of man and the world must include this element of the unpredictable in its image of the world and of mankind's possible future.

The very existence of the phenomenon of compensation in the wholeness of the individual human being and still more in the unconscious of mankind, makes all the mere-ego's linear thinking, fearfulness, and pessimism appear utterly misguided. We are acquainted with spontaneous manifestations of the collective unconscious in history, movements which apparently run through all of mankind, for instance the advent of rational consciousness in the first millennium before the Christian era. We know all about the upheaval called modernism which for the past one hundred and fifty years has had the entire world and ourselves as well in its grasp. And yet people still dignify with the name of cultural philosophy their anxious attempts to project present negative experiences into the future; they fail to consider the reaction every illness and every upheaval in the human psyche calls forth, both collectively and individually.

Man's capacity for adaptation is so great that it should inspire awe mixed with horror. It is simply unspeakable what a human being, reduced to an animal-like condition, can endure, and what heights he can later attain, by means of the regenerative powers of the psyche, sometimes without his even having come to terms yet with what he has suffered.

This is not the place to speak of the terrible damage such occurrences can cause. I wish rather to discuss the creative power present in us all which in the course of human development has more and more surmounted the threats posed by external nature and which also has the ability to tame our inner nature. Just as earthquakes, floods, and epidemics failed to wipe out uncomprehending humanity, so, too, terror, collectivization, and even demented individuals will be unable to destroy mankind, now steadily gaining insight into its own situation.

Here, too, the "compact" between God and Noah of which the Old Testament speaks comes into play; in it, mankind is promised that no new flood will destroy mankind. This compact sealed between the Divinity and mankind is an expression of the link between the ego and the self. This unity of the creative divine principle with creative mankind and the creative man which every individual is cannot be lost or forgotten, because it constitutes the actual structure of man and of mankind.

The profound oneness of humankind rests on the paradoxical unity within which whatever the individual experiences as self, so to speak as "his" self, connects with the self of every other individual. For if individuality is the unique form of the divine in man, representing the ego before the split, then the self as a spaceless and timeless non-point is never "my divine aspect" but simply "the divine." And this divine aspect, the self, which represents the creative dimension of mankind in every man, constellates a profound connection among all men, a connection which, in such personal phenomena as the transference, *participation mystique* and a wealth of parapsychological phenomena, approaches identity.[5]

The interconnectedness of mankind and the connectedness of mankind with the divine is also the connectedness of the human and the divine with the world. What we call the psyche is a web in which worldly, human, and divine elements are inextricably interwoven. Our ego-consciousness attempts—and indeed must do so—to separate the strands of that which is experienced in the depths of the psyche as seamless reality. But the formation of the living being does not take place in a retort outside the world, but within the world itself, and the world is within man not only substantially but also functionally. Man is inseparably connected with the world; this connection is the prerequisite for his continuous exchange with the world, for his development within the world and for his coming to know it.

This profound connection between man and the world rests on what we call the self, and in the unitary reality this creative self constitutes not only the unity of the human being but also the unity of the human and the divine and of man and the world. Therefore the relationship of man to the world always corresponds to that between man and his self, and accepting the world not only means affirming the world as something divine,

5. See above, Essay I.

but also affirming man as something residing in and
with the divine. For experience of the world whenever
it is a genuine "Great Experience" of the self in the
world and the world in the self, is the creative confir-
mation of the unity of man and the world in divine
being.

The "mere-world" of the senses, on the other hand,
is a functional construct of our conscious; when the
whole person perceives the world, every "Great Experience" transcends this mere-world of our isolated mere-
ego. Hence the sickness, despair, and longing that characterize any existence cut out for life in the mere-world,
itself only a partial world, and consequently cut off from
true being. Each vital moment, each vital contact, contains a fullness of being that infinitely transcends the
bloodless mere-world of isolated ego-consciousness.

We require no initiation, however, into the mystery
of the unitary reality, for from the outset we are initiated
into it and remain so, even if we are unaware of this.
That is why Lao-tse's saying is so true, in contrast to the
usual Western misunderstanding:

> Who in his self honors the world
> To him we may well entrust the world.
> Who in his self loves the world
> To him we may well surrender the world.[6]

The problem of the alleged "Fall from Divine Grace"
thus appears as the problem of "man's fall from himself," and there is much evidence that the fragmented

---

6. [Translated from Neumann's modified version of Richard Wilhelm's translation of the *Tao Tê Ching*.]

condition of modern man and his "mere-ego-ness" signify the fall from the divine in modern dress. Doubtless modern man's status as a rational mere-ego seems to be that of a "godless" being, and the characteristic anxiety and despair into which he has hurtled can easily be interpreted as the abyss of hell, into which he has fallen as a result of his godlessness and his loss of God. That this "fallen man" regards himself as fallen into the world forms part of the same hellish situation in which the world and nature are viewed as primarily hostile elements.

But to reject the world as a fallen world is tantamount to rejecting man as fallen. When man fails to honor and love himself, he fails to honor and love the world, as well as the divine principle that resides in the world and in himself; and when he thinks of himself as remote from the divine, he indeed removes himself from it.

But in reality man, because he is alive, can never be remote from the divine, which—even if he is unaware of the fact—constitutes the root of his being. Even the rational mere-ego, in its despair seeking ways where apparently there is no way out, ways which may be digressions and deviations, still remains in its search connected with the fundamental creativity of man.

Thus even the fatal process of collectivization, which reduces the individual to one utilitarian aspect of his possibilities, also contains creative elements. For what we fear as the atomization of modern man already carries the seeds of a new revolution. When man finds himself exploited, listless, meaningless, he becomes the revolutionary of the future, even if all he accomplishes is to call attention through his failure to his humanness.

"Collectivization" is only the primitive and undifferentiated beginning of a future development, of a new unification of mankind. In scientific research the necessity for "teamwork" is becoming increasingly apparent; this teamwork should not be viewed as the dissolution, limitation, or extermination of individuality but as the first productive manifestation of what one might describe as co-individuality.

The unity of culture and of cultural development was always determined by the interaction of widely varying individualities. Only an ensemble of the heterogeneous qualities of the leading figures, the men of deeds and the contemplatives, the founders of religions and the priests, the artists and the philosophers, can shape the culture of a people, a time, or of mankind. While this "ensemble" was previously unconscious, it is gradually becoming the object of awareness; as a result, the multiplicity of human individuality can be intentionally put to good use. Today the initial manifestations of this development appear awkward, for they are still largely guided by the perceptions of the goal-oriented rational ego. But when, for instance, scientific research teams hire a psychologist to apply group-therapeutic methods for mediating among differing points of view and temperaments, biases, and prejudices, this already constitutes a genuine form of highly promising co-individualization.

Individuality does, after all, normally imply one-sidedness. It can be seen as a unique selection from among all existing possibilities, for the consciousness of any given personality is determined by the bias of the attitude and function type to which it belongs. If one realizes that many of the difficulties people experience when they must live together, for instance in a marriage, grow out of such unconscious bias, one can imagine how these difficulties multiply when it is a question of achieving cooperation in large organizations such as an army or a factory, and even more when it is a question of the heterogeneity of large masses of people, or even of peoples and races. Therefore it is precisely the individual differences among human beings that produce those attempts to achieve uniformity that result in the atomization of the individual.

But the moment creative participation and individual accomplishment become burdensome tasks, suppression of the individual must cease. More and more mankind sees the need to make the individual productive, whether in the name of increasing industrial productivity or of competition among the superpowers. It is easy to predict that in the future mankind will choose its teachers from among those with a gift for teaching, as it will choose its technicians from among the technically gifted and its psychologists from among the psychologically gifted. Within these individual groups, those who show gifts for particular lines of work will be promoted, and the overall collaboration will be steered by persons whose own individuality imbues them with the conviction that creating the "ensemble" is an important productive goal. At present this development is slowed by lack of insight into its desirability, but the necessity to "care for" in every sense the steadily increasing numbers of human beings tends to further the emergence of natural talents from among the likewise steadily growing fund of human potential, which expands as the human race expands.

It is thus by no means utopian to assume that the humanity of the future will recognize more clearly than today's the extent to which it depends on the accomplishments of its creative individuals, and that it will protect these accomplishments and coordinate them through co-individual group activity. In the process, however, the nature of the individual human psyche will prevail in its uniqueness, as it always has, for when the collectivity recognizes that an individual's creativeness is necessary and fruitful to the community, it will voluntarily or involuntarily provide the conditions that the individual requires in order to remain creative; and this implies that standardization will yield to reindividualization.

The seemingly insignificant personal observation that in Israel the initially purely rational collectivization of the communal settlements is beginning to succumb to pressure for individuality points to a fundamental law of human existence. One need not fear for the individual, for in the individual resides the only available creative reality. But in every land and in every school the word must be spread that no terror, no industrialization, no state, no religion, no social order—in short, nothing—can destroy the creative divine principle in man. Times of peril pass, totalitarian states fall just as democracies do; what remains is man, forever changing and creative; the transformations of his consciousness merely demonstrate the invincibility of the human psyche, which transcends the old, destroying it that it may be reborn in a new form.

The imperishable connection between the ego and the self is the decisive phenomenon of human existence, and in a period when man inclines to self-negation, it seems important to stress that this connection survives, remains valid and is indestructible, regardless of whether a person is believing or despairing, conscious or unconscious.

Modern man's feeling that he is an isolated, sinful, or lost creature in a fallen world must be dispelled. This is not to say that one should simply ignore the problem of evil as if it had disappeared in the general inflation of values, or that one should deny the process by which man acquires consciousness. For the acquisition of consciousness is actually a specifically human form of creativity, and more and more the emphasis is shifting toward understanding and realizing man as creative man, indeed as a creature that is by nature creative.

2

What a topic, this quest for meaning! One could apply the words of Lao-tse: "The Tao that can be expressed is not the eternal Tao."[7]

When I had reached this point in writing my paper, I asked the *I Ching* whether, since I have been trying for so many years to fulfill my expectations and those of the people I am addressing, I might not force myself to reach some conclusion. I received the reply "Limitation" (No. 60) ䷻ , with six at the top. The commentary says, "Here at the end of the time of limitation, one should not attempt forcibly to continue limitation. This line is

7. [*Tao Tê Ching*, tr. Ch'u Ta-Kao (5th ed., London, 1959), p. 11.]

weak and at the top of the trigram is K'an, danger. Anything attempted here by force has a galling effect and
cannot be continued. Hence a new direction must be
taken, and thereupon remorse will disappear."[8]

With a sigh of relief I put aside what I had previously
planned as the continuation of this paper. But I realized
at once how difficult it would be to abandon this self-
imposed limitation, for it represents the actual source of
Western man's needs, and the impulse to self-limitation
is as present in me as in all of us. It is the need of consciousness, of the ordered ego, limited by its super-ego,
which always cherishes the false belief that it must cling
to itself, which fears collapsing into itself precisely because it secretly harbors the fear-inspiring belief that it
is a fallen being in a fallen world. Why do we believe
our false belief? Does not our very clinging to it always
hurl us into an abyss of despair? Why do we believe in
a non-existent destruction, in an unreal crisis, in an un-
founded guilt? Why do we speak of self-alienation as
our characteristic experience if allegedly we never were
close to ourselves and therefore cannot know what self-
alienation really is?

We speak of a lack of orientation and meaning and
we can, and in fact do, experience constantly how precisely this alleged lack of meaning can provide guidance,
so long as we do not lock ourselves into the prison of our
consciousness. We speak of secularization, and certainly
many will interpret my message as follows: the old religious values—God, freedom, immortality—no longer
carry any validity for modern man. Indeed, even some-

8. *I Ching*, p. 698.

one as concerned for the individual as Kahler can assert, citing Rilke and Simone Weil (and he might draw on many other witnesses): "We no longer live our days in nearness to the divine."[9]

But how could we live at all if not in "nearness to the divine," for in fact that is the only kind of "nearness" there is! It is our consciousness that repeatedly allows itself to be persuaded of our remoteness from God. Yet perhaps even a criminal devouring a piece of bread that stills his hunger is near to the divine. The divine is so much more reliable than anything else; we tend to forget this, but only because we have heard so much about the demands the divine places upon us and have allowed ourselves to be persuaded that it will be remote from us if we fail to fulfill them. Without doubt such tales have a pedagogic function, but what a wretched sort of pedagogy! What father would dream of telling his child, "Do thus and so, and if you do not—I will disappear"? What a strange divine Father this must be who is always making demands, when properly speaking the divine asks no questions and makes no demands, giving and taking, within us and outside us, irrespective of our attitude. This "irrespective of our attitude" does not suggest that the divine does not see us; but we are, so to speak, contained in the eyes of the divine in such a way that being looked upon, looked over, overlooked and overseen almost coincide with one another—to be sure, irrespective of us; but that does not imply that it is without consequence for us whether we look to the divine or not.

9. *The Tower and the Abyss*, p. 195.

We hear those great and terrible tales of the Divinity who throws man out of Paradise, who demands the death of His son and yet forbids killing, so many confusing and therefore so human and human-seeming assertions about a Divinity which allows us to covet and forbids covetousness, which wants to save man and hands him over to the devil—great and terrible and certainly true, but at the same time confusing tales, and man, when he allows himself to be confused by them, suffers punishment and death, and after death he is hurled into the seething cauldron, and so on and so forth. Great tales, very human tales, born from the depths of the human psyche—what wonder if modern man no longer believes these revelations, what wonder if an Asian visiting the West is amazed when he encounters *this particular religious-spiritual universe!* And how untouched by all this the Divinity remains, that Divinity we know not, but *are*, that we constantly experience, that tells us strange tales and then nullifies them. But we cling to these tales and sorrow when the material left behind by the Divinity crumbles between the fingers of our soul.

What excessive demands have been placed upon us by our likeness to God, how we have been punished for it, how it has been driven out of us! Created in God's image—and fallen. Who can believe that a good God-Father would treat us in such a fashion! It is true and understandable that we should feel we have been treated in this fashion, because we did lose the world of our origin, Paradise, when we became an ego, but we should take comfort or try to regain our origin and stop believing that we are fallen and must be punished. We should take comfort, or rather, be comforted; we should open our inner and outer senses to the infinite comfort of the divine which is one with the world.

Oh no, it cannot be forgotten: man is a murderer, he is evil—at least a murderer and evil in addition to everything else; how can one be comforted? We know that the East (and the East is very wise, much wiser than we) thinks and teaches that a point can be reached where joy and sorrow are no more—and here, of course, there is no need for comfort; surely the presence of the divine must be very great there. Alas, I know nothing of this and am much in need of comforting, as are all the people with whom I am acquainted and who come to me. And how greatly I fail at comforting; the spirit-wind of the divine is in my breath, and yet I so often remain inconsolable and incapable of offering comfort!

Our likeness to God is so clouded when it reaches us, to the extent we are an ego, although God-likeness is actively present in the ego as well—indeed, especially in the ego. The God-likeness is clouded and opaque when we are a "mere-ego," but the "mere-ego" is never the true ego. For as a "mere-ego" we are encapsulated and imprisoned, and the Western rational ego is precisely such a poor, crippled mere-ego. But that is not sufficient reason for cursing this mere-ego, or, like the East, wanting to be rid of it. This poor ego also needs comforting. It must be told that as a mere-ego it is not itself. For not until we experience ourselves as a self-ego do we arrive at what we are.

The mere-ego exists in anxiety and despair, it experiences itself as lost in a world of the non-ego, as inadequate and "fallen" in relation to an absolute obligation, as atomized in a collectivized world. As if man in his real being could be collectivized, as if anything in the world could alienate him from his self-ego-integrity! Even when the mere-ego is crushed by concentration camps, by hunger and torture, and man is hurled back into pure creatureliness, he remains what he is: a divine being, descended from the divine and belonging to the divine.

One of our crucial tasks is to illuminate the darkness into which we stumble as a "mere-ego." Here "task" means nothing more nor less than experiencing ourselves in our humanness, for only as a self-ego do we transcend the boundaries of ourselves as ego and become *Homo humanus* in our and his authenticity. Independently of our individual circumstances, we remain, in our common self-ness, saved and open, connected with the world and world-creative. The temporarily relative ego stands side by side with the eternal self. The ego represents man as a historic being in time, while as a self-ego he simultaneously exists in eternity.

When we speak of the archetypes and the self of the human psyche which become creative in man, the implication is that in this realm man extends into his eternity, into himself as eternity. But this eternal self-ego-integrity is not an "authenticity" which must be distinguished from the non-authenticity of the ego and defended against it. Nor must one be "sublimated" or elevated to the other. Man always exists in the realm of the authentic, lives from it, is one with it. There are merely differences in the transparency of this authenticity, not differences in the authenticity itself or in our nearness to it. We in the Western world are so Judaeo-

Christian, so overstrained and overworked; as a result we are more or less cheated out of ourselves. We do understand and respect the cultic dance of primitive man, but we look askance at a person dancing to jazz because we think his enjoyment superficial. But here, too, a divine element enters in and moves the world creatively; the infinite "corporeal world," which embraces the entire world, and the archetypal forces are circling and moving in couples dancing the rumba as they move in the stars and the atoms.

Certainly with man something more enters in than with the natural world; but "known or unknown, the divine is always present." Certainly there are degrees of the divine, and a Bach Passion represents something different from the sentimental melody of a popular tune. But mountains and grains of sand also coexist without our feeling a need to assign them relative values, and everything in the world, including the sentimental melody, is still divine, capable of achieving divine effects, heightening them and revealing them creatively to man. And when, for instance, the corporeal self hops and slides, and when the little girlfriend, who meets none of the requirements of the decalogue, dances along, a divine event takes place; archetypal elements come to life, human ancestral lines and universal connections come into play, that the event may eventuate. — It remains a sacred and divine event like the dance of Krishna with Radha at the middle of the middle.[10] And it remains this quite independently of whether the dancers or any of the onlookers know it.

10. See above, Essay III.

But if every dance, every step, every meal, but also every glance of a living eye is full of the divine, why should anyone want to make us think we live remote from the divine? And that something within us which we are as a self knows of this, for if I can know of it even as an ego, how should my self-ego not know of it? And how can there be boundaries between it and me, except when I am locked up inside myself as a mere-ego? Thus this knowledge is everywhere and at hand, and this knowledge alone supports life and supports us all.

Then does this lament that man has fallen from meaning merely constitute a lament over his "egoification"? And is all congruence with the movement of the self a recovery, a return? But how can one recover that which can never be lost? For that is what I think I understand Zen to mean by the "imperishable nature of the Buddha." Does that suggest that our suffering as ego-suffering, as the suffering of the mere-ego, is actually an illusion, and does it not seem the most logical thing to want to be free of this ego, this annoying ballast, these obscuring glasses which we must put aside if we wish to experience ourselves as self-ego?

Without question this would appear, at least theoretically, to be the solution chosen by the East, but it seems not to apply to Zen, for the egos of these masters are as mighty as lions. As little as I accept the idea of man as fallen and the world as fallen do I believe that the divine erred when it created me as an ego. But if it did not err, what, then, is the significance of this ego?

I fear I am not a good Jew, although I am not quite certain, but on my path through life I have learned to experience and to venerate the divine as something formless and creative. This path in life has perhaps brought me closer to an understanding of the self-revelation of YHWH, in whose sign the Exodus from Egypt took place and every exodus from Egypt takes place, namely the strange divine name *Ehyeh asher ehyeh*: I am who I am.[11] Since every human being can speak only of his own experience when the question of meaning arises, I, too, can speak only of my personal experience and say what this *Ehyeh* means to me in this connection.

I cannot believe that our consciousness can impart consciousness to the divine. After all, was it not this divine principle which gave *me* consciousness, if one can speak at all of giving and receiving in such a context. But I am convinced that the point of consciousness with which I as an ego am endowed springs directly from this *Ehyeh asher ehyeh*, I am who I am, which is the name of God. This numinous I-point of consciousness which has me, which engenders me in every moment as an ego, is the actual self-ego-structure of my imperishable being. And this timeless point of the "I am" is a supremely numinous presence and actuality, expressed through my ego, which not only "pro-jects" [*entwirft*] me myself and the world in consciousness, but, as a "pro-jecting" agent, is also simultaneously a "pro-jected" ego. And this ego-self, in which the ego joins with the self, always transcends itself in a transcendent self-ego, a joining of the self with the ego. If anywhere, then here man's likeness to God achieves lasting reality in that creative force which created the world in light and continually creates

11. The "I am" remains the core of this name, regardless of whether one interprets it as present, future, or "I am here."

it anew. Here the "dual nature" of man, of which it is written, "God and Man are like unto twins,"[12] finds its fulfillment and unity, for the ego does not exist except in its linkage with the self and is rooted in the self as in a non-ego, with which it is identical, with and without its own awareness. The motto "vocatus atque non vocatus aderit deus"[13] applies here, in the formulation: known or unknown, here is the "I am." Even if the human ego seems to lock itself up as a mere-ego and to cut itself off from the self, by its very being it is always unknowingly linked with the self and identical with it.

In psychology we speak of the "genesis of the ego," even, in a certain sense, of the genesis of the self as it appears to the ego; we do so in order to describe and understand events in time, i.e., in history and in the fate of the individual. Yet in fact the creative original state, the self-ego-identity, is present from the very beginning; it is a given of human existence. And the basis of the ego-self constellation is that we must start with ourselves as the smaller ego, and not as the larger self. Only when we experience ourselves as a totality can we actualize the unity of ego and self in ourselves; we must *be* it in ego-actuality, but we can never *have* it.

Even in saying that this ego-point is "pro-jected" by the self, we have already formulated it wrong, precisely because we tried to formulate something for which language does not suffice. For if I as ego experience myself as something projected, as a self I am simultaneously

---

12. *Talmud Sanhedrin* 46b.

13. ["Called or uncalled, the god is present": a Delphic oracle, translated into Latin by Erasmus. C. G. Jung had this carved above the doorway of his house (1909).]

also that which "pro-jects" myself. Therefore the possibility exists that as an ego I can say of myself: "I am a stranger to myself," for that condition is the source of all self-knowledge. But if the self appears to the ego as something "completely different" and as a "thou" that demands to be recognized, then I am at the same time the recognizing ego and also the self-ego, which is present within me as the ego desirous of experience.

This state of affairs forms the basis for the view that the Divinity attains its own consciousness in human consciousness. But it does not "attain" consciousness, for that is not, or is only seemingly, a matter of a process within time; rather this consciousness-point of the "I am who I am" is like a static flash of lightning, a consciousness outside of time, which seen "from the vantage point of the self" exists outside time, and seen from the vantage point of the ego steps into time in the temporal moment. But even this creative moment of consciousness is "atemporal"; one might also say "eternal" or "in God," in which case the spatial "in" corresponds not to the creative moment itself but to its temporal-spatial dimension as seen from the vantage point of the ego.

This connection between the ego and the self should not be understood in pantheistic terms. The very fact that the formless divine principle appears within the human structure as an "I am there" and "I am who I am," and not as an "it," is the root of Western man's human ego-ness, the root of human individuality and individuation. Any view of the world that excludes the divine must somehow account for this "I am" which has become actuality in mankind. If it attempts in the existentialist manner to reduce this "I am" to pure subjectivity, it necessarily incurs the misfortune of being plunged into despair and absurdity, for while the "I am" does feed into the human ego, it is not rooted in it.

In the limitation of the ego to a "mere-ego," we are only part of a world consisting of related parts—human beings, animals, and things. But this "mere-ego" has lost the experience of its own numinosity, of its "I am who I am." As this "mere-ego" we are integrated into the merely temporal-spatial world, and a substantial measure of the ego's despair in its isolation stems from this limitation, which expresses itself in the loss of a relationship to the unconscious, to the self, and to the unitary reality, likewise the loss of the world-self linkage with which the latter is identical. When that happens, the mere-ego has lost its character as an ego which, as part of the ego-self unity, is a creative and not only a rational ego.

The rational ego, as part of the consciousness-ego, exercises a highly significant partial function, providing an organ for grasping the world through the conscious; as such, it forms a part of the system by which the personality operates. But it is a different matter with the will, the function of decision. It, too, can be part of the mere-ego and in its interests can aim for all that is useful, purposeful, collectively necessary, etc., but its actual source derives from the creatively numinous "I am" point. For although we do not adequately realize it, the will has the hidden function of achieving wholeness. Since the "I will" springs from the creative "I am," the body and the psyche obediently place themselves at its disposal in an act of unity located on the edge of space-and-timelessness. In the "I will" point of the "I am," this act becomes creative and quits the space-and-timelessness of the "I am who I am" to enter the spatial-temporal world.

The individual self, i.e., that "part" of the self belonging to the individual's individuality, always appears in conjunction with an ego, in which it "filializes" itself, in which it represents, in the form of the "I am" and the "I will" point of nothingness, the actual creative force. But if one goes so far as to speak of a "part," clearly it is no longer a question of the actual self, of the self of the self, so to speak; rather one implies that the individual self is already an "incarnation," a temporal and spatial embodiment of the space-and-timeless self. We find here a correspondence between space- and timelessness and entrance into the space-time dimension, analogous to that connection which exists between the space-and-timeless point-of-nothingness typical of the creative divine element and the extended spatial-temporal world. Individuality, too, the self, is present in the extratemporal moment of birth as a complete, creative "I am" and "I will," but at that very moment it enters time and must develop, take on shape and fulfill itself within the temporality and spatiality of the world.

The creative point-of-nothingness of the individual self, to which the world belongs, and that point to which the individual's unfolding destiny belongs are one and the same; they manifest themselves with the aid of the spaceless and timeless "I am" that springs up in the ego and to which the world becomes visible in its temporality and spatiality. Assigned to the spatial-temporal extension of time yet to be experienced in which the ego experiences the world, as well as to the spatial-temporal extension in which the ego experiences its own life as destiny, are creative points-of-nothingness of the "I am who I am," which coincide with each other or are identical with each other, points-of-nothingness out of which arise as conjoined realities the existence of the world and events-as-destiny.

That is to say: the spatial-temporal unfolding of individuality and the ego always harbors the creative point-of-nothingness of space-and-timelessness. The "I am here" of the individual self and the "I am" of the ego exist, if one may say so, in every moment in simultaneity with the continuing present of the central creative nothingness, out of which and "in which" all of unfolded being lives. The ego-time of the ego and its world and the world's time in its extended aspect are continuously embraced by the timelessness and the worldlessness of the self that is conjoined with the ego and belongs to the unitary reality whose being does not exist "behind" or "in" everything spatial and temporal but *as* everything spatial and temporal.

While difficult to express conceptually, this unity of being-in-time and being-outside-of-time, of the inner-worldly and outer-worldly existence of the creative element, which at the same time is that of existence itself, can, nonetheless, be grasped concretely. For apparently the point-of-conception of the work of art corresponds precisely to that of individuality; both are extra-worldly, extra-temporal, and extra-spatial; both must manifest themselves creatively within the categories of space and time and must take on form. In the "I will" point of the artist's creative conception, the psyche as a whole places itself at the disposal of the self-ego as it expresses itself. Thus a symphony, as Mozart reported, can be simultaneously present, with all its details and relationships, in the timeless moment of conception, only later to unfold successively in the temporal dimension as a stream of note-pictures, graphic symbols lined up in space. That means: here, too, as in the birth-moment of the horoscope, the "I will" comes into being in the creative "I am" and brings forth a world out of the point-of-nothingness of space-and-timelessness.

Here, too, we confront a phenomenon which one might describe or circumscribe as the "timelessness" of a moment in time. The moment in time, be it that of a life or, for instance, of a piece of music, is built into a progression of time in which it finds itself between a before and an after and leads from one to the other. Yet each of these moments-in-time exists as an "ever-present present" in timelessness; it is not only not conditioned by any before; it is a unique one-time occurrence, just as the individual is not only a product of his ancestors but also a unique one-time being. The music that fills me, presently alive in timelessness, is indivisible as present from my "I am present" in its capacity as my timeless present-point—and this present that unfolds in time never really enters the stream of time, although it fulfills itself within time.

If I intend to write something, this creative ego-will remains present throughout the process by which conception becomes realization. Although I write in time, the creative moment of this writing is timelessly present in every moment. In that creative and wholly unforeseeable moment my ego's "I am" and "I will" are conjoined in such a way with the self which includes my ego that it is the self's extra-temporal creative force that guides me, starting with the instant of mental conception and continuing through my word-seeking and pen-pushing existence. Often as an ego I must perform extraordinarily extensive feats of the conscious, and these feats remain permanently incorporated into the connection that transcends the ego, for every idea and every unforeseen and unforeseeable turn of the creative process depends on this superiority of the self over the ego. Within the purely logical thought process this ego-self connection seems to carry less weight, but to the extent that a creative process is involved, the connection is likewise superior to the ego and the conscious. Even in mathematics intuition plays a decisive role—as the intuitionists' school attests. Yet intuition must always rely on the connection with the psyche's supraconsciousness and unconscious forces.[14]

The same holds true for my life in time, in which I fulfill myself as a self, as myself, although I am always also an ego at a world-and-time point of my inner-worldly existence. But in the fulfilled moment I am whole and indivisible, although this moment appears as a part of my life occurring in space and time, of my self-realization. Here, too, the indivisible unity of simultaneity can be found, a unity within which I exist as an "I am," an "I will," and an "I am self" in the creative extra-spatial and extra-temporal point-of-nothingness of the unitary reality, at the same time unfolding my living being spatially and temporally in the world.

Yet it is not, as my earlier oversimplified formulation might suggest, that the ego exists in time and the self in

14. Jung, *Psychological Types*, CW 6, Def. 35, "Intuition."

timelessness. The numinous "I am" core of the ego in its indissoluble unity with the self, with the "I am present" of the self, is also linked to the creative extra-temporal and extra-worldly element, out of which time and the world are continually being generated. For as an ego-self/self-ego unity I am an inseparable part of the extra-temporal unitary reality to which I belong in every creative moment of my existence.

In this sense the temporality experienced by the ego is at once real and unreal, and existence is, whether I know it or not, as much a spatial-temporal continuum as a creation which sporadically flares up in every extra-temporal "moment" of the everlasting present. In regard to this fact, too, the old statement holds true: "God renews the Creation every morning," which may be explicated as "God renews the Creation every moment." But the divine renews the Creation not only in every moment, but in the moment of every existing being and existence. And the atemporality of the creative element paradoxically by no means contradicts the living-in-time of the living being, which manifests itself as pure spontaneity in a world of infinite spontaneities. Only an ego that shuts itself off and thereby shuts itself up achieves the illusion of an exclusively temporal-spatial and closed reality consisting of "parts" to which the human individual belongs as a part of this spatial-temporal existence.

Refutation of this error, so essential if modern man is to overcome his sense of catastrophe, must not be sought in the direction repeatedly taken by the wrong-headed humanism of the West when it ascribes eternal religious, metaphysical, philosophical, and moral validity to the split introduced into the world by the rational mere-ego. This eternalization almost always occurs in the name of distinctions that confront the "false" world of the ego with the "true" world. Here one can clearly see the frightful misunderstanding introduced into Western thought with the assertion that "being" is opposed to "seeming," "authentic" to "fallen, inauthentic."

Just as one cannot say that the self "is" and the ego "seems" or that the "ego" is a fallen self, one cannot claim that the ego-world is a world of appearances and inauthentic. For the ego-world is the periphery belonging to the creatorly self-ego unity of the "I am who I am" in the creative nothingness. The ego-world is the outside of this inside. Yet at the same time this outside is in reality no outside, since it functions only for the ego as an outside vis-à-vis an inside, nor is it an inside, since the "inner" creatorly nothingness continuously manifests itself as something that creates the world and the outside. But as ego-consciousness we cannot grasp this seamless reality, which corresponds to the alchemical *solve et coagula*, other than by dividing it and putting it together again.

Precisely, once it has become transparent how easily the ego-self dual structure of the human psyche can mislead us into distinguishing between a world of appearances, a fallen world, and a world of essence, an authentic world of the self, one cannot emphasize too strongly that this dual nature is a unity appearing in twin-form.

The division of the world into being and seeming, or into pure and impure, authentic and inauthentic, not only gives rise to the catastrophic split in the Western world, but also to the fundamental inhumanity of its misguided humanism, whose abstractness culminates in disdain for merely human, merely worldly life. This misguided humanism with its predilection for the "noble," the "genuine," and the "elevated" can assume many forms; all of them lead to contempt for natural man and natural, un-"elevated" life.

So, for example, an excellent book on Rilke and Heidegger[15] states, in an interpretation of Rilke's lines

> Gieb mir, oh Erde, den reinen
> Thon für den Tränenkrug[16]
> (Give me, oh earth, pure
> clay for my jug of tears—)

"But the 'weeping,' 'that which is held back' is actually non-form; it has not transcended the purely subjective realm of experience, which extends into nowhere and everywhere. It is itself non-being, a 'nowhere'—'all nowhere is evil'—a disruptive, alarming element. It is 'unleashed' only by the mere-experience; it is 'leashed' only when it has been given form. But that which is formed, whatever and however it may be, is 'being' pure and simple, of which one can say: 'All being is appropriate.' "

In these sentences something inhumane finds expression; aside from the fact that Rilke is here profoundly misunderstood and misinterpreted, this view imperils the very existence of the Western world. Man's "weeping" is in no sense non-being and a "nowhere"; rather it

15. Else Buddeberg, *Denker und Dichter des Seins: Heidegger, Rilke* (Stuttgart, 1956), p. 22.
16. Rainer Maria Rilke, *Gedichte 1906-1926* (Wiesbaden, 1953), p. 294.

is existence at its most vital and lives, even when in-
choate and unable to reach man's ear, in the heart of the
divine. Rilke's plea to the earth for a pure jug of tears
does not issue from the "nowhereness" of this weeping,
but from his eternal living-in-the-divine. When he asks
the earth to give him clay for the jug of tears, this re-
quest for a form that will contain and retain the world's
infinite tears signifies the wish that the invisible-infinite
may become something visible and finite intended for
man, whose closed heart should more readily open up to
the form of the poem—so the poet hopes—and whose
blindness should be made seeing again. At issue is the
power of the creative to unlock, a power which uses
form as its instrument, as a key, to unlock man's stonily
closed heart and cause it to beat again.

This misunderstanding of the poem reveals with es-
pecial clarity the false conception, derived from the
Greeks, of a closed "corporeal form of being," in contrast to the formless open form of the East, which sees
the true task of the artist as consisting in portraying the
divine as the living movement of spiritual spontaneity
and of the creative moment.[17] Weeping as a figure in
infinite motion within the internal space of existence is
an archetypal human melody which for all its formlessness is eternal form and creative reality.

The tears of him who weeps in reality need no jug to
contain them, and the poet who celebrates those tears
liberates them when his pen lends form to the formless-
infinite. Certainly he does not transform a "nowhere"

17. Mai-mai Sze, *The Tao of Painting* (New York, 1956; 2nd ed.,
1963) [Vol. 1, p. 86].

into "being," but by virtue of his own inner motion he makes something that is moved in the divine into something that moves man.

Whether a person is "authentic" or "inauthentic," whether he lives "genuinely" or not, and regardless of his usefulness to collective processes and cultural developments, the life of a single individual is *the* "great treasure" in its uniqueness, and everyone is "eternal man" in the "eternal world." Since every individual's ego-self contains the "I am here" of the "I am," the life and world of every individual also embraces the entire world and the entire creation. The important issue placed before consciousness has to do not with whether man "is" something or "is not" something, but with whether his real being is transparent or opaque to him.

In this sense the story of my life is the story of every human being, the story of mankind. And this is true not only because every ego-self carries within it not only humanity but all of history and history's ego-presentness. All forces, all elements of existence, all landscapes and passions, the seasons and the timelessness of nothingness are woven into my life, created for me, offered to me, and when I fulfill myself they are fulfilled. As fulfilled being flows into my life, known and unknown it reveals itself as the divine element that moves the Creation. In every individual this creative world undergoes transformation and comes to itself, and as an ego-self I participate in this occurrence when I open myself up and let it fulfill itself in me; I am creator, creature and creative force at once. I am these things not only as something both divinely creative and humanly individual, but also as a world unique unto myself. In the self-ness of my individuality not only am I whole, but the Creation becomes whole, and as a self existing in the unitary reality I transcend and fulfill my "I am-ness" at the same time as my "world-ness."

This all-embracing character of my existence transcends the historically relative nature of my ego-ness in time, although I do not exist outside of it. If I am the "whole person" and my world is the "whole world," my life is also the "whole of life." But it becomes both these things precisely by virtue of my mortality; and death, properly understood, is the actual symbol of my individuality, for death alone makes me something unique.

Modern man's fear of death is the heritage of the religion that has already died within him, whose sense of guilt he has inherited, but whose vehicles for mercy he has lost. Kahler's sentence, "We no longer live our days in nearness to the divine," is the last reflection of that separation of the human from the divine which has cast a pall of fear over Western man. The fallen ego was left in the cruelly paradoxical situation that the survival of its authentic immortal soul in the realm of authenticity, the beyond, depended on the conduct of its "inauthentic" ego in this "inauthentic" world. The ego, oppressed by the impossibility of fulfilling the demands placed upon it, found the sword of fear dangling over it and was tortured with the *memento mori* that in one's "final hour" death and hell coincided. Death and the Judgment Day became a threat; the ego's suffering might be prolonged into eternity.

One cannot deny the pedagogic significance this cruel threat can have for taming the evil in man, any more than one can overlook the fatal effect the split induced by this threat has on Western man. Now evil must be stamped out at all cost, since it leads in the future to hell. In reality, however, confronting and assimilating evil constitutes a never-to-be-completed task, a task for a lifetime. Accordingly, when man finds himself threatened with punishment in hell, he has little choice but to split off evil, his own evil, and not merely suppress it but take the more radical step of repressing it. But this splitting-off of evil necessarily leads one to experience it as something "foreign" to oneself—and project it onto that which is foreign. In the last analysis, this projection of evil onto the foreign Other[18] has, as any survey of the two-thousand-year history of the West will show, not exactly improved the white man. Nor is that all; man attributed the cruelty of this fear that was poisoning him to the Divinity, following that strange law prevailing in the West that may describe such cruelty as "inhumane" but apparently views it as readily reconcilable with the image of the divine.

This fear felt by supposedly secularized modern man is the heritage of the threat implied by the *memento mori* in a world dominated by evil. That means: the devil, guilt, and death have remained, while God, mercy, and the eternal life have vanished. This catastrophic and absurd existence threatens man, who has come to experience himself as a "mere-ego," cut off from the divine, and as a result hurls himself into himself, into the abyss ripped open by the split within him. This fall into the abyss is our destiny, at once our undoing and our salvation. The existentialist experience of our times has many

18. Neumann, *Depth Psychology and a New Ethic*.

shadings, but the experience of man's loneliness forms a common motif. When thus thrown back on himself, man confounds the ego-ness of his ego in fatal fashion with the wholeness of his ego-self-integrity. But when the ego is cut off from the self, its desperate efforts at achieving equilibrium lead to inflation of the ego, to Luciferian pride in absurd existence, or to the megalomaniac claim that the ego "pro-jects" itself and the world.

This is not intended as criticism of the assertions of a particular philosophy or person, but as a criticism of the ego-sense of each and every one of us, a sense to which these assertions testify. Each of us in his isolation clings to this Luciferian "nevertheless" in the face of the threat of existence, each of us must throw himself into the world as part of his life project. And the ego's defiant "nevertheless" is by no means the worst mode for life in this world, for in the ego's attempt at self-sufficiency, the "I am here" of the self in the ego is at work, without, however, the ego's being aware of it. That means that in its defiance against loneliness and lostness, the ego draws the will to live and affirmation of its paradoxical existence from the divine element within it, the divine element which "pro-jects" the world and the ego and affirms the paradoxical absurdity of existence.

This paradox rests on the genuine paradox fundamental to the human situation: that divine and human elements, self and ego, coexist in man as a unity. This unity can be lived and adumbrated, but never formulated except in paradoxes. That is why such a great misunderstanding is perpetrated when theologians criticize modern man's attempts to regain the unity of ego and self, i.e., the unity of the human with the divine, as "deification" of man. Even when Western man ceases to experience himself only as an ego, he certainly does not experience himself as a self, as we rightly or wrongly assume Asian man does.

The touchstones for any experience of our ego-self-integrity are two basic problems, two challenges: death and evil. They are the *aqua fortis* which reveals definitively whether something within us has preserved or restored the alchemical quality of the gold of our innermost nature; but they are also the *aqua fortis* which reveals that we are a compound, of which only a part is gold, the other part changeable lead.

As an ego-self I myself am the task that has been set for me. That means that precisely as an individuality and as an ego-ness situated in time I must come to terms not only with myself, with my gold and my lead, my good and bad elements, but also with the world, which has been laid upon me as a task. The unique ego of my ego-self, which is identical with my mortality, with my transitory nature, guarantees that I have a unique task to accomplish as an individual.

My experience is the irrevocably unique experience of the divine within me. The world created only for me, that can be experienced and creatively realized only by me, corresponds to my ego-self in its likeness to God. The unity of the unique world, consisting of myself as an individual with the creative world that is created for me and evolves in my life, corresponds to the irrevocable task of my self-discovery and self-becoming. This irrevocability pertains to me and my intransitoriness as well as to my transitoriness, for both are as inseparable as the

transitory-intransitory nature of the everlasting presentness of every moment and of the divine itself.

Yet at issue here is less a matter of mortality and immortality, of good and evil, than of the invincibility of
the divine, creatively present within everything and
above and beyond everything. If today we seem to experience chaos, terror, and man's inhumanity to man
more than in any previous period, we should not lose
sight of this invincibility, which is alive even in the sui-
cide who, with his leap into death, not only takes a stand
against negativity, but, paradoxically, by saying *no* refutes the *no*, as if unwittingly he were certain of his in-
destructibility even as he blotted himself out.

Through my ego's creative "I am" and "I will" I am
constantly being forced to make choices, am constantly
positing yes and no, good and evil. Such choices between
opposites are as good as identical with my ego-ness, for
even when I do not choose, that constitutes a choice.
This process of choice coincides with my freedom and
my suffering; yet my ego's suffering from evil, from my
evil, from the evil in man and in the world, says not the
slightest thing about the existence of evil outside of my
ego in the throes of choice.

Blaming this problem on the divine merely compounds the error, unavoidable, to be sure, which leads
us to personalize the image of the divine and picture it
as something like our ego, faced with moral choices. But
when we assert that the creative-divine element engenders both good and evil, life and death, light and darkness, we are already exceeding the limits of an ego that
makes choices as we do and capturing that aspect of the
divine which is not choice-oriented but creative. The

creative, however, is beyond good and evil. Without realizing it, we acknowledge this principle when, for instance, we do not hold a poet or writer morally responsible for what he creates, but on the contrary measure him by whether he succeeds—like Shakespeare—in creating both good and evil and portraying them with creative objectivity.

The conviction that the patriarchal Divinity is a sort of moral super-ego remains so strong in Western man that we either blame the thus diminished Divinity completely for evil or foolishly try to defend it as "exclusively good."

But any attribute we must remove from the divine falls to the lot of man, and we must learn to endure living as an "I am" and to make choices in a world created by the creative-divine element, which itself transcends all choices. In the process we constantly experience through our likeness to God, as manifested in our ego-self-integrity, that this choice-making aspect of our "ego" does not merely exist in contrast to the creative but is contained within it, for it embraces all opposites.

We ourselves, as a form of being that creatively forges its own life, are infinitely more than our choice-making ego. As an entity bound up with the world and humanity, we create our own fate with its good and evil, ourselves functioning as creatures of nature and instinct, as well as of spirit. We must, to be sure, say yes or no to ourselves, we must accept or reject ourselves as good and evil, but we are uninterruptedly compelled to do that which an Other in ourselves or we as an ego would ourselves condemn as evil. Similarly we must sometimes do something good by way of self-sacrifice, even as we strain against it with all the intensity inspired by man's instinct for self-preservation. Yet we are incapable of limiting the creative wholeness of our being to exclusively "good" actions, aside from the fact that the necessity for our ego to reach moral decisions by no means always assures our ability to judge whether the good we do is really good and the evil we do really evil. That the contents of the choices which we as an ego must make are relative in no way changes the absoluteness of the necessity imposed upon us to choose. And furthermore, as an ego we suffer, which is part and parcel of our nature as a creative entity doing both good and evil, and of our ego passing judgment on good and evil. Knowledge of the creative necessity for our being evil as well as good neither obviates the necessity for our moral choices nor our suffering over them. We know enough—more than enough—about the relative way in which choices vary, according to the situation of the person involved, his cultural canon and the limits of his consciousness; but nevertheless no ego can escape the necessity for such choice.

The ego confronted with a choice is always lonely, but it makes a difference whether it chooses as an isolated "mere-ego" and mere-part of its group or in full awareness of the numinosity of the "I am." Yet this awareness does not shield man from guilt and error; it does not relieve him of either the choice or the risk of incurring guilt. Both are givens that accompany the necessary bias and transitoriness of our ego-ness, by virtue of which we are included in that creative form of being that embraces good and evil.

But for the human being who has found a new relationship to the good and evil in human reality, a transformation occurs in his relationship to himself, once he has acted. He can understand his action, which independently of his will has turned out to be good or evil, and the consequences of his action, as part of destiny, and accept it as a necessary part, not only of the realization of his ego-self but also of the realization of the world that is inextricably bound up with the former.

Here, too, it becomes apparent, without any diminution of the ego, that my fateful choice, which is inextricably bound up with that of my fellow human beings, can be experienced as meaningful in terms of good and of evil. Moreover, my creative being, which, for instance, compels me to be unconscious and to follow my instincts, is by no means always evil, nor is my consciously repressing ego by any means always good. (It is obvious that the reverse is likewise by no means an absolute law.) Here, too, each unique and unforeseeable choice forms part of the destiny of an individual who, as a creative ego-self, must constantly choose his path and follow it as a freely choosing ego in every creative moment, even if his path should be prescribed for him by his unknown self.

This experience of the unity of our ego-self-integrity, which creatively engenders good and evil, morally judges and suffers, does not result in any sort of god-like situation beyond good and evil, nor does it any longer result in the guilt feelings of an isolated ego, continually succumbing to the excessive demands of a terrifying super-ego. I am saved neither from my ego-ness nor from my evil-ness, not even through my own efforts or the experience of my ego-self-integrity, but I experience as meaningful the necessity of my ego-self-ness in the form of ego-ness and self-ness in guilt and innocence; and in the finality implied in every moment of my life by my ego-ness and my mortality, this meaning confers a new sort of innocence, which applies to us as well as to the world which is linked with us and was created at the same time as we were.

In the *I Ching* the sign of "The Wanderer" ☲☶ is followed by the sign of "The Gentle" ☴☴. The commentary, which links both signs, says, "The wanderer has nothing that might receive him; hence there follows the hexagram of THE GENTLE, THE PENETRATING. The Gentle means going into. / This means that the wanderer in his forlornness has no place to stay in, and that hence there follows Sun, the hexagram of homecoming."[19]

The abandoned condition of the Wanderer, which is our own, leads to the homecoming, the return to the Gentle, which penetrates the world, the divine, the self, ourselves. In his homecoming, man's wandering ego-self accepts being. And in this acceptance man experiences the world as the emanation of the creative, which as unitary reality presents itself as that to which we must come home, even though we have never been released from it. It is the homecoming of a prodigal son who was never lost, and the return is no reentry and no turning point, but only a process whereby he becomes aware of having gone forth and being home again.

Only when the idea that there is such a thing as a

19. *I Ching*, pp. 674, 679. [The full title of the hexagram Sun, according to Wilhelm/Baynes, is "The Gentle (The Penetrating Wind)."]

"false" and "inauthentic" life has been recognized for an error, only when being has become transparent as the being of the divine in lust as in asceticism, in giving as in receiving, in the cloud as in the poem that captures it, only then does being-in-the-world become more than merely a loneliness in which the Wanderer has nothing that would receive him, but a return to a shelter that was in fact never lost. Here being lost and being sheltered coincide, for just as in our ego-ness we are lost, and must be lost, since we do not experience any personal form of the divine Other as an "external reality," so in our ego-self-integrity we are sheltered, since we have stepped outside our proximity to the divine. Not until we return home to this sheltered state do we really begin to live in this divine world. And to live in it is identical with feeling in the very soles of our feet that our paths are eternal paths.

Psychology calls part of this encounter with the eternal "archetypal experience." But today we encounter this experience not in a discrete, sacred realm but wherever and whenever we are capable of experiencing as whole persons the whole world. For the non-fallen world is the world of the "Great Experience" which is always accessible; it is the world in which the difference between great and small, correct and incorrect vanishes, because the personal becomes transparent as the transpersonal, and the transpersonal limits itself to the personal. This self-limitation to the personal makes possible a return to the wholeness of the world's wholeness as experienced in every individual. In something supposedly transitory and inauthentic the eternal and the authentic manifests itself, and a simple little song resounds with love for man, the divine, the world. As life's eternal paths are illuminated, life beyond the ego's experience of chaos comes into focus as a world of the preordained, and we need only follow these paths to be able to experience our course as eternal and sheltered. In that instant the time of our travelling melts to an eternal moment, in which no path and no order are visible to the walker, because no more time is visible, but only the meaningfulness of the present moment.

But this fulfilled present is not based on some futureless, amoral, or hedonistic form of being; suffering remains, as well as the agony of choice. But the resonance of the depths, the archetypal resonance in which vibrate both the background of the world as a unitary reality and the background of the ego as self, confers on everything unique, seemingly inadequate and isolated, the meaning which reveals life as creative and indestructible. Although not the slightest thing has "changed," everything is new; the abstract character of temporal succession is superseded by the eternity of the moment, and the abandoned state of the ego by the shelteredness of the ego-self, from which, thanks to the unity of the creative-divine with my "I am," I can never be expelled.

Here "encounter" as well as identity, the non-selfness of the ego as well as the ego-self unity of the personality, are inextricably linked in the twin-nature of God's image. In the experience of "congruence" human life becomes meaningful. I am congruent with the world, I am congruent with my self, the ego-self and the world are congruent, belong together, are one, are omnipresent and ever-present.

When the individual person experiences his life thus

as destiny, as the "whole world" and as filled with meaning, he fulfills himself not only in time but also outside of time. In the temporal succession of events, in the experience of destiny, he realizes himself not only as a unity of ego and self, of conscious and unconscious, but also as a projection of himself and of his self in the unity of internal and external happenings. The people who happen to me and I myself as a person happening to myself are one in an overall pattern, and that which unfolds in the unfolding of time's passage is also something real beyond time. This "beyond time" is experienced both as "planned from the outset"—as, for instance, in the horoscope—and as something unique and eternal, which disguises itself in the temporal. Each person is born into the uniqueness of his origin, his landscape, his times and his type and must bear all the limitations that go along with this condition, and fulfill them. But "besides"—as we say—we experience the world *and* ourselves not as something unique and limited, but as something unique and eternal. As an ego and as consciousness I may be temporal and limited, but as a self and something beyond consciousness I am eternal. Each spring is a unique event, an "I am here" in the now, but its uniqueness and special characteristics also emit a double gleam, that of the uniqueness of the ego and its "never-again," and also that of the eternity of the self and its "always here" and its "forever and ever, Amen." Only this twin-like experience of unity confers meaning in the divine image. This experience of the divine as a creative "enthusiasm," of creative being-in-God, affirms existence as an infinite finitude, whose eternity stems from the creative. This enthusiasm of the divine, of the creative nothingness that flows forth from itself, compels all human beings to undergo the transformation of becoming, so that it may prove itself eternal in the midst of transformation.

This belonging-together in the twin unity of existence is as obvious when experienced as it appears paradoxical when formulated. As an ego we must speak of the non-ego, of the Thou, and of the self, because their unity is possible only in the completeness of the experienced creative moment; it falls apart in the "statement" of the ego. If we point out this meaning-conferring "knowledge without knowledge" that grows out of our ego-self experience, the ego's statement may cancel itself out, but our experience of it remains, although it cannot be adequately expressed, as the inalienable possession of our existence.

V

PEACE AS THE SYMBOL
OF LIFE

I

What is peace? At first glance this may seem a topic very
close to the heart of everyone today, in a time of wars,
rioting, coups d'état, and revolutions in every sphere of
life. Not until we look more closely and ponder more
deeply—not until we actually meditate on this theme—
do we realize that in reality we have no idea what peace
is. Or to put it a little more circumspectly: I very seldom
know the meaning of this word "peace."

We habitually use the word "peace" to mean the opposite of war. At first glance it may appear that this
interpretation is the only one possible. But it is bound to
give us pause when we recall that the longing for peace
is so universally human that it is inadequate to regard
peace as merely the opposite of war. The ideal of
peace—future peace, eternal peace, heavenly peace—appears to be an archetypal hope of mankind. In other
words it seems related to something so quintessential in

"Frieden als Symbol des Lebens," in *Der schöpferische Mensch* (Zurich, 1959); revised from the version in *Eranos-Jahrbuch 1958*, on
"Man and Peace." Translated by Jan van Heurck.

man that it is not enough to interpret "peace" simply as one term in the polarity "war-peace."

Perhaps, in the course of our deliberations, the meaning of man's authentic longing for peace will become apparent. We may also come to understand peace not merely as a symbol of something all mankind feels is important, but as something more concrete and substantial. But our point of departure must be the ideal which attaches to the word "peace."

The word "peace" is frequently used as a synonym for "quiet," but verbal constructions employing "peace" to mean "rest, quiet," are highly ambivalent. That is, in addition to its profound and legitimate use, the word is also used in a way which is illegitimate and suspect. Take the phrase "to make one's peace." It can express an authentic development, although even in this case, if we are punctilious about language, we would have to consider the implications of the verb "to make." However, the expression "to make one's peace" can also describe a penchant for easy compromise, the abandonment of legitimate demands, the making of wrong concessions. For decades now we have ceaselessly borne witness to the fact that one can "make one's peace" even with the Devil and destruction, which in reality is just another way of saying that one wants to be "left in peace" or wants—in a sense which can only lead to disaster—to "have peace."

In contrast to this "will to peace," which constitutes a will to retreat and to hold onto a false sense of security, there are the remarkable words of Jesus: "I came not to send peace, but a sword" (Matthew 11:34). Doubtless nothing was further from his mind than that his words should be fulfilled in such ghastly and literal terms, in the bloodbaths which ensued throughout millennia of Christian wars and persecutions. Nevertheless, in this statement Christ clearly declared his opposition to man's propensity to strive to be left in peace at any price, and to make his peace with everything which threatens this counterfeit peace. In this case the desire for "peace and quiet" is equivalent to the misguided detachment of the man who stands on the sidelines, who does not want to "get involved."

And yet a question arises: Aren't these things—detachment, quiet, peace, and even the refusal to get involved—among the highest of philosophical ideals? How are we to determine when we are seeing an authentic case of "standing above the fray" (*au-dessus de la mêlée*) and when someone is just "deserting the colors"? Indeed, is it possible to decide this at all? This brings us to another question: What do we really mean by the military expression "to desert the colors"? In the past the colors, the flag we swear by and die for, were a sacred symbol, and in a sense they still are. But how many flags, banners, eagles, crests, and standards men have already died for, and how often deviltry, cloaked in these symbols, has driven them to despair and death! And yet the idea of deserting the colors still remains a moral, not a military concept, and the concept of "fighting for" something, "standing up" for something, refusing to "admit defeat," and countless other such sentiments, hold a universal human appeal that transcends the military. "War is ... father of all,"[1] and "For he was a man, and that

1. Heraclitus, fr. 53, in K. Freeman, *Ancilla to the Pre-Socratic Phi-*

means a fighter."² So what are we to make of this desire, integral to human nature, to "have peace" and to be "left in peace"?

If peace is the polar opposite of war and these two poles determine life, which unfolds by swinging back and forth between them, then the desire for peace signifies something impossible and senseless, namely the desire to cling to a state which is necessarily transitory and fleeting. It would appear that what brings man to desire peace is, quite simply, the suffering which is a basic constituent of life as an enantiodromian, dialectical process which unfolds through the action of contraries—that is, a life involving war. But in this case the desire for peace would be equivalent to the desire for the cessation of life, and the equation "the peace and quiet of the grave" truly plays a paramount role in human life.

But what does this equation mean, and what is the meaning of the wish, which strikes us as so natural that we do not think twice about it, *Requiescat in pace*, "May he rest in peace," which we voice when we lay a dead man in his grave? In this, as in all life-and-death matters, men reveal themselves for what they really are; we can see what is truly important to them and what are their true commitments, which are often the direct opposite of the ideologies and faiths to which they consciously adhere. Thus for most moderns, death appears equivalent to the end, to ultimate dissolution. That is,

---

losophers (1948). ["War is both king of all and father of all, and it has revealed some as gods, others as men; some it has made slaves, others free."]

2. Goethe, *Westöstlicher Diwan* ["Einlass," XII, 4, 15-16 of the collection *Chuld Nameh, Buch des Paradieses.*]

without knowing it they are materialists for whom life and soul are synonymous with the body and its continued existence. For them, to rest in peace and to be dead actually mean: finally it's all over. They feel weary and worn out and have had enough of life's sufferings and disappointments, and of the struggle for survival. In itself this form of "desire for peace" is perfectly understandable. The remarkable thing is merely its inconsistency, the unrelatedness of the attitude to modern man's worldview as a whole and to the very different beliefs he ostensibly holds.

It is notable how slight a role the concept of a "life after death"—a concept championed by all religions—plays in the life of modern man. But it is not hard to understand why this is so if we look at the contrast between the millennia-old ideas of heaven and hell and the modern state of mind. Our views about life after death depend on our attitudes toward deity and the soul, and when one of these constellations sinks beneath our horizon, it takes with it an entire star-filled firmament. The messianic age following upon the Last Judgment, and the ideal of salvation—regardless of whether this consists in the pure contemplation of God, the gratification of earthly desires projected onto a higher plane, the pleasurable sight of the sufferings of the unredeemed, and so on—arouses in modern man the protest that all this would bore him to tears. It seems to me that this reaction is anything but cynical, for in reality it expresses the fact that man does not equate happiness either with pleasure, with passive contemplation, or with peace, and that in the absence of some contrary force there is not only no life, but also no joy and no salvation—salvation being truly present only if it saves one from something which, at the same time, it remains possible for one to really *experience*.

But if, for modern man, even the theological concept of life after death is no longer valid, and if he equates death with peace and the cessation of life, and life with the struggle for survival, why does he feel such a dread of death? Why is the human soul so disinclined to allow its mortal terror to be dispelled by the ancient and compelling argument of the materialists and rationalists, who claim that there is nothing to fear because after death there no longer exists anything capable of experiencing fear?

So, does clinging to life, loving life, and the desire to postpone death and its peace, really mean that the human soul, by its very nature, is ready to accept war as the father of all things and to involve itself in life and the struggle synonymous with it; and that the life impulse and the will to live, in a higher sense, involve the readiness to take up the struggle and to be "a fighter"?

If we look into the etymology of the word "peace" [*Frieden*] in German,[3] we make the surprising discovery that, at least in the beginning, the word had a very narrow meaning. Those for whom the word implies something general and universal, something which indeed transcends the human, will find it almost disappointing—but also illuminating—to learn that "peace" [*Frieden*] is related to "free" [*frei*], "friend" [*Freund*], and with *frei* is related to love.[4] In other words, peace is that

3. F. Kluge, *Etymologisches Wörterbuch der deutschen Sprache*, ed. A. Goetze (1948).
4. [Cf. German *freien*, formerly "to marry," now "to court."—Tr.]

which belongs to a person and which he must treat with consideration. Friends are "free" men, as opposed to those who are not of one's group and who are made slaves, and only with these friends whom one loves— "free" and "to court" [*frei* and *freien*] derive from the same root—does one live "in peace" [*in Frieden*]. Here, as so often in the biological realm, it seems as if the zone of freedom consists exclusively of a territory comprising things affiliated to oneself, cut out of an intrinsically hostile world dominated by war and by martial law.[5]

If, now, we try to approach peace as a *symbol* signifying more than the absence of war, conflict, and turmoil, we encounter peace in the sense of *concordia*, equilibrium between opposing forces. But now it is no longer possible to equate a unity such as "peace," which transcends all opposites, with simple quiet. For what we might call a "living peace," appertaining as it does to life, is in perpetual motion. A state of being, it is at the same time an activity which unites contraries. This living peace is threatened not only by the war, destruction, and the chaos of life, but also by the "dead peace" which signifies stagnation and rigidity and can likewise lead to chaos, disintegration, and death.

Thus (without my wishing to be overly systematic) the true quaternity of these symbols would be a polarity consisting of dead peace and life-generating war on the one hand, and living peace and death-dealing chaos on the other.

5. [The derivation of "peace" and "pact" suggests a similar relation to the idea of a stockade, of demarcating an area. See *The Oxford Dictionary of English Etymology*, ed. C. T. Onions (1966), s.v. "peace" and "pact."—Tr.]

This living peace betokens concord, the balance of forces, and harmony. The concept which most clearly corresponds to this symbol is, I believe, the biological concept of "dynamic equilibrium."[6] As the name makes clear, what is involved here is a state which, lacking stationary character, nevertheless maintains its equilibrium, while its constituent materials, as well as the contents, forces, and tensions which make it up, continually flow away from it as others flow in to take their place. This concept—originally formulated to describe the living organism, the cell, and the cell systems, and for physics—is also valid in the psychic realm, for there too there is a process of internal regulation which integrates and gives cohesion to the "dynamic equilibrium" of the personality and the psychic system, maintaining them in a state of "living peace." But the essential trait of dynamic equilibrium is that it applies only to "open" systems such as a living organism, and not to closed systems.

If we expand this concept and speak in terms of a "creative dynamic equilibrium," we are referring to a situation in which the equilibrium between inflow and outflow is not only perpetually reproduced and preserved, but which also enables the entity which exists in this state of equilibrium—regardless of whether it is an organism or a biopsychic unit—to grow and develop internally and externally on the foundation of this equilibrium, and to expand its living area by admitting into it new territories in which it can live in new ways.

The term "open" system has already been applied to

6. Ludwig von Bertalanffy, *Das biologische Weltbild* (Bern, 1949).

the biological and physical planes. The same openness, but operating on another plane, distinguishes man's position vis-à-vis the instinct-bound animal kingdom, and that of the creative man vis-à-vis his ordinary, tradition-bound fellows.

Closely linked to the openness, and to the dynamic, mobile character of the flux or stream to which this openness is perpetually exposed, is what in another context[7] we called the "characteristic superabundance" of existence. On the one hand this "superabundance" confers on the open entity its creativity, its capacity to expand and change. But at the same time it also threatens to flood an all-too-open system which is not capable—to keep to our metaphor—of regulating inflow and outflow by means of various sluices and regulatory systems, and of insuring the productivity of its own territory through controlled irrigation.

For the concept of creative dynamic equilibrium involves not only openness but also the very fact that a system is open, that is, that it is an organic unit, regardless of the position this unit occupies on the life-scale and regardless of the nature of those regulatory mechanisms which enable it to exist and unite its parts.

A territory, constituting a living and open system which actively regulates ingress to and egress from its borders, represents the fundamental pattern and template basic to all human civilization. It is not straying from the point to remind ourselves that all the high civilizations—Assyrian, Babylonian, Egyptian, Indian, Chinese, American—have been based on irrigation.

7. See above, Essay III.

Whether we interpret this as the external manifestation of an internal image or only as a metaphor, the fact remains that human civilization manifests itself as the realization of being in a state of creative equilibrium-in-flux.

A concomitant of this being is what we have described as "living peace." So "living peace" is linked to an equilibrium, an accord, a harmony of opposites which is transcends and brings into balance in such a way that in this war and competition of contraries the coexistence and relationship of these contraries is perpetually preserved. Peace, as its etymology indicates, is limited to a territory, i.e., is valid for a system which, although open, employs self-limiting boundaries and thus "fences in"[8] its territory. In other words, limitation and the setting of boundaries are a precondition of living peace, just as openness is.

Clearly this living peace does not rule out war. In other words, it can by no means be equated with a phase of peaceful repose and "uncontestedness," but on the contrary can involve a host of "military confrontations" whether within the pacified system or along its borders. Nevertheless, as long as the constructive and creative character implied by the concept of equilibrium is preserved, the quality of living peace reigns inviolate, above and beyond these confrontations. And as long as this peace reigns, the existence whose equilibrium it maintains is also in harmony with the vital stream which goes on flowing in and out of it, no matter how vast or how small the stream may be, or how primitive or complex

8. [German *umfriedet*, literally "encircles with peace."—Tr.]

the regulatory and system-building forces and mechanisms which determine its flow within the "fenced-in" territory.

Peace, equilibrium, harmony—what do these terms or symbols mean in the psychical realm? Taking as our starting point consciousness and the ego, we ask: How does consciousness relate to war, the dialectical principle, and the polarity war-and-peace? The moment we ask this question we become aware of the peace-making function of consciousness. The conscious ego is an organ whose task it is to establish a dynamic equilibrium between the inner world and the outer. It makes clear to us, as perhaps nothing else does to this extent, the fact that stimuli, contents, and demands flow into consciousness from the outside world (which includes the body), to be regulated and adapted by consciousness, while at the same time material flows into it from the inner world of the unconscious. It is an essential function of the central nervous system and of its supreme exponent, ego-consciousness, to harmonize and equilibrate this influx and efflux effected between conscious and unconscious, and consciousness and the external world. Adaptation, harmonization, and equilibration constitute a paramount demand of existence, and consciousness presupposes the successful functioning of this "living peace." For in a sense both the external and the internal worlds are on the attack, and we have good reason to speak of the danger that consciousness may be "overwhelmed." But consciousness can prevent itself from being overwhelmed by maintaining its territory in a state of living peace; for although on the one hand the territory is open, on the other its defensive systems, regulatory systems, and sluices enable it to hold its own as a territory, keeping it from being flooded by the vital stream which issues from the world or the unconscious.

An essential function of consciousness makes possible this "inner peace": detachment. It is the detachment achieved by consciousness which enables it to exist as a distinct, coherent unit in the first place. In other words, detachment corresponds to the cell wall in the cell, the skin in the living organism. All represent boundaries and limitations, that is, enclosures within whose confines alone "dynamic equilibrium" can exist.

To clarify this we need only remember the opposite of detachment, namely participation, ranging from unconscious *participation mystique* and total participation (identification) to the diverse forms of sharing and sympathy. What they all have in common—for worse as well as for better—is the loss of segregation. But this also means the loss of peace, brought about by the intensification of affective sympathy and the intensified experience of pleasure and pain synonymous with it.

The achievement of peace through the avoidance of pleasure and pain, through segregation, and through detachment is a basic form of the urge to achieve salvation, and is intimately linked to the nature of consciousness. For unquestionably one precondition of consciousness and its maintenance of a peace based on detachment is "cooling off." The ability of consciousness to form abstractions also derives from this "cleansing," which divests the contents of consciousness of their intense and perilous emotionality.

It is not necessary to repeat what we have said elsewhere concerning the detached attitude of consciousness, the breakdown of emotional components, and the process of becoming conscious and of rationalization.[9] The purpose of all these developments and mechanisms is, among other things, to establish boundaries and, by modifying the world as it presses in on consciousness and the ego, to give them the chance to function in peace. For the organic system of the conscious ego works right only if one "keeps cool," and it always tends to break down when its harmonious detachment is disrupted by emotion, affect, passionate concern, and so on. All invasions from within or without act as a military invasion. A disruption of consciousness which annuls its ability to effect balance can be very dangerous and lead to the destruction of the individual. It is immaterial whether the undermining of consciousness, and thus of the objective judgment whose function it is to supervise the work of adaptation, occurs as the result of an invasion from outside (such as a flood of stimuli), an internal invasion, an affect, or—as is the case, for example, in physical illness—a biological debilitation of the substratum within which the central nervous system, and with it consciousness, has its roots.

Thus the configuration of a detached "living peace," with all that is, is fundamental to the conscious ego in its labor to achieve objectivity. That is, it is integral to cognitive functioning, which is not only wholly dependent on the peace of consciousness but itself is a peacemaking element. At the beginning consciousness is overwhelmed and threatened; in the end it finds the ordering principle of knowledge.

9. Neumann, *Origins and History*.

But the knowing consciousness does not merely make peace with the passions and instinctual claims of the unconscious; it brings order into the amorphous and overwhelming world, and by the knowledge of principle, grasps the point of rest in the fleeting phenomenal realm. The fact that knowledge affords "satisfaction"[10] means that in knowledge the unrest of being in the world and of being at the mercy of the world becomes rest. In this sense, truth gives peace and truth *is* peace as the known principle of being. The peace found in the satisfaction of knowledge is the fruit of the victory of knowledge, which has brought form into the perilous chaos of existence and thus enclosed it. Thus whenever this world of peace, achieved by the knowledge of principle and thus given form, is disturbed—that is, whenever conscious cognition proves inadequate—the result is dissatisfaction communicated to the ego as disquiet and danger. The ego, experiencing this as an invasion of its peace, reacts with fear.

At this point the ego, which does not want its peace disturbed, marshals its defenses and attempts to ensure its safety by cutting off the influx of stimuli. In other words, the regulation necessary for the self-preservation of the ego and the system of consciousness is stepped up to such a degree that it threatens the openness of the system whose dynamic equilibrium it is supposed to preserve. Detachment turns into defensiveness, resistance, and exclusion, taking the familiar forms of suppression and repression.

This defensive peace of the closed-off consciousness is

10. [German *Befriedigung*, literally "pacification."—Tr.]

a "little peace" which, for the sake of peace, tries to hold at bay substantial areas of the world and the unconscious. This attitude of "appeasement" is as widespread as it is dangerous. We encounter it even on the highest levels, in the form of intellectual, aesthetic, and religious neutrality and "disinterest" in the sense of a *détachement*. The decision as to what, in this phenomenon, should be regarded as legitimate and what as illegitimate is extremely difficult for anyone who does not want to get overly caught up either in contemporary politics or in a radical religious quietism. Notably, the concept of taking up or occupying a position belongs to military terminology, and the "defense" of the "little peace" of the conscious ego is an act of war. This is why any instance of intellectual detachment and failure to take a position, every act of disinterested aesthetic contemplation, and every act, on religious grounds, of refusal to get involved, is suspect. It is suspect not only because this little "peace at any price" is impossible and breaks down every time there is a genuine crisis, but above all because it actually magnifies and intensifies the danger it is intended to quell and hold at bay.

The stoical detachment advocated by philosophical individualism, like the ivory tower of the individualistic artist, fails to confer security and peace, for no individual can exist without being rooted in the collective, and no consciousness can exist that is not rooted in the unconscious. Yet the ego tries, by maintaining a defensive, isolationist peace, to screen itself from its relatedness to the collective and the world, as well as to the unconscious.

A consciousness closed off from the unconscious simply activates the unconscious, and the isolation of a per-

sonality within its own consciousness activates the unconscious in the world around it. Such an isolation of
consciousness can be achieved only by repression and
suppression, so it has disastrous psychological and ethical repercussions,[11] and the "little peace" (which only appears to be peace) is more than compensated by the intensification of the struggle with the environment. The
unconscious negative effect radiating from this kind of
isolationist, defensive peace is proof of the material relatedness of every individual to his unconscious and to
the world around him, in which the family circle, being
closest to him, is the most prevalent locus of the disor-
ders described here. This relatedness exists even if the
conscious ego knows nothing about it, i.e., irrespective
of any isolationist tendency of the ego, which tries to
eliminate awareness of its relatedness in order to defend
its little peace.

This problem is the same as that which has confronted us in psychotherapy with the problem of transference. In the original psychoanalytic version of transference, the analyst, in his role as disinterested observing
ego, had to defend his peace and refrain from getting
involved in the real battleground, the patient's psyche,
while at the same time his conscious mind remained
open and receptive. Not until Jung and the post-Freud-
ian elaboration of psychoanalysis did analysts learn to
understand the analytic situation as a *relationship* in
which healing peace arises only out of the interaction of
two personalities, and in which the egos of both partners
remain open, and in openness give themselves, to the

11. Neumann, *Depth Psychology and a New Ethic.*

Thou of the external world, as well as to that of the inner world, the self.

Openness simply means an unbiased attitude towards reality—that is, readiness to see the truth, which, without regard for rules, can appear in unexpected forms and unpredictable guises. The best can turn out to be the worst, the worst to be the most precious. Our paths are almost always different from what we expect, and often the expected is only the first step into the unexpected. But this unexpectedness affects both partners. Thus their openness always simultaneously involves exposure, and the slight advantage the analyst derives from his greater experience, and from what at first appears to be his less clouded vantage point, is more than cancelled out by the bewildering projections of the patient. In the beginning it seems as inevitable for the analyst to become entangled in this web of unconscious participation as it is necessary for him to unravel it.

Failure to secure one's position leads to war, wounds, and defeat, but also to victory and change. In the same way, preserving one's security and detachment, although it appears to bring peace, in reality results in failure to acquire new knowledge, and in the exclusion of new experience capable of transforming both partners. Naturally the analyst's openness to his own unconscious and nonresistance of his own affects are signs neither of blindness nor of abreaction. Yet the serpentine path he must follow, keeping his balance along with his openness, will not allow him completely to avoid either, for often the darkness of his personal blindness is the foil which, by contrast, helps illuminate a situation, and abreaction supplies the vital shock of amicable conflict

which drives a breach through the patient's defensive
wall. For the analyst's openness and self-exposure image
the human condition and make it impossible for the
analysand (if he is sufficiently mature) to employ defensive armor which has now been revealed as grotesque
and inhuman.

Thus openness is equivalent to the surrender of the
"little peace" in which the conscious ego seeks security.
But behind this loss looms the image of another and
greater peace which now embraces not only the conscious ego, but the entire psyche.

The Hebrew root שלום, "shalom" or "peace," involves the idea of being well, whole, complete, perfect,
and the word *schlemut*, in which the root *shalom* is central, also means "consummation." As we have already
emphasized, the principle of creative equilibrium is also
valid for the psyche, and the basic law of compensation,
which regulates the relations between conscious and unconscious and whose task it is to guarantee the unitary
functioning of the psyche, is, in the highest sense, the
expression of a propensity to heal the personality and
keep it healthy. In other words it works to ensure the
welfare of the personality, for which "peace" is a central
concern.

Unquestionably this same "great peace" has been the
goal of ethical and philosophical imperatives and efforts
to secure "emotional calm" and the peace of mind that
goes with it. But not until the findings of depth psychology revealed this did we know why the little peace of
the conscious mind has often substituted (and *had* to
substitute) for the great peace. Only when, as in the mystery religions, the world of gods and demons—that is,

the powers of the psyche—has been included in confrontation and in peace, has it been possible to achieve
something more than the defensive peace of the conscious mind.

The individual, embedded as he is in the psyche of
mankind and in the world, is necessarily exposed to all
the perils and suffering involved in a life which flows
like water and is pounded by the waves of enantiodromian forces. Thus the psyche, representing the place
where this life, in the form of inner and outer world, is
manifested to the ego, is the primary and authentic
arena of human decision. How, in this world in which
war is the father of all things, is it possible for man to
achieve what may legitimately bear the name of peace?
Heraclitus says of this great peace: "They do not comprehend how, being at variance but in accord with itself,
it is a harmony of opposing forces like that of the bow
and the lyre."[12]

In this passage we see the "great peace" of the psyche
in the form of being "in accord with itself," a state which
is possible despite the dominant principle of opposition.
Here the goal of the "harmony of opposing forces" is no
longer confined to the conscious mind, but extends to
the whole of the psyche as the unity of conscious and
unconscious.

Thus this great peace, as the final term in a developmental process, would await us at the end of the war

12. Heraclitus, fr. 51. [Here the author interposed a parenthesis
justifying his modification of the Diels-Krantz rendering of this
fragment. Neumann's version is translated above. The rendering in
Freeman, *Ancilla*: "They do not understand how that which differs
with itself is in agreement: harmony consists of opposing tension,
like that of the bow and the lyre."]

which we know as the confrontation of the ego with the unconscious, and the question arises as to whether we may justly designate this "end" (assuming that it exists) as "peace."

How can we reconcile the perpetual confrontation (that is, the perpetual war) which ensues when the conscious ego is open to the unconscious and the world, and the openness of the personality to a storm-tossed and mobile existence, with a peace that is not based on a self-demarcating defensive peace?

Initially the ego's conflict with the unconscious always involves war, for the first and never-ending encounter of the ego is with the shadow. It cannot be emphasized often enough that the "acceptance" of the shadow has nothing to do with its passive *appeasement*. In terms of the New Ethic,[13] which will not tolerate the suppression and repression of the shadow, this pact with the shadow, perilous for both parties, which is made at the conclusion of the confrontation, represents a kind of creative equilibrium which must be fought for and defended over and over again. After all, the point here is not for me to make peace with my shadow in such a way that I "rest content"[14] with it. My acceptance of the evil in myself as something which befalls me, but also as that which is my due, is the same thing as to accept my limitations and my suffering from them. The aim of the combat with the shadow is not the hubristic desire to leave my humanity behind me, cease to have a shadow, and do away with my limitations, but neither is it to "determine"[15] these limitations and make peace with them

13. Neumann, *Depth Psychology and a New Ethic.*
14. [*zu-frieden*, literally "(am) at peace."—Tr.]
15. [*fest-zu-stellen*, "fix limits of."—Tr.]

by accepting them as a given. I can accept the shadow only if, in the course of our battle with the dragon, the shadow has been so soundly trounced that it ceases to be a devouring dragon and becomes my dark brother. But this victory cannot be won if, by an act of repression, I behave as if the dragon did not exist simply because I am sitting in the fortress of my closed-off consciousness and my moral certainty. It is equally impossible to win victory if I suppress the dragon and chain him up as the Olympian gods did the Titans, so that the world above is continually under threat of a subterranean earthquake, a rebellion of the suppressed material, and my ostensibly serene existence is forever overshadowed by the apocalyptic vision of a twilight of the gods in which all supreme values must topple and fall. For this too is a kind of defensive and exclusionary peace which eliminates the possibility of achieving that greater peace which includes the darkness.

The hero's battle with the shadow-dragon, culminating in the conclusion of peace between himself and his dark brother, leads not only to the transformation of the shadow-foe but also to the transformation of the hero. To be a hero, at least on this plane, also involves the decision and the capacity to be evil. The situation is different in the higher forms of the battle with the dragon, in which the principle of struggle has been overcome, and in which a saint may associate with predators and dragons as if they were his own kind, and they willingly obey him. But on the level of the battle with the dragon as evil, a phase of all "holy wars" regardless of where and how they are waged, the hero achieves victory only if he receives and assimilates the demonic surplus lost by the shadow-dragon in the course of its transformation into the dark brother. Early in his career Jung pointed out that the hero has the eyes of the dragon he is fighting.[16] In giving battle, inflicting wounds and killing, i.e., in using his sword, the hero is "evil." The sword is the dragon's tooth transformed, and the necessity and the desire to be the stronger contain, in hidden form, the principle of power which is the evil principle of the dragon itself. But the acceptance of this evil as a meaningful weapon in the struggle to win the greater peace deprives the evil of its power to do harm. The fact that for the hero warfare and the sword do not, as they do for the dragon, represent power for power's sake and the supreme meaning and goal of his life, but are an instrument in the service of a greater meaning and integration, makes the armed and fighting hero a hero of peace, and his defanged and disarmed foe becomes the dark brother who, without denying his darkness, is revealed as the ally of the hero of light.

The fact that the purpose of the battle with the dragon is the achievement of a greater peace is evident from the result of the struggle: the hero's liberation of the princess and conquest of the treasure. This second phase of the ego's confrontation with the unconscious—that with the anima, the princess freed from the dragon—is the symbolic expression of the conquest of the soul as the creative quality of the psyche.[17]

The little peace of the segregated consciousness, in which the principle of openness has been restricted or

16. Jung, *Symbols of Transformation*, CW 5, pars. 574f.
17. Ibid., passim, and Neumann, *Origins and History*, passim.

abandoned in the interests of self-defense, brings with it the danger of inflexibility, that is, of lack of creativity. But when—to stick to an appropriate metaphor—the hero of consciousness leaves his castle and its secure peace and sets out on a journey to adventure which begins with the quest for and combat with the dragon, the ego's confrontation with the unconscious starts to get dangerous and dangerously creative.

The conquest of the anima and the hero's union with her creates a new integration, and a new unity of peace, of which the *hierosgamos*, the sacred connubium of the hero and the princess, is the symbolic expression. This new unity and new potential for expanding and enlarging the realm of peace—the encounter with the female counter-principle—stands under a different star and involves a different creative possibility and a different danger (i.e., from those involved in the encounter with the shadow alone). To deal with the overwhelming power of the unconscious demands the all-out mobilization of the combative powers of consciousness. In the more difficult confrontation between the hero of the conscious ego and the female aspect of the psyche, the anima, the hero must release this psychic aspect from its fusion both with the shadow and with the mother archetype in the unconscious.[18]

The breaking down of compounds into their separate components, the polarization of what is ambivalent and

18. The uroboric bisexual character of the dreadfulness of the feminine-maternal principle is shown by the fact that the male shadow, which is its companion, plays a phallic-murderer role, just as the dreadfulness of the masculine-paternal is shown by the fact that its associate, the female shadow, appears in its devouring and disintegrating form.

unclear, is a paramount task of consciousness; and the stages of the confrontation with the unconscious unfold in such a way that each time a different part or aspect of a previously compound entity, overwhelming and impossible to picture clearly, is examined and dealt with. The first stage in the liberation of the anima involves overcoming its fusion with the shadow, during which process its negative, destructive masculinity, which seeks to subjugate the male principle to its own demand for power, is overcome by the increased valor of the conscious ego. He is the Siegfried of myth who subdues the Brunhild whom Gunther had tied to the bedpost.

The characteristic expression of this negative-feminine anima, behind which we glimpse the dreadful mother, is the fusion of the seductive with the devouring and murderous. The feminine, as the sorceress who brings intoxication and death, weakens and disintegrates the masculine principle. The hero must resist her as Odysseus did Circe and the Sirens, for if he does not he will be overpowered by her as Samson was by Delilah.[19]

But it is possible to overcome a pair of opposites or establish a peace that embraces two antagonistic forces only if there occurs a process of transformation in which the contraries lose themselves in each other, and each is victorious through the other. In his conquest of the shadow the hero must rely on his heroic masculinity. The risk he takes is that of defeat and death in battle, that is, a form of destruction appropriate to the male. By the same token victory and the accompanying transformation in which the hero reveals his dragon nature leads

19. Neumann, *The Great Mother*.

to an intensification of the masculine principle which suits his nature.

The confrontation with the liberated anima, the feminine-creative principle of the psyche, demands something else of the hero. The freeing of the anima requires a discriminating militant male heroism, but *union* with it requires a transformation, indeed a conversion, of his nature. Whereas the liberated anima is transformed from a passively feminine principle into a positively active "in-spirational" feminine principle united with his spiritual side, the masculine principle must now set aside his warrior's ways. As the lover of Venus, Mars carries no weapons. During its contact with and acceptance of the anima, the ego has not only to prove its masculinity but also to realize its own femininity. The conscious ego changes from an active to a receptive principle which hearkens to the message of the unconscious. But because it is no longer exclusively active, it is also, in a new way, defenseless before the female. In the confrontation with the deeper layer of the psyche which the anima represents, the principle confronting the anima can no longer rely on the valorous, well-armored masculinity of the conscious ego, which is accustomed to the conquest and self-defense of battle. Instead it must possess a core of inner security, deriving from its new intimacy with the unconscious, which enables it to relate to the anima without armor, in other words with a new openness that is without protection. This involves the risk that the openness and receptivity of the listener can abruptly change into a state of bondage, and that the masculine principle may be emasculated as Hercules was by Omphale or Samson by Delilah, either by the loss of his radiant, consecrated masculinity (Samson's loss of his hair) or by being forced to don women's clothing like Hercules. In both cases the masculine principle is overwhelmed, the internal as well as external balance between male and female is lost, and the peace of the marriage between the hero and the liberated anima undergoes regression and is dissolved.

The creative peace between hero and anima is the peace of two transformed beings. One partner, the anima, is the liberated psychical principle with is actively, creatively, inspirationally, devoted to consciousness and the ego, and which, being feminine, simultaneously receives into itself the activity of the ego-hero and makes it fruitful. The other partner is the conscious ego which openly receives the activity of the psyche through the anima and which gives form to the psychic material. In the process the conscious ego, through its activity and openness, effects a mutual bond between conscious and unconscious under a sign of peace in which masculine and feminine exist in creative equilibrium.

Two forces threaten this equilibrium and peace. There can be a fortification and closing-off of consciousness, and an overpowering of the anima, which is now made a prisoner and brought into the hero's castle (the patriarchal world of consciousness), thereby losing its inspirational function. This retreat of the ego to its initial position is equivalent to the loss of the feminine, listening component of the hero; the counterfeit increase of his masculinity; and the abandonment of his creative relationship with the unconscious. The second danger is the subjection of the masculine and the preponderance of the hero's feminine side, i.e., a regressive victory of the anima leading to a victory of the unconscious and to a debilitation or separation of the components of consciousness, which may take the form of castration or dis-memberment, impotence, addiction, neurotic disorder, or psychosis. In both cases the peace, the "harmony of opposing forces" in the male-female union of marriage, is dissolved as one of the poles gains ascendancy over the other.

We may not be masters of the *I Ching*, but we are its disciples, for we use the *I Ching*. Hence we may and must attempt to rely on it. The sign Tai, "Peace," ☷☰ , is composed of two signs. The lower half is the sign for the creative principle, the upper for the receptive. The direction from which they approach each other—the creative moving upward from below, the receptive downward from above—leads to a penetration and fer-tilization whose product is termed peace.

The creativity of this peace is shown by the fact that it is a sign of the coming of spring and that its opposite is the sign for "Standstill."[20] Standstill is the inversion of peace because here the creative sign is above and the re-ceptive below, so that when they move they must move away from each other, and the sky rises as the earth sinks down.

The sign for creative peace is the exact counterpart of the star of David ✡ , the union of two triangles repre-senting male and female, heaven and earth, whose cen-teredness, imaged by the space in the middle, is a symbol of the godhead.

First we should turn our attention to two aspects of this sign: the creative aspect and the center. The two belong together, for they are united by the symbol of peace. Often a psychologically fruitful approach is to in-

20. *I Ching*, hexagram 12.

terpret the lower sign of the *I Ching* as the unconscious, the upper as the conscious. The relationship between the two then enables us to grasp the meaning the sign possesses for the dominant psychical configuration and arrive at that concrete interpretation in which the upper part equals heaven and the lower equals earth. By this interpretation of the sign of creative peace, consciousness is viewed as feminine and descending, the unconscious as masculine and ascending. Thus a creative unconscious is joined to a receptive conscious. This is, on another plane, the same configuration which we interpreted as that of the ego-hero laying down his arms and wedding the inspirational-creative anima. Their marriage signifies creative peace.

If, in addition, we look at the nuclear trigrams, we see that (as the commentary shows)[21] the upper one, "the Arousing" or eldest son, united with the lower, the "Joyous" or youngest daughter, compensates for the quite different union of the creative anima and the feminine, receptive consciousness. We find here a host of symbols of coherence in which the union of contraries, creativity and peace, forms a miraculous unity which becomes reality only in that blessed time when our salvation is fulfilled.

2

In the confrontation between ego and unconscious, the entire personality undergoes a transformation in which the opposition of conscious and unconscious, which is

21. [Ibid., commentary for hexagram 11 (Wilhelm/Baynes, p. 445).]

present at the beginning, starts to change character. In this process, which has been described as a process of integration and centering, something is formed which, in the advances and retreats of battle in which peace is won and lost again, exists as a center of change beyond change. This formation or becoming visible of a point of rest betokens that the ego is beginning to find support in something which, present from the outset, is little by little revealed as fundamental reality. The revelation of the unity of the self produces a new source of peace, a new order. This totality, absolutely unrelated to the little peace of consciousness, is the root of the greater peace which shows itself as the goal of the union of contraries within the psyche.

The psychical function of equilibration, of bringing what is unbalanced into balance over and over, and always on a different plane, compensating for any deviation from creative health and striving to effect the wholeness of the psyche, is a form of centroversion: this is evident from the fact that for the ego it becomes perceptible as a central principle of order. Thus in alchemy it is said that this center represents the "mediator, making peace between the enemies or elements."[22]

Through this center, or through the unified field established around it, the psyche becomes a unitary territory which is now governed by the creative peace of dynamic equilibrium. The becoming visible of the midpoint, of the self, as and in the center of the psyche, is regarded as the final stage in the individuation pro-

22. *Theatrum chemicum* IV (1613), p. 601 ["Tractatus aureua"], quoted by Jung, *Aion*, CW 9 ii, par. 377, n. 57.

cess. At this point the personality seems, in a sense, to have arrived at "its own" individual peace.

Two questions now confront us. First: Does this "arrival at one's own peace" really take place, and what does it mean? Second: Is such a peace even permissible? Does not every peace, in a time of strife, represent a refusal to get involved that is opposed to the fundamental unity between the individual and the Thou of his fellow human beings—the individual and the times into which he was born?

Even the mandala is a fortress. Even the psychical totality it represents is a walled-off territory in which the same laws apply, with respect to peace and war, as in the territory of consciousness. The mandala has a compensatory quality which is the salvation of a disintegrated and threatened psyche. The integration of alchemy is a way of transformation for the man who has lost his natural integration through emphasis and overemphasis of his ego and consciousness. Thus the mandala is a mantra, an instrument. As a collective image and as a spontaneous product of the psyche, its aim is to promote the healing, wholeness, and peace of the diseased and fragmented man who has no peace. Just as ego and consciousness are products of the psyche which created them to act as centering forces, smoothing relations between antagonistic drives and instincts, so too the mandala and the image of the self are products of the psyche which act as centering and harmonizing forces, preventing conflict between conscious and unconscious. The participation of the ego, and thereby of the whole personality, in the symbol of totality bestows peace. It is a way of centering and stabilization which secures man against overwhelming and disintegrating forces from within and without, from above and below. Thus the mandala, as fortress and city, as temenos and sacred precinct, represents a clearly segregated abode of peace in the midst of a world overrun with the raging strife of opposites—heaven and hell, gods and demons.

It is by no means accidental that the mandala, in its character as fortress, resembles consciousness. Looking at primitives, as well as at children and sick people, we must often interpret the protective mandala as a protective consciousness, and its midpoint as the sacred ego at the center of consciousness. For the ego, with its four functions of consciousness,[23] is the middle of a circle, the balance of contraries, the point of the mediator, and the lord of peace. That the intimate connection of ego and self is the central phenomenon of psychical life is shown by the dual significance of the mandala and its center.

But the image of the fortress, as the closed-off territory which must be defended, is only *one* image of the mandala, only *one* symbol of consciousness and psychical totality. Whether we are speaking of the little peace of consciousness or the greater peace of the psyche, defensive peace never represents the highest form of peace attainable.

Creative peace and its potential growth are dependent on the openness of a system, that is, also on the potential risk. The openness of the whole personality—openness of the whole to the whole—is tantamount to surrender: not simply to self-exposure but to self-abandonment, to the (unconditional) giving over of self.

23. [Sensation, thinking, feeling, intuition. Cf. Jung, *Psychological Types*, CW 6, par. 7 (introduction) and passim.]

But how is it possible for this self-abandoned open-ness not to result in disintegration and destruction? The conscious ego, in its openness and self-surrender, has an invisible support in the totality of the psyche, the symbol of which is the self; but what supports the psyche in *its* openness and self-surrender? What happens to the open and creative mandala—the mandala, that is, at risk? How can the mandala be protected when it is self-aban-doned? How can it remain at peace when it is open to the contrary powers, the gods and demons? What ren-ders the golden flower of the center inviolate, when all the other blossoms of reality fall victim to every rude grasping hand?

The final phase in the psychical development of the personality always involves its discovery not only of peace but of "meaning." At first meaning and the dis-covery of meaning appear dependent on ego and con-sciousness, which must act as heroes, actively experienc-ing and bestowing meaning, transforming what is chaotic, meaningless, and capricious, and imparting sense to the seemingly senseless. But this heroic, active posture cannot adequately deal with an overwhelming reality which cannot be composed and mastered by means of any experience involving only the conscious mind. Nothing less than the mobilization of the entire personality (and this barely) will suffice to master what cannot be mastered. This engagement of the total per-sonality ensues in the course of the ego's confrontation with the unconscious, which at the same time is the world. In this confrontation the *bestowal* of meaning by consciousness, is transformed into the *discovery* of mean-ing by the (total) personality. Not until this discovery of meaning does something come to rest which up to now has always been without rest; and something which has always been driven by the longing for peace, finally approaches it.

This central peace, the peace of totality, is the product of a growth process whose roots lie in time and in the world, but whose fruit reaches into the timeless and into a reality which, as unitary reality, is beyond the dichotomy of outer and inner. Like all growth, this growth is a perpetual flux, perpetual motion, a building up and withering away, war and peace at once; and yet its essence is peace and timeless harmony. So too, despite the war between life and death, construction and disintegration, that is perpetually taking place within us as it does in every organism, we are as whole totalities beyond all this, in the peace of a balanced harmony of opposing forces.

The opposition between the *being* of peace and the *existence* among contraries, or between being and becoming, does not apply here, for our paradoxical reality is always both at the same time, or rather is one within the other. This unity of "one within the other" can also be found in the symbol of the circle, which is the unity of center and periphery. The center—being in peace—belongs to a periphery of warring contraries, of dialectical life involving two or four forces, and joins with it to form a totality.

This unity within contraries is a priori, for from the very beginning it is a given of psycho-organic existence; and at the same time is the fruit of a growth process. An unindividuated psyche does not fall apart. Indeed, the unconscious primitive and the child are less fragmented, in their unconscious functioning, than the adult Western man. In primitives and children the a priori totality of primordial peace, which comes into being with the unity of every living being,[24] is still a living thing.

Primordial peace, which being untroubled by consciousness is experienced as self-evident, does, to be sure, disappear with the development of the conscious ego, which necessarily experiences life as the war of contraries. But in reality this peace is not lost because, as the guiding principle of the psyche, it exists beyond its vicissitudes. The experience of this peace and the recollection of its eternal being appear intimately related to the experience of the center, which is revealed not only as mediator between the contraries and as the fountainhead and source of the flow, but also as the goal and ocean where the flow empties out.[25]

But is it possible to attain this "recollection" of primordial peace? For by now it is clear that the peace we are seeking cannot be the little peace of consciousness or any form of defensive peace based on refusal to get involved. And the mandala, in the form of a closed-off fortress which defends and systematizes the totality and is supposed to protect the center at its own midpoint, also appears to be a defensive peace. But what is this

24. [Da-Sein, literally "being there." Dasein = "being, existence."—Tr.]

25. This image is used in the *Theatrum chemicum* concerning the illustration of an inner circle, A, and an outer circle with the four opposing poles, B, C, D, E: "A is the inside, as it were the origin and source from which the other letters flow, and likewise the final goal to which all the others flow back, as rivers flow into the ocean or into the great sea." Quoted in Jung, *Aion*, par. 378 (with diagram).

center, which we customarily describe as ego and as self, and what in the center must be defended?

The link between ego and self is rooted in a fundamental paradox which consciousness experiences as identity and non-identity with itself. Man, in his sense of being alien to himself, of not being identical to himself, relies on his self as on another, a Thou which as that-which-is-not-I is wholly other, and yet is he himself as self. To be sure, this paradox exists for the ego in the act of reflection, but it does not apply to creative, spontaneous existence. For if the ego were not grounded in the self, and if the self did not serve as creative source within the ego, the ego could never open itself up and be creative and, emerging from itself, experience itself as belonging to self. But what is the meaning of the center and being centered, if I as ego am not ego at all, and if I become myself only when my ego abandons me? And what is this self whose I-am-that-I-am does indeed exist beyond the ego, but reveals itself, and is experienced as existent, only in its union with the ego?

These deliberations seem to border on what we are accustomed to call mysticism. Indeed, it seems to me that they are, to a large extent, consistent with mystical testimony; but they are also valid in terms of the more modest assertion of psychology, for here we are speaking only of man's attempt to make sense of himself. To be sure, the fact that this sense always leads him to the same sense (i.e., meaning) as all philosophy and all religion, should surprise no one who makes the effort to see man for what he is: the paradoxical unity of ego and self which constitutes the core of what is human, while at the same time transcending it.

Our existence as ego-selves is so fundamentally rooted in openness that the act of closing oneself off signifies a loss of one's essence. In other words, a man who experiences himself only as ego thereby forfeits his true existence as unity of ego and self. On the other hand, only by establishing its limits can the ego become aware of itself as ego, and so experience the self as self. Ego and consciousness are unthinkable without self-delimitation and the formation of a territory. But in this act of determinative knowledge and clarification, that which is known is at the same time lost, whereas that state of vitality in which the ego opens itself up and abandons demarcation, produces creative unity, although this unity cannot be reflected upon. At first it may seem that we have once again run into the same old indeterminacy principle which allows us either to define clearly and thus distort the ego-self phenomenon in the course of observing it and making it conscious, or to embody it in an open creative existence, but without the ability to make it conscious.

This raises the question of whether our experience of the ego and ego-self actually corresponds to the experience of a "center," as the archetypal symbol of the circle suggests, and whether even this "determination" (in the true sense of the word),[26] meaningful and lucid as it may be, does not fence us in. The symbol of the circle is unsurpassed as a defensive formula of concentration and coherence. But as a symbol of creative life it is inadequate and needs supplementation. We experience ourselves as living beings, not as "points" and not as a center

26. [*Festlegung*, "fixing the limits."—Tr.]

(or not exclusively as a center). And when we speak of ourselves as ego, in reality we mean something which, although it is indeed form, is *living* form which, in addition to that totality which limits and is limited by form, always embraces the flowing openness of the totality, and that surplus which leaves all form behind. Here, as in other ways, our Greek heritage of overemphasis on form has distorted Western thought about man, giving it a false "de-termination."

Although in the past I myself never understood the Oriental assertion that ego does not exist, gradually I am coming to understand more and more the justice of the protest lodged in this claim. Just as the physical organism possesses a center without our being aware of any center, so the psyche is a totality without center, in other words a "field," which as a field has an integrated and hierarchical order. It is natural to choose, as a simplified description of this order, the geometrical "symbol" of the circle and its center, for it is easier for the conscious mind to grasp this image than the non-graphic image of the field.

I am not implying that the mandala is not an adequate symbol of the psyche. The psyche, which not only produces this symbol but always accords it the significance due things supremely sacred, does not make mistakes. But more perhaps than in the past, we must understand that on the one hand the mandala is a protective, defensive, concentrative symbol; and on the other, that its meaning lies in what I have called the "anthropocentric accent" in the development of consciousness.[27]

27. Neumann, *Origins and History*, [pp. 25, 126, and passim].

Initially man orients himself in the world by ordering it in relation to himself, establishing himself as its center, and describing the midpoint of this orientation system as "I" (ego). Even when he begins to move beyond this and to experience himself as the image or likeness of something else—that is, as an ego-self—he experiences the divine as that creative force which makes the world and man: so to speak, as a creative center to which man, in his role as *homo creator* and *homo faber*, as world-creator and world-transformer, represents the equivalent.

Understandably, this establishing of a center brings with it the tendency to interpret what is experienced and that which does the experiencing as a *person* more or less like a human being, so that a personal ego is introduced into situations which actually imply "man" in general. The same law governs the concept of the personal God, and we often say "the god" and "the goddess" when we really mean "the divine."

The Judiac prohibition against making a "graven image" of the divine results from the perception that no anthropomorphic personalization can adequately represent the divine and numinous. In this regard, unlike Buber with his overemphasis on the I-Thou, Scholem has stressed the tendency of Jewish mysticism to avoid minimizing the distance between man and God with inadequate personalizations.[28] In other words, even in the experience of God as a Thou, Jewish mysticism always retains its awareness of the gulf separating what it is possible to experience from the reality of a divine inacces-

28. Gershom Scholem, *Major Trends in Jewish Mysticism* (New York, 2nd ed., 1946).

sible to experience. Elsewhere, in an analogous case,[29] we have attempted to show that psychologically the "self" ought properly to be interpreted as a supervisory field which, from the perspective of the ego-structure of consciousness, is manifested in the image not of the field but of the personal center.

The emergence of the imageless image of a totality without center makes us experience the closed-in circle as a prison in relation to that openness wherein the flowing, creative aspect of living existence remains more adequately maintained. Just as the living totality of a tree is more powerful than that found in the geometrical figure of the circle, and the harmony of a landscape more powerful that that of a structure which is merely symmetrical, so man in his creative openness is more alive than in a closed-off pseudo-centeredness which often masks unapproachable inhibition.

That simplified orientation in which we regard the ego as the center of consciousness and the self as the center of the psyche remains valid from a psychologically "microcosmic" perspective, as does the idea of the ego-self *axis* of the personality. But from the "macrocosmic" perspective in which man is perceived as a being existing in the world and beyond it, in unitary reality, we must— to keep to our metaphor—"open up" the axis, taking it as a pipe through which creative life flows in and out.[30] The same life which acts in the field of totality that is unitary reality, and which we venerate there, in its per-

29. See above, Essay I.

30. One is tempted to interpret this image as the return of the "solar phallus," the procreative spirit-wind emanating from the radiant sun which begets life in the form of the Holy Spirit.

sonified form, as "creative divinity," is revealed to us, in the field of totality that is the psyche, in the form of the self and in the field of consciousness in the form of the ego.

If we experience and try to formulate the "open" structure of being in this way, we need not abandon, but only relativize, that orientation by the center which is necessary to our understanding of the structure of the psyche. The human personality is viewed from its creative aspect, and is placed within that context of openness in which alone it is capable of existing. That experience of creative excess which characterizes life predominates here to such a degree that the vocabulary of attack and defense, of life as war, pales by comparison, although it can never be eliminated altogether because it belongs to the essence of life.

In this openness of the personality as an entity in which the union of ego and self exists as an open, creative force within an open world, we arrive at a new form of peace, the lower levels of which, at least from time to time, are accessible to experience.

Unlike the defensive peace based on the preservation of detachment, this open peace is possible only where there is abundance and affirmation of life. Within open receptivity operates something beyond all contraries, in which man swims along with the stream of life between the opposing banks of Yes and No, identifying neither with the one nor the other in any permanent way. To be sure, openness towards the flow of the stream presupposes the formal unity of the personality, but the reflecting ego which takes up positions is embraced by a higher order in which the stream is more important than its right bank or its left.

The freedom found in this openness is the expression of a knowledge linked to peace and based on openness to the flowing stream. Whereas consciousness, like a ray of light emanating from the ego, is capable of illuminating only isolated segments of the world, the knowledge belonging to this peace constitutes an unchanging light source which illuminates everything uniformly.

At this point, it appears, the relationship between openness and emptiness begins to acquire some clarity, in a new and positive sense, for European man. For the most part the indeterminate openness of exposure to life, representing unchannelled spontaneity, can only be described "negatively." In his struggle with the demons, the Buddha's invincibility is shown by the fact that the throne they attack is empty. At first we are inclined to interpret this emptiness as the impregnability of ascetic, world-renouncing meditation. But the intriguing and enriching element found in the incomprehensible material of Zen may well consist in that shock, leading to greater openness, which enables us to experience emptiness as fullness and fullness as emptiness; what is wide open as a stream of abundance; and the flow of life as the unity of the intangible and invisible with the tangible and visible.

This emptiness is equivalent to the "ether" (atmosphere) of the older physics, which was regarded as the basis of all physical processes and from whose vibration light supposedly derived. Regardless of whether the element is ether or air, there always exists something invisibly in motion, something empty: the essence which offers itself to us in the fragrance of a world in bloom, which vibrates in the melody of Krishna and of the magic flute, or in the rustling wind in which divinity reveals itself.

When we, as open beings, are moved by this emptiness-in-motion, we experience life as existence suspended within a free-floating peace. This peace, whether we call it the Tao or something else, is revealed as a universal condition which suffuses the most troubled, bloody and evil phenomena as well as the stillness of the stones and the beauty of living things. Perhaps this gives us a clue to the assertion of Zen that "all things are at rest from eternity"—meaning that in the paradox of unitary reality, this eternal repose is not in any way disrupted by the eternal flux of becoming and passing away.

All this is like the image of the wave. We perceive a linear wave as a perpetual motion, yet at the same time we claim that it consists of oscillating points which never leave their places. Our conscious mind perceives an essentially unreal motion—the linear wave—but not the eternally animated repose of the individual point.

Open participation in the world of becoming is the precondition for the equally open participation in that primordial peace in which all things are at rest from eternity. Here too we could cite Lao-tse's image of the hub of the turning wheel which remains at rest in the midst of its revolutions. Independence from the rise and fall of the turning wheel does not consist in detachment from them, but rather in the fact that one remains at the center of the motion. This pliant participation is the essential factor in physical techniques like Japanese jiu-jitsu as well as, for example, the artistic technique of ink-painting. This "being in the center of the motion" presupposes the perpetual openness of a state of attention in which consciousness is free-floating, not directed towards a goal.

This attentive openness is linked to an absolute spontaneity about the way in which one relates to things, resulting in an unbroken flow between the world and man which is not disrupted by any intervention of conscious thought and which represents that direct "response" on which the Zen masters lay such stress. This spontaneity is by no means an unfamiliar phenomenon. We experience it not only in the unconscious coordinated interaction of our body in its instinctually governed behavior and in its immediate response to every act of our will, but also, in the mental-emotional sphere, in every act of speech, and in every exchange of speech in which the productivity of the unconscious expresses things which the ego has never thought about before.

In the creative process this element of surprise is even greater. This is true not only of the archaic, somnambulistic-matriarchal form of creativity, but also of the higher and later kind which also embraces the consciousness. The intimate dialogue between conscious ego and unconscious involves a flowing and immediate response of one to the other. That is, in mental work, even of a mathematical-logical kind, it is characteristic for the conscious ego to respond to the problem-posing of the unconscious, just as it is for the unconscious to respond to that of the conscious. This process of creative dialogue is grounded in the fact that the total man responds to a stimulus, and the healing property of all creative work lies in the fact that when man is open to this kind of total response, he also experiences himself, subjectively, as a totality embracing both conscious and unconscious.

Perpetually experiencing this totality, the personality experiences itself, as we commonly say, as "centered." But in reality what is going on here is an experience of unity by a totality open to another totality which is likewise open. The term "to be in the Tao" best expresses this experience of oneness with a unitary reality which embraces both what is within and what is without.

The Latin word for peace is *pax*, which derives from the same root as the German word *Fuge* ("joint, that which fits into something else") in the sense of *fügen, zusammenfügen* ("to fit, to fit together") Latin *com-pages* = *Fuge*, "joint, connection." Things which belong together and which suit each other, fit themselves to each other, and that which suitably fitted together is at peace. To fit oneself [*sich fügen*] means to adapt to what is suitable, and "dispensation" [*Fügung*] is the fate which belongs to and is fitting to me. The root *feg* is related to *fagor*, "fitting," and to *fagar, fair*, "beautiful." But in Greek to be adapted, to be fitted together [*zusammengefügt*], is ἁρμονίζειν, a verb whose substantive form means "harmony." To be at peace, to be in harmony, to be in the Tao means to fit oneself to what is fitting [*sich der Fügung fügen*]. This state of being in accord and being in harmony bestows peace in the central sense of the word "satisfaction" [*Zufriedenheit*, from *Frieden*, "peace"]. Man, as an open, animated being, is in accord with what, being living, is quickened and quickens. This accord, as a state of adaptedness and fittedness [*Eingefügtsein*] characterized by openness toward world

307

and self, at the same time means being "at peace" both with oneself and the world. This being at peace with the world requires neither withdrawal from the world nor the renunciation of active intervention in its affairs to bring about change. It includes the possibility of refraining from intervention in a particular situation and the possibility of "retreat," just as it may include the necessity of plunging into the midst of danger. To do the right thing (in German) is to do it *mit Fug und Recht*, that is, fittingly and correctly. This "fitted-together" quality of harmony, and this alone, expresses peace in accord with creative existence.

Unlike uncreative, self-satisfied satisfaction [*selbstzufriedene Zufriedenheit*], the highest form of peace means creative participation in the everyday circumstances of life, as well as creative independence from life. In other words, it constitutes a form of autarky in which creative life experiences itself as a source and a stream which, on its course through the world, flows through the most diverse landscapes without being hindered in its flow, and at the same time reflects the most varied images of the world without thereby losing its own transparency.

The word "autarky," the Greek equivalent of German *Zufriedenheit* ["satisfaction, contentment"],[31] brings us perilously close to the defensive philosophy of the Stoics and quietists. But true autarky is opposed to such attempts to avoid involvement in the world in order to be left in peace. Plato's description of autarky in the *Timaeus* states: "And turning in its circular orbit it was

31. ["Self-sufficiency" is a more usual sense of *Autarkie*/autarky in both languages. Cf. *Origins and History*, pp. 9f. and 33f., where the inexact translation "autarchy" was used.]

thus constituted as the one, absolutely self-contained universe, and because of its excellence, it was satisfied with its own company and needed no one else, having sufficient acquaintance and friendship with itself."[32] The same work comments concerning the autarkic nature of the world as a circular, self-enclosed uroboros:[33] "For thanks to its artful construction it makes of its own decomposition the source of its own nourishment, and all suffering and action is accomplished in and through itself."

To achieve this autarky possessed by nature requires of man that he become like nature. Abandoning his emphasis on the segregation of his personality as a fortress made up of ego and self, and maintaining an open, dynamic equilibrium, he must form part of the world through which the world, as self-transforming Tao, can flow. By displaying this supreme penetrability, man becomes part of unitary reality. The outer and inner worlds are fitted together, and both, revealing themselves as one and the same, reveal a single meaning. When this state is attained, the reign of primordial peace is regained, bringing with it a knowledge which man lacks in the archaic state of *participation mystique*, the unconscious participation in the world.

There are many ways to arrive at this knowledge, which is an expression of that "great experience" which we have discussed in relation to the nature of creativity. We will briefly allude to a few of these possible ways, which involve a vital union of creative peace and knowledge.

32. [*Timaeus* 34b; the passage cited next is at 33c.]
33. Neumann, *Origins and History*, [as above, n. 31].

In his significant essay "On the Nature of the Psyche," Jung stated that the archetype determines the course of the configurational process "with seeming foreknowledge, or as though it were already in possession of the goal to be circumscribed by the centering process."[34] This foreknowledge is not only characteristic with regard to a particular archetype; representing, as it does, the "absolute knowledge" to which Jung alludes in the same work, it belongs to the world of archetypes in general.

In harmony with the world of archetypes and with foreknowledge, man experiences himself in the Tao and arrives at a feeling of peace in which the crucial experience is the accord between the inner world and the outer. Contact with archetypal knowledge releases in man an existential security which he otherwise lacks, and the lack of which keeps him in a state of perpetual unrest. This state is a form of "rightness" which is not only overwhelmingly numinous, but also produces a feeling of self-evidentness, a feeling that everything is as it should be, which rules out any hint of the dramatic. The more powerful the experience of rightness which accompanies it, the more clearly this feeling is revealed to be a modulation of living harmony which goes hand in hand with stillness, serenity, and peace.

This "harmonious turmoil" can coexist with falling ill or getting well, with crisis or crisis-solving. Perhaps this can most easily be demonstrated with reference to the accord experienced between an *I Ching* oracle and events accompanying and following it. Regardless of

34. CW 8, par. 411.

whether the oracle is "positive" or "negative," regardless of the sign which reveals its meaning, its emphases, and its modalities, this state of being-in-harmony produces what we call stillness, serenity, and peace. The fact that the *I Ching* gives an answer and that this answer is experienced as meaningful, as "fitting," reveals that the individual fits into a whole to whose befittingness he has fitted himself. But this "making oneself fit" is not an action, above all not an action of the ego and consciousness; rather, it is a being-discovered by what was there all along. A man discovers himself in his self-evident, matter-of-fact unity with the totality of the world, and learns that he not only belongs to what is beyond himself as an ego, but at the most profound level—i.e., in the depths where he really exists but where his conscious mind cannot reach—he actually *is* this ever-changing being. In this state of harmony with the world of archetypes, it becomes evident that he belongs to those "things" which are "at rest from eternity." That is, he experiences himself beyond the strife of the times and beyond the momentary configuration of existence, as "fitted in" and at the same time as free. The psychical states described by the symbols of stillness, serenity, and peace are revealed as contingencies of the world which at the same time are contingencies of being.

The existence which dwells in open harmony with the ever-changing whole rests in peace. It is calm and unruffled even by that never-ending transformation of transformations which is accomplished within it, and within which it is accomplished. For this reason this peace is also stillness. Within it breathes a creative vitality in the form of motion which, paradoxically, is untroubled by its own mobility and is not driven from its stillness.

Thus the symbols of this configuration are light and emptiness. Light, which illuminates everything involved in creative change without itself being altered by this change; and "emptiness" as the space where all changes take place, but which cannot be affected and filled up by these changes, for the emptiness of space always remains that all-embracing thing "in" which all changes undergo change.

Light and space here are not symbols of the physical, material world but symbols of "spirit." But our own experience of being-in-harmony tells us that there is nothing abstract and conceptual about this "spirit." We experience our psyche and the world as a unity cohering in peace and in stillness. Not only we ourselves, but the world as unitary reality, exists in peace and in stillness. Indeed, it almost seems that we can arrive at "our" peace and "our" stillness only when we have become sufficiently open to reality to allow *its* peace and stillness to pass into and through us.

Within this peace operates a living creative openness, and the motion characterizing this being-in-harmony is free and, in the highest sense, spontaneous. There is no contradiction between remaining open as one rests in the stillness of being whole, and pursuing the play of opposites, mobile and moved. Such still serenity can be found even during severe emotional distress, in situations in which one genuinely cannot act and desires not to know anything more, for in the stillness dwells the peace of a higher insight: that despite everything, things are "right" just as they are. This is why, in our strife-ridden age which often gives us cause for despair, this peace can be attained by the individual without withdrawal from active involvement in life and from life itself being either possible or permissible. Man's experience of being-in-harmony is the experience of his harmony with nature; but this does not imply harmony with any and all forms of human society.

Nature is always filled with unknowing knowledge. Its creative life is always fitted into the unity of an order, harmony with which constitutes the self-evident being of everything in nature. Just as, in the Book of Changes, that which exists outside the Tao is also subject to the law of the Tao, so even where nature is unnatural, it is nevertheless the Tao itself as the reality of life as motion-in-change. Thus nature is by its very nature still and at peace, and within this being-in-harmony-with-oneself the raging of the waterfall and the roaring of the fire are just as still as the calm of the sea or the drifting clouds.

Nature's being-in-the-Tao is the state where the creative principle is realized as the indwelling spirit of living things, which moves them from within. Because this unity of life and spirit in nature-as-Tao is at the same time a being-at-peace, union with nature means being embedded in nature, and to go with nature means to achieve peace and the spirit which animates this peace. But the conscious ego stands apart from nature-as-world as well as from nature-as-unconscious, and thus if man is to arrive at nature and its peace, he must be transformed, and his ego-consciousness must discover its relativity in order that he may rediscover his link with his own great nature as an ego-self, and with the even greater nature of which his own forms a part.

But in this peace in which man experiences the true and authentic nature of what is, peace and stillness are revealed as a spiritual-psychical element dwelling in nature, which we feel as serenity.

The German word *heiter*, "serene," derives from the clear cloudless sky. It is related to the (German) suffix *heit*, meaning "species" or "essence" and found in compound substantives, as well as to the Indo-European root **ketu* meaning "radiance, brightness, shine."[35] Thus the sky, that which shines brightly with a radiance drawn from itself, is the true symbol of serenity. Its radiance is of untarnished purity and remains untouched by the dark clouds which gather beneath it and then dissolve again. Here the unity of sky, light, and emptiness becomes evident. In the *Tibetan Book of the Dead* we read: "Thine own consciousness, shining, void, and inseparable from the Great Body of Radiance, hath no birth, nor death, and is the Immutable Light."[36] By now it will be obvious that what in this passage is translated as "consciousness," does not correspond to what we normally call "consciousness." Only in its transformed state is our consciousness revealed as part of that "free-floating" knowledge, inseparable from all events, which, as it is shining and empty, is peace, stillness, and serenity. It contains the creative turmoil of its own transformations and illuminates this turmoil without dimming the peace, stillness, and serene clarity of its own reality. This "true" being of the world, illuminated and at the same time giving off light from within itself, appears to us in

35. Kluge, *Etymologisches Wörterbuch*.
36. W. Y. Evans-Wentz, ed., *The Tibetan Book of the Dead*, tr. Lama Kazi Dawa-Samdup (3rd ed., London, 1957), p. 96.

the form of beauty; and in art the essence of the world-as-beauty becomes the "Great Experience."

But is it not purely arbitrary to relate that vast ocean which is art to the symbol of serenity? What do tragedy, Gothic architecture and Indian sculpture, Picasso, Shakespeare, and Kafka have to do with serenity?

Let us not forget: Our attempt to see the essence of life as serenity, stillness, and peace does not mean that death and misfortune, evil and suffering, do not exist. We associate beauty as much with the lucidity of Bach and the might of Beethoven, as with the dread of Goya and the torment of Van Gogh. Simple, balanced, symmetrical order is not the only element of what we perceive as beauty. To an even greater extent it is the manifold and complex harmony of a balanced asymmetry which also contains dissonance. The creation of and search for the beautiful is an expression of that same detached serenity in which, beyond all the darkness and dread of the subject shaped by artistic craft, the disciplining power, the proportion and the rhythm of form, achieve an unassailable transcendence. This transcendence subjugates the contrariety of a life spanning pain and pleasure, light and darkness. All art, regardless of whether it affirms the harmoniously beautiful or, as in the modern period, denies it, is a play of forms. At its highest it makes evident the unity of life as play-with-form, and life becomes the arena of a supreme beauty whose radiance embraces the whole of the play in serenity, stillness, and peace.

We perceive this serenity, within the gravity of a Bach fugue, as a playful law governing that which, ever-fleeting, ever reassembles; but equally it can transform itself into the solemn and numinous. In Bach ardent emotion pulses like blood through the detachment of form, and a mastery of craft which subdues disorder appears as celebration and solemnity, and at the same time as the supreme, religious form of clarity, stillness, and serenity. On the other hand, the divine serenity of Mozart, in its sublime sympathy with all that lives—a serenity most closely akin to the smile—is simultaneously secular and religious. Here emotion and form achieve a supreme harmony which, illuminating itself, becomes evident to itself.

Yet the serenity of the game is also evident in artists like Picasso, in that creative spontaneity which creates a formless chaos and is savage almost past bearing. Anyone who has seen the film of Picasso during an improvisation session, driven by his inspirations, in every stroke of the brush and every erasure the very incarnation of that spontaneity-at-play which is the creative process, will understand that this is true.

The serenity of the creative principle is not the same thing as gaiety, but neither is it in any way the contrary of seriousness. It can even take tragic form, as it does, for example, in Rembrandt's final self-portrait. But even here, the beauty of color and form, and the openness-*cum*-detachment from the self as ego which makes the self-portrait possible in the first place, enable us to glimpse the serenity of being at home with one's self which includes tragedy and overcomes it. This serenity and stillness can be found in every example of supreme craftsmanship, in the all-embracing vision of the creative man. Such a man pits the gods and the Powers against the hero. He does justice to Iago's malice as well as to the noble savagery of Othello. He lends a voice to the innocence of Ophelia just as to the brooding of Hamlet. With an openness that is without bias the artist assigns its place to everything that lives. If, in allowing reality to emerge, he allows the good to be destroyed and evil to triumph, he himself, as the creative source behind all that happens, remains at the same time moving and unmoved. He possesses that supreme serenity which floats above all, which is detached and knowing like the all-illuminating light and yet which at the same time is profoundly identified and in sympathy with the darkness which opposes the light and with the human which itself has been set between the light and the darkness.

The dissonant element in life becomes apparent in that serenity which embraces tragedy, and in the farcical and grotesque nature of the clown and the fool the dissonance turns into a source of laughter whose strident quality—as at the end of Verdi's *Falstaff*—is rendered serene in the wisdom of humor. But on the highest level the dissonant is transposed, as in the art of Klee, into a spiritual element in which all dissonance is dissolved into music or, as in the late work of Bartók is outshone by a light in which it is impossible to distinguish between harmony and discord.

That creative principle—at the same time serene—which we encounter in the beauty of nature and art, is life and spirit in one, and it is this very oneness which we experience as peace. Its most familiar emblem is the smile of the Buddha in which the unity of sympathy and detachment appears as a symbol of the divine itself.

Suzuki tells of a Chinese art critic who lived in the year 500 and who cites, as the essential trait of the su-

preme artist, the ability to express "the cosmic spirit in
its rhythmic motion." This critic was the subject of the
following commentary by another Chinese: "The other
five essentials are acquired by studious application; as to
the cosmic spirit, it is an inborn quality and no amount
of craftsmanship, however closely followed, enables one
to attain it; nor can the mere elapsing of years qualify
one to be its owner. (No conscious efforts, no designed
strivings will lead the artist to the realization of the
spirit.) It is only recognized in the mystic silence of his
Unconscious (the original Chinese word for this is beyond literal translation). He comes to it without knowing how, when or where. . . ."[37]

But this "inborn quality" must not be misinterpreted
as an innate aptitude. The inborn quality of creative life
is the source of all living things in the nature outside, as
well as in the psyche within. It exists in every blade of
grass as well as in every individual person. The open
bond with this inborn quality, and a life based on identity with it, appears to be a grace; and yet at the same
time it constitutes the true task of man, who wants to
come to his right mind and to a state of creative peace
in harmony with the world. We too are the expression
of this eternally serene and creative force within us, and
as ego we are its instrument. The fact that our inalienable unity with the creative principle is distorted again
and again and thus appears to have been lost, seems to
be part of the game which we are playing at the same
time that it is playing with us. The wind which, both

37. D. T. Suzuki, "Sengai: Zen and Art," *Art News Annual* (New
York), XXVII (1958), p. 193.

outside and inside us, bloweth where it listeth, plays with us and tosses us about like balls for as long as we resist it. If we open ourselves up and let it pass through us, we attain to the innermost life of the world and of ourselves, and arrive at the unitary reality in which we and the world together belong.

Only when he arrives at this unitary reality does man lose the feeling of being exposed and lost. He becomes a "wanderer" who yields himself utterly to the wind of events, which no longer represent an alien force but are that which belongs to him, which he follows after. This fitting-oneself-in is not fatalism in the negative sense, for *amor fati, amor dei*, and *amor sui* are one. Harmony with all that befalls becomes harmony with the innermost part of our own being and with our guiding numen, and these three are revealed as one and the same. Our inmost being is creative life and peace with ourselves, is serenity and stillness within the compass of life and death. It is "shining" and "empty" and has "neither birth nor death and is the unalterable light." At the same time it indwells the transformations of the creative and the receptive, light and darkness, heaven and earth. It is outside us and within us and beyond us as we ourselves. Of it can be said what Heraclitus said concerning the etheric fire in the human body: μεταβάλλον ἀναπαύεται, "Changing, it is at rest."[38]

38. Fr. 84a. [Freeman, *Ancilla*: "It rests from change."]

VI

THE PSYCHE AS THE PLACE
OF CREATION

I

The word *Gestaltung*, translated by "creation" in this context, combines two areas of connotation which are by no means identical or synonymous. In the first place, "creation" stands for creative power, i.e., the capacity and the ability to create works of art; when we talk about the psyche as the place of creation, we may mean that it is a locus of creative capacity and activity in this sense. At the same time, however, "creation" also connotes the actual product of creation, the result of the creative process, the figure creatively realized in art. When we finally become aware that "creating" and "creation" are inseparably bound up with forming, giving form to, and form itself, we shall have some idea of the problem that confronts us.

The symbolic concept of "creation" is so rich in associational content that we are tempted to restrict its usage from the outset to our particular subject, creation in the human psyche, and perhaps even to confine it to that

---

"Die Psyche als Ort der Gestaltung," *Eranos-Jahrbuch 1960*, on "Man and Creation." Translated by Eugene Rolfe.

power in the psyche which creates and forms all our symbols and works of art. But here again, as so often, this narrowing of connotation and the gain in distinctness of reference which it brings are purchased all too dearly at the cost of an excessive impoverishment in the range of the associations. It seems particularly important to recognize that the shaping and form-building capacity of the creative psyche is intimately connected with the reality of the world, of nature, and of the living process. The creative and formative power of this reality not only precedes the creative power of the psyche in time, but it also provides the context through which and in which this psychic creativity came into being in the first place.

When we distinguish in nature between the "living" and the "dead" and characterize as "living" plants, animals, and human beings, but as "dead" the "things" of the world, we are following the guidance of "appearance," that age-old teacher of the human race in its thoughts and musings about itself and the world.

Basing itself on "appearance" in this way, the human psyche teaches us to distinguish not only objects, such as animals and stones, human beings and trees, but also movements and forms. However, from the point of view of these "appearances," moving clouds and the wind that drives them, streaming water and rising flame, are all equally "alive." The life of plants is seen as the earth itself assuming living form, animals as living forms that belong to the forest which envelops, shelters, and nourishes them; and stones and brooks in the same way, like plants and animals and human beings, appear as parts of the mountain that is the center of their existence. It would seem, therefore, that the human psyche tends from the outset not only to apprehend forms and the transformation of forms, but also, and more particularly, to perceive and recognize the essential unity of everything that is real. This implies that from the earliest times man, as he observes, tries to order and assimilate the abundance of the forms and movements that surround him.

The mythologies and the mythical cosmologies, with their teachings about the powers that create and shape heaven and earth, nature and life, animals and human beings, are the earliest expression of man's thoughts and musings about this capacity for self-transformation which is inherent in reality. And when the biblical story of creation speaks of God as the Creator and Former of heaven and earth, light and water, in the same sense as he is Creator of plants, animals, and man, this expresses the truth that man experiences the whole world—including nature and the living beings that animate nature—as a single, coherent unity of creations and created forms.

Let us not forget that the philosophy of the four elements, fire, water, air, and earth, which was already no longer naïve, continued to exert a determining influence on Western thought—e.g., in medicine—right up into the eighteenth century. Yet as symbols of psychic experience of the world, how different these "elements" are from the elements of modern physics and chemistry and from the way in which we now describe their various forms and transformations! This world of natural science is a construction erected by human thought, in which the appearances registered by our senses are progressively overcome by abstraction. But the unitariness of the overflowing abundance of forms that make up the infinite multiplicity of our world is in this way ultimately compressed into a single mathematical formula, in which nothing is left either of the abundance of forms or of the multiplicity of the world.

At first sight, it might seem as if the ultimate goal of natural science was actually to overcome the appearances which are crucially involved in the organization of our senses and hence, also, of the psyche, and as if the extrusion of the abundance of forms would at the same time involve the exclusion of the psyche itself, i.e., of the organ that actually perceives this abundance. At this point, the question even arises as to whether form itself is not a product of the psyche and an "improper" illusion about the world, which must in fact be overcome. Yet even the world of abstraction and of the mathematical formula, however high it may ride and however "detached" and abstracted it may seem to be, still remains fastened to that matrix of "experience" which we apprehend with and through our senses.

Are we dealing here with a conceptual world that is adequate to reality or with a world based on illusion? This is a question that can only be decided by experiment, but experiment involves an interrogation of nature which itself starts out from appearance.

Moreover, even the world of physics and chemistry which lies behind these initial appearances is a world of form and organization. When we are told that "solid bodies in the strict sense of the word are always crystals"[1] and that, still deeper down in the center of

---

1. C. F. von Weizsäcker and J. Juilfs, *Contemporary Physics*, tr. A. J. Pomerans (New York and London, 1962), p. 137.

matter, in the atom, there is "a tendency to form closed shells,"[2] a tendency which determines the position of an element and the type of its reaction in the chemical system of the elements, we realize that even in the realm of so-called dead and inorganic matter, the principle of form and organization prevails. Whether and to what extent the "models" of modern physics, by whose aid the infinite and inconceivable abundance of reality is reduced to order and made intelligible to us, are imposed by the conscious mind as the forming power of cognition in the psyche,[3] or obversely whether these images of the sphere, the nucleus and the shell, and of openness and closedness, are actually operative in what we call matter and reach out from there into the image-making power of the psyche, may be left as an open question in this context. In any case, however, we discover these images as images in and of the psyche; and the psyche, as we know and as the mandala demonstrates, also has a tendency to form "constellations," which is clearly analogous to the tendency to form "closed shells."

These images correspond to constellations of order that control certain forces or dynamisms which—whether in what we call matter or in what we call psyche—produce shaped and ordered realities out of elements that are neither shaped nor ordered.

The question as to whether these "images" represent a process in which a reality in itself inexpressible in fact assumes a graphic form remains undecided—but also

2. Ibid., p. 135.
3. Cf. Wolfgang Pauli, "The Influence of Archetypal Ideas on the Scientific Theories of Kepler," in *The Interpretation of Nature and the Psyche*, by Pauli and C. G. Jung (New York and London, 1955).

unimportant. The decisive factor is that these images are adequate in relation to what we call outer and inner reality. However, in this context "adequate" means not only that in this way something becomes graphically visible and therefore intelligible to man, but that with the aid of these images man can actually live in reality and achieve an adaptation to life and an enhanced capacity for living. At the same time, this clearly implies that the order to which a particular image relates and which is perceived within the image and therefore apprehended as a truth of reality is not projected by the psyche but is actually present in the reality concerned—even though in itself it may be inexpressible in graphic terms. The image may in fact be a projection, but the dynamic order that is perceived by means of the image is not. If it were not the case that the image were an illusion in the sense that nothing real could be apprehended by means of it, then no orientation within the framework of the real world could come about through the agency of the image. The image would then be a delusory phantasm, and we know that the collision of such an image with reality makes the victim of such a delusion incapable of living and leads straight to a psychic and emotional breakdown.

Even if it is true, as science tells us, that disorder is statistically "probable" and order statistically "improbable," the fact remains that we live in a world in which we are confronted by both order and disorder. The human psyche, and the vital process in which and from which it takes its origin, actually apprehends life in this way as a perpetual confrontation between order and disorder—between form and a trend that is hostile to form.

It is typical of man, stamped as he is with the character of the psychic, that he experiences reality with wonder and reverence as a world of order, while at the same time he encounters disorder and hostility to form with feelings of anxiety and horror. The truth is that order or the creation of form and its capacity for transformation are experienced in terms of the symbol of life, while disorder and hostility to form are experienced in terms of death and of the chaos that destroys and dissolves form.

Yet form as the principle of order and life and of defense against death and dissolution is not simply a psychic image, not simply something "designed" by the psyche (such as, for example, a picture by an artist). On the contrary, the experience of form is in a certain sense an a priori datum of the psyche; it is derived from the biological level which precedes the psyche, if not directly from the physical level. However, at the physical level, the "form-conserving function" of the filled, saturated, and therefore closed shells (e.g., of inert gases) is, I take it, if we assume that more is involved than a simply analogy, a passive occurrence in *natura naturata*.[4] But the vital process in an unicellular organism, considered as a form that insulates itself from the world by means of the cellular membrane, already represents the active self-formation of *natura naturans*.[5] In both the inorganic and the organic kingdoms a fixed form operates to conserve its own existence. However, while in the inorganic king-

4. [Literally, "nature natured," a process in which nature is passively determined.—Tr.]

5. ["Nature naturing," a process in which nature actively forms itself.—Tr.]

dom there is only one way in which a given form can be conserved, and a change in the fixed form is exactly the same as a chemical compound involving a basic alteration of the elements or a transformation into another element, the active process of self-transformation which characterizes the vital process involves a constant ongoing change in its components and contents.

But even when man experiences the world of the vital process as a world of ascending orders of being, he is not simply projecting psychic images. On the contrary, he is apprehending a series of connections that are outside the human psyche. It was the nineteenth-century theory of evolution which first provided an objective basis for this concept and metaphor of an "ascent" from the lower to the high. It taught us that the "lower" represents an earlier and the "high" a later stage of development, and that one stage evolved out of the other. Yet the conceptual image of an ascending order from the inorganic to the organic kingdom and from plants and animals to man is historically far more ancient than this; for example, it is already to be found as a picture image of the world in the biblical myth of creation, in spite of the fact that the Bible not only "knew" nothing about the theory of evolution but actually provided the basis for a diametrically opposite concept of the creation of species, which was only finally "superseded" by the theory of evolution.

Nowadays we experience the world of reality as an ascent, at the beginning of which so-called "dead" nature appears as something passively shaped and formed, which then, in the realm of the living organism, rises to the level of living forms that carry the process of differentiation further and further forward. In these forms the dominant role is initially played by the nature of the species; the single creature is a "preformed form" in which the species is vitally involved as an anonymous controlling and directing agency. At the same time, however, this anonymity and the absorption of the single creature in the nature of the species do not prevent the occurrence of endless variations in the outer form, as we can see, for example, in the case of the radiolaria.

At this stage, the characteristic superabundance of creative forms is already a striking feature. This has been described by Professor Portmann as "undirected self-representation,"[6] i.e., as the "phenomenon" that the vital process emerges and expresses itself in forms that bring no visible or demonstrable advantage to the organism. Here Portmann introduces his concept of "inwardness," which in his view is to be found in all forms of life; as a psychologist, I should prefer to reserve this term for the higher ranges of living creatures, though it is possible that rudimentary stages or analogous developments are to be found far earlier, even in the inorganic kingdom. But it is among the higher living creatures that inwardness is clearly discernible in the sense that there is at work in the individual not only an agency that directs development in accordance with the nature of the species (in the form, that is, of an anonymous authority to which the single creature is passively subjected), but that this effective agency also takes the form of something which in man we describe as "psychic" or

6. Adolf Portmann, "Unterwegs zu einem neuen Bild vom Organismus," in *Die Welt in neuer Sicht* (Munich, 1957), p. 43.

as "inwardness"—that is to say, as a temperament or disposition. This disposition is itself still largely conditioned by the nature of the species, but it does not take possession of all members of the species automatically, in a passive way; the possessor of this disposition is now the individual, in whom the disposition prescribed by the nature of the species varies in a unique way.

There remains one final stage in creative development, in which the vital process, shaped and formed, becomes itself a "continual shaper and former." Not only is this function of the biopsyche which has been shaped and formed in accordance with the nature of the species now incorporated in the being of the single creature, but the vital process becomes a form of existence that is itself capable of creation and able to produce created forms out of its own being. This creative production of created forms is the unique happening that is typical and characteristic of the human psyche alone.

Before we turn our attention to the psyche as the place of formative creation, we must once again ask ourselves whether this ascending concatenation of the vital process which reaches its culmination in the psyche represents a projection of the human psyche upon nature or whether it corresponds to an objective sequential situation in which the creative and formative function of the psyche becomes visible as the final result of a process of ascent in life itself. It is my opinion that we are confronted here by a metapsychological aspect, i.e., by a conception of the vital process which, though it certainly arises out of the specifically creative experience peculiar to the human psyche, is by no means a projection. While natural science is primarily concerned with causal chains in "dead nature," i.e., in a reality passively created, psychology is—among other things—the reflected inwardness of the creative and formative processes that take place in the human psyche. However, as this creative potency of the psyche becomes conscious, psychology also becomes aware of those developments in the history of life which precede and prepare the way for this creative potency of the psyche.

This means that the metapsychological aspect, which discloses especially the ascent of this same creative potency in the biophysical dimension of the living creatures that preceded man in evolution, actually relates to a real objective situation, just as much as the biological aspect, which, for example, discerns in the evolution of earlier living creatures a preparation for the sense-organs and the nervous system of man.

So we must ask ourselves, "What is there, in the ascending sequence of living creatures, that anticipates the creative vitality of the human psyche, its reflected inwardness, the cognitive function of the conscious mind, and the relative freedom of the human ego?"

"Species" are the great master-configurations in which we find the vital process in reality. They are "orders" whose genesis and mode of operation are unknown to us; what we do know, however, is that for the individuals in which they are exemplified they are transpersonal in character. The species is a datum prior to the individual which determines its configuration and its behavior. This determining agency, which is inherited principally in the nuclei of the cells, but probably also in the protoplasm, orders and controls not only the structural development of the body but also the behavior of the individual in its relationship to other members of its own species as a member of a group, a sexual partner, and a descendant; furthermore, this agency also largely determines its behavior towards all those plant and animal species that as friends, enemies, or victims form part of the life of this particular species. But this relationship to the living environment is only a part or segment of a larger environment that is also "ordered," since landscape, place of origin, element (e.g., water and air), and, if we think of the migrations of animals, an entire geography of the earth's surface, must be included in the span of the world of perception and action which is ordered and monitored for the benefit of the species.

This implies, however, that the creative and formative agency which determines the "species" contains a priori something quasi "inner" that is related to something quasi "outer" and something quasi "outer" that relates to something quasi "inner" and that these two aspects are intertwined with one another. The configuration of the species is always a form that provides "order" and security at one and the same time. From the overwhelming and destructive multiplicity of the vital process, it cuts out a segment of reality that in a unicellular organism seems tiny but which continually increases in size as the evolution of living creatures progresses. This segment is the specific range of experience that is open to the species in question. But the lower we descend in the scale of evolution, the more we shall find that the single unit—the single cell, for example—has a far larger potential for a multiplicity of reactions than it retains later on. However, in relation to the species it is dependent; it does not exist as a single, self-differentiating creature. The single unit derives its security in life essentially from its being in accordance with the species, within which it is, in a sense, enclosed, whereas what we call the "individual" is not yet fixed, even as regards space and time.

It follows that the directing agency is still, initially, nothing "inner." And here we must have recourse, once again, to the example of the slime mold, which at first occurs in the form of unicellular organisms that exist independently of each other.[7] These then undergo a curious change. They mobilize toward a number of centers, streaming in to each center—each organism at first retaining its own individuality. However, after changing their positions in space in various ways, they proceed to constitute the slime mold and its different organs and become cells of the larger organism.

What concerns us here is the "ordering" and assembling of many unicellular organisms around centers situated outside themselves, by means of which the *slime mold* comes into existence, constituting as it does an organic whole. We have to imagine this co-ordination, and the future "order" that the later individual slime mold possesses, is present in the form of a built-in plan in the unicellular organisms that precede the formation of the slime mold. But we can only imagine this on the following assumption. In the multicellular higher organisms which are known to us, each single cell as it develops takes up the place and the function assigned to it in the total organism in a way which is beyond our understanding. We have to assume that each single cell carries

7. See the citation of Sinnott above, in Essay II, n. 4.

an overall plan of the organism and of its own place within that organism. It must contain, too, a tendency to differentiate and a technique of differentiation which make it possible for the originally polyvalent cell that had existed at the beginning of the process to develop into the highly differentiated cell that finally achieves its effective function as an exceedingly small part of a special organ or organic system within the superordinate totality of the organism.

In the higher organisms there is a continuous connection linking one cell and another in the form of tissue, etc.; the differentiating, precipitating, and co-ordinating effect, e.g., of a chemical agent on the single cell, coming as it were from outside, is actually situated within an organic continuum to which the cell itself belongs (i.e., the body). In the case of our slime mold, however, this continuum only comes into existence at the end, and we have to assume that in the blueprint for the genesis of the slime mold that is carried in the unicellular organisms the division into "really outer" and "relatively outer" is not valid, since the directing centers are spatially external to the unicellular organisms and are not inside a physical continuum to which the unicellular organism belongs. In other words, these centers are situated at a spot outside their physical existence, which is nevertheless included in the blueprint carried by the unicellular organisms. The multicellular configuration of the slime mold, which we finally apprehend as a total configuration removed from the sphere of the outside world, arises out of a unitary "field," in which "outside space with centers" and unicellular organisms distributed in the field are brought together in an orderly arrangement under unitary direction.

The centers that direct the unicellular organisms in the outside space are unquestionably part of the blueprint of the slime mold, and as a result it is impossible to determine whether they are to be allocated to an outer or an inner space. It follows that in this "species" it is difficult to determine what is really to be regarded as the carrier or representative of the species—the unicellular organisms or the slime mold. Correspondingly, the allocation of the space as "outer" and "inner" and the time as "after" the end of the unicellular organisms or "before" the beginning of the slime mold is problematic in the extreme. And we find the same kind of indeterminacy in far higher species. In the configurations of larva, chrysalis, and butterfly, it is impossible to identify which of these is the individual that is the representative and carrier of the species. Here again we find that different forms of life, different lifetimes, and different living spaces may belong to different stages in the life of a single species. The species is not yet embodied in individuals with a single, continuing formative development in a single, continuing living space and a single, continuing life span; but the species still controls and dominates the particular, individual phases of the development.

On the other hand, we know that membership of a species implies participation in a specific world of observation and action and specific patterns of behavior that are based on a knowledge of the world and its reactions. Yet it is impossible to ascribe this kind of knowledge and this kind of meaningful direction, by means of which the species is guided in its adjustment, simply to the individual, as seems to be the case with psychological knowledge. On the contrary, as we said at the beginning, this is unconscious and uncentered knowledge that does not belong to the individual. We have already spoken more than once of a "field" knowledge and of the "extraneous" knowledge that is not incorporated in the individual. One example of this is the "knowing" orderly arrangement which directs the unicellular organisms of the future slime mold. Another is the rabies virus described by Portmann, in what we might even call its "behavior" towards man and in its differentiated "knowledge" of the functioning of the human nervous system.[8]

A "field" is a transpersonal configuration of the vital process; individuals, whose dynamic relationships with one another are determined by the field, are contained within this configuration. The relationships of the parts of this field (e.g., of the individual members of a species) are determined by the totality of the field, e.g., by the "character" of the living creature which is peculiar to its species and by the connections between its vital "field" and the vital fields of other living creatures. Thus the character which is peculiar to a given species forms part of the environment of that species, so that, for example, in the case of the rabies virus, man, dogs, and water, too, are essential constituents of its vital unity.

Here again, it is possible that the conception of the world which we derive from our conscious mind and its polarized viewpoint may be misleading us when it

8. Portmann, "Die Bedeutung der Bilder in der lebendigen Energiewandlung," *EJ 1952.*

speaks in terms of a living creature here and an environment over there and of the effect of the one upon the other. This separation between subject and object—valid though it is for our conscious mind—is, if at all, less valid when applied to lower forms of life. Yet the concept of a field, in which the living creature and its environment are regarded as a continuum, may perhaps bring us a stage further.

The knowledge of the world incorporated in the species makes it possible for the species to live in the world; it is the expression of that unknown quantity which we describe as "adaptation." But it is remarkable, and typical of our attitude, how strongly within this concept our basic presupposition of the separation between object and subject comes out and is represented. The concept presupposes that a living thing which is cut off from what is outside exists independently in its own right and adapts to something outside. But that is quite simply impossible. The truth is that living creatures are already, a priori, "in a state of adaptation" in this sense; moreover, the further back we go in the scale of evolution, the less do we find a living creature that is "independent" and a "subject," cut off from the world outside.

As I see it, what is known as adaptation is generally understood as a process that runs its course in time and is to be explained in terms, e.g., of mutation, the struggle for existence, and natural selection. But the basic question as to why living creatures do not become extinct before they have achieved this "adaptation" has never been answered in this context.

However, we cannot neglect the problem of origin, which is still awaiting a solution. A question of principle is involved here. How are we to conceive of life's capacity for relationship with other living creatures—a capacity which is common to all species? If we locate this capacity for relationship, which assumes a different form and character in every species, right at the beginning of evolution—and in my view it extends beyond organic life—then we must date back the typical mode of "being-in-the-world" and "being-with-the-world" which characterizes the vital process to a primordial situation at the origin of things. We cannot first "posit" a vital process and then proceed to enquire into its relationship with the world. The implication here is that every species, and every living creature out of which a species evolves, must necessarily be equipped from the outset with a basic order of attributes and arrangements which constitute a "set" that guarantees its capacity to live. Once granted the presence of this basic order, the species can "adapt," mutate, and evolve or perish in the struggle for existence. However, this basic order cannot be explained in the same manner as those attempts to explain the evolution of existing basic orders, that is, of established living creatures. Nuclear structures that condition inheritance and all structures that are present in the body are, of course, already arranged and ordered by the basic directive structure of the species. If we banish from our minds this "inner aspect" which applies to already existing hereditary structures, but is not valid for the early stages of life, and look for the creativity in the openness of a directive field which embraces both inner and outer aspects, the problem will appear in a somewhat different light.

As a species, every form of life contains only a particular tiny segment of reality in its world of observation and action. It is true that as evolution ascends, this segment grows larger; yet it always remains, relatively speaking, small or even tiny. Nevertheless, it is always shaped and ordered in such a way that however different it may be in different species, it still makes possible the existence of life in a world that is to a large extent beyond the experience and the capacity for experience of a single living creature. In other words, however tiny and incomplete the segment of reality of the species may be in relation to the total range of reality, it still remains an adequate "totality for life" in the sense that it is sufficient for existence and "omits" nothing in its scheme of reactions which could lead to its extinction as a species.

On closer examination we can see that this is a truly remarkable phenomenon. It implies that the concept of the "preservation of life" actually plays, in some respects, a subordinate role in nature. Of course, every species fulfils the law of self-preservation; yet apparently, in the course of evolution, nature, in her creation of species, "has at heart" something other than the simple preservation of life. On the face of it, we can interpret this statement as anthropomorphic and as questionable for that reason. Personally, however, I am convinced that it is justified and that it brings us closer to the center of the range of problems that concern us. It seems to me that from the very beginning there is a superabundance of creativity at work, and that the effect of this principle is by no means simply to give rise to self-preserving species. The ascending evolution of these species is always closely bound up with a widening in the scope of their creative and formative activity. This means that the vital process is gaining a more comprehensive experience of reality. We know in fact that the ascent of evolution corresponds to an increasingly comprehensive grasp by the vital process of the world of observation and action.

At this point, the problem of anthropomorphism and the problem of circular reasoning both come clearly into view. We naturally see the evolution of the vital process from the vantage point of the level of awareness which has been achieved by the human psyche. In man, for the first time, knowledge has become conscious, and this has happened not only in the form of self-knowledge but also as the will to a progressive knowledge of reality. From this point of view we see nature as the unfolding of a kind of creativity, which not only produces new forms but in and through these forms is continually reaching out to new extensions of the segment of reality that is open to knowledge.

On the other hand, from the point of view of the preservation of the life of the species, no extension of the knowledge of reality is necessary. Once the basic "set" governing the preservation of life is present, the existence of a species can only be endangered by fundamental changes in the environment, and we know that there are species of animals which have remained unchanged for immensely long periods and have still preserved their existence. The sea, probably the origin of life, still typically provides the securest environment. Yet the very fact that life has literally begun to "ascend," to emerge out of the water and to conquer the earth and the air, has brought with it an increasing experience of the world that necessarily also involves life in ever-increas-

339

ing perils. Here, too, the typical overflowing superabundance of creativity is clearly at work from the beginning. There can be no doubt that the sea provides an inexhaustible environment for life. This means that the principle of the preservation of life does not in any way demand that the vital process should forsake the world of its primordial origin.

Let us return to the problem of circular reasoning. We started out from the human psyche and from the principle of creativity and progressive knowledge which is becoming conscious in that psyche and we went on to understand the totality of life from an anthropomorphic point of view. We necessarily apprehend the vital process from the standpoint which is peculiar to ourselves, and if creativity is a basic category of human existence, we experience what is happening in and around us in the light of this category. Yet this admission on our part may be definitely limited and possibly even invalidated. The fact is that it was not psychology which discovered and investigated the world of nature and its evolution. Man's age-old striving to grasp reality has never consciously started out from the point of view of creativity; nor has this aspect ever determined the results of research. On the contrary, it would appear that this creative, formative, and cognitive process is really present in the unfolding of life, but that the human psyche is the organ that arose in the course of this evolution—the organ, in fact, in which this tendency is apprehended by an "ego" as "inwardness." Here, too, it may be possible to identify a type of evolution which aims in its ascent toward such an ego-knowledge as this, in the form of a centered and self-reflecting knowledge of inwardness. If the ascent of species is characterized by the fact that larger and larger segments of reality emerge as the world of observation and action, then we may perhaps assume that what began as a largely extraneous and "field" knowledge, in which no fixed co-ordination with space and time had existed for an "individual," gradually migrated into the interior, as it were, and at first appeared as knowledge in the biopsyche of a living creature that had been shaped and formed in accordance with the species. This migration-into-the-interior of knowledge, which has been as it were "incorporated" into the organism, corresponds to the evolution of the sense organs, the nervous system, and their rudimentary precursors. At this stage, formation in accordance with the species implies a form already largely preformed and "given," with an effect that is prescribed and invariable.

Among higher forms of life, where incorporation has proceeded much further and where there is a capacity for co-ordinating space and time and a well-developed nervous system, the process of being directed by a field knowledge that embraces both an inner and an outer aspect is much less in evidence; a new form of direction carried out by structures, instincts, etc., incorporated *in the individual* now becomes effectively operative. At the same time, this kind of incorporated autonomy represents a relative independence from the outside world and brings with it the possibility of a greater freedom, which becomes increasingly obvious, for the higher forms of life. At first, this greater freedom represents no more than a widening of the segment of the world that is open to experience; there is still no question of an "inner" freedom. The biological and biopsychical determinants that direct behavior and disposition still achieve their effect as "preformed forms"; they constitute an a priori given order that determines the life of each single specimen of the species. Yet although each single specimen is nothing but a "representative of the species," the fact that the structure of the species varies slightly in every specimen signifies nothing less than the dawn of individuality, and with the ascent of species this development begins to play an increasingly vital role.[9]

This means that among the higher forms of life and, finally, in man, we find, in addition to biopsychic determination by the species, a steadily growing contribution which is made by sociopsychic and individual influences. The narrower or larger social grouping begins to become increasingly important and inserts itself between the biopsychic dimension determined by the species and the environment. On the other hand, there is a process of individualization which emerges more and more clearly, and is connected with the appearance of what Portmann has described as inwardness and disposition. At first, these factors too are still, by and large, biopsychically determined. We find rudiments of individualization among living creatures, for example in the development of psychosexual differentiation, attitudes of

9. It must not be assumed that these developments are in the direct line of ascent and proceed logically and schematically in conformity with the evolution of species. As we have already seen, what is to some extent a reversal of the process of individualization is to be found in, e.g., the evolution of insects from larva through pupa to butterfly, which seems to have vanished already in the early species; and also the individualization of the species through single specimens, e.g., among ants, bees, and termites, is abandoned or restricted in favor of the other principles, such as, a team of individualities.

leadership and subordination, etc.; yet the phenomenon of freedom is still scarcely to be found, if it exists at all, and, apart perhaps from the primates, there is still no formative or cognitive spontaneity. Preformed formation in the sense of a rigidly determined structure of behavior and cognition remains the dominant characteristic.

With the human psyche, the case is different. For the human psyche, as the typical phenomenon of man, is no longer merely a preformed form, but an agency of continual creative formation. Yet this continually creative agency of the human psyche is apparently (however enigmatic this fact may seem to us) a relatively recent manifestation. We are not referring here to the abrupt, almost instantaneous emergence of high cultures some six thousand years ago, but to a much earlier and more astonishing phenomenon. The stone tools of prehistoric and early man, which are the most important records we possess of those periods and in terms of the technology of their production and employment provide us with our most illuminating sources of evidence, point clearly to the fact that man, in this prehistoric era, was an exceedingly conservative and uninventive creature. Over a period of some three hundred thousand years, during which man's environment underwent the extremes of change involved in two glacial and two interglacial epochs, man's tools remained absolutely unchanged; approximately two more millennia had to pass before an improved toolmaking technology won the day. In other words, the evolution of the specific tools that characterize man, from their crudest to their most refined form, required a period of half a million years.

It is only in the last forty thousand years—possibly or probably coinciding with the emergence of new types of man—that technical evolution has begun to progress with more than ordinary speed, in the last ten thousand years with very great speed, and in the last five thousand years with an almost manic rapidity which has brought about a continuous and unceasing change in the human situation.

This means, however, that until about forty thousand years ago man did not by any means possess that psyche characterized by "continuous creative formation" which we regard as characteristic of the human species. However, since the emergence of the individual conscious mind also unquestionably falls within this most recent epoch, we must associate the special quality of those creative and formative processes which continually renew themselves with this newly emerging tension in the psyche—the tension, that is, between the ego of the conscious mind and the unconscious.

The evolution of prehistoric and early man, which is exceedingly slow in comparison with our own, relates him more closely with the psychic constellation of the higher animals, in which the role of the individual is still almost entirely undeveloped and the determining part is played by the species. It is true that the beginnings of social differentiation and of the dependence of the single human being on his social group are already to be found in this period. Yet the striking uniformity of the technical capability of early man, from Africa to eastern Asia (which probably also applies to his overall level of evolution), contrasts in the most emphatic way with the cultural evolution of man in the most recent epoch, which is characterized by an immense abundance of varying low and high cultures among the most diverse races in all the different continents of the globe.

If, psychologically, we point out the contrast between man's most recent, "patriarchal" epoch, centered as it is in masculine ego-consciousness, and a matriarchal epoch with a matriarchal consciousness, we are implying that, in the latter case, ego activity is still relatively lacking in independence and that the constellating activity of the unconscious, of the instincts and of archetypal structures, that is to say, the collective, not yet individualized tendencies, are dominant.[10]

In all probability, the epoch of "matriarchal consciousness," with its relatively weak ego, did not produce any "tradition." No doubt its experience was in the main confined to an inspirational and mantic psychic activity constellated by a given situation, though this activity was already fully capable of forming morality and producing rituals. In sharp contrast to this stage, the beginning of the patriarchal epoch everywhere inaugurated a great age of myth formation. The matriarchal, inspirational, mantic dimension was still present in this epoch, but it was now not only "let through" by an ego in a momentary situation, but held fast, worked upon, and handed down in a tradition. At first, it was probably in the men's group, the place of origin of the future patriarchal domination, that the significance of the individual became institutionalized. This means that we now witness the evolution of the "Great Individual," in

10. Neumann, "Über den Mond und das matriarchale Bewusstsein," in *Zur Psychologie des Weiblichen* (U. d. M. 2). [Cf. tr. Hildegard Nagel in *Spring 1954.*]

the form just as much of a leader and chieftain as of a magician and medicine man, a seer and a poet, a sacral king and lawgiver.

This function of the "Great Individual" was already evolving in the prehistory of mankind when the "Great Individuals" were for the group the representatives of the ego, the self, and the super-ego, that is to say, of the authorities of the human psyche which were still, at that stage, largely unconscious. As we know, in prehuman and early human times, the small group, which probably at first consisted of a few single families, formed the sociopsychic unit. The earliest human beings, whose stone tools were better adapted for woodworking than for use as weapons, were trappers,[11] that is to say, they lived as a group which needed "leaders" just as much as the later Ice Age, with its emphasis on magic, needed magicians and artists, painters and sculptors, shamans, prophets, and priests.

The fact that in this primeval period the volitional, aggressive and constructive activity of the patriarchal ego, the lawgiving activity of the super-ego, and the more passively observant and visionary activity of the matriarchal ego must necessarily still have appeared unseparated from one another as a single instrument of the self will not surprise us if we remember that even in the early historical period all these functions—visions and dealings with the supernatural powers, lawgiving, administration, and warfare, to name but a few—were united in the person of the sacral king, who was the "Great Individual." And even today the atavistic figure

11. *L'Homme avant l'existence* (Paris: Armand Colin, 1959).

of the dictator and sovereign ruler is still most intimately connected with the basic archaic conception of the "Great Individual."

And so, in the stadial development of the psychic, in the psyche of the higher animals and of the matriarchal and patriarchal consciousness in man, we find, not only a growing independence of the ego and, with the ego, of individuality, but also a growing tension between, on the one hand, the increasingly independent ego and the self-organizing and systematizing conscious mind, and, on the other hand, the unconscious as the representative of the collective unconscious, the structure of the species, and the instincts. In contrast to the "preformed form" of the biopsyche which characterizes the higher animals, man has reached the phase of the actively creative and formative psyche, which involves a completely new kind of takeover of the process of creation from the biopsyche into the psyche of man. Hand in hand with this potency of the human psyche, which now appears as a directly creative inwardness that is becoming conscious, there is a tendency towards individualization, spearheaded by its outstanding exponent in evolution, the ego-consciousness of man. We now observe a "psychization" of the structure of the species and of its instincts and drives, and at last, very gradually, they become conscious in an ego. At the same time the instincts, as rigid structures conditioned by the species, recede in importance, and the greater, though admittedly more conflict-ridden, autonomy and freedom of the individual in relation to the social group and the species are no longer grounded simply on the development of the ego but also on the process whereby the ego becomes a self. In this process the ego stands revealed as the exponent of the basic totality of the individual, that is to say of the ego-self structure, which is the axis of the actively creative potentialities of the individual.

We find that in the composition of the human psyche all the stages in the history of the evolution of life which have led up to man as he is today are still in a certain sense very much alive. What we have to regard as the deepest level is the level of "conformity with the species." From the purely biological and biopsychical viewpoint, every man—independently of race and nation and also, to a large extent, independently of the historical period—must, as man, conform to the nature of the species. Among many other features, this includes the instinctive structure common to all men and the images in the form of archetypes and symbols which correspond to this instinctive structure. An essential part of this basic structure of human experience is made up of symbolism derived from nature: abyss and cave, wellspring and tree, stone and star, river crossing and sea, desert or wilderness, mountain peak and green meadow. All these—apart from geographical variants—are images and atmospheric feelings about the world that are common to the human race. The animal symbolism which represents the sexual instinct is another example of a fundamental archetypal structure of the psyche. When the animal appears—whether as a snake, a bull or a ram, a buck or a horse, a dog or a cat—that is already a "filling in" of the basic schema, and depends on the regional experience of the group in which the symbol or the underlying instinctual constellation emerges. This means that the layer of the biopsychic is overlaid by the sociopsychic layer which is, admittedly, also collective, but which has to be co-ordinated with the individual group, in all its geographical, historical, political, and social particularity.

And so, while the great polyvalent archetypal structure belongs to the collective unconscious of mankind, the filling in of this structure and its realization in terms of symbolic images is co-determined from the outset by the sociopsychic dimension of the group or nation, which relates it to a specific historical and geographical time and space. For example, the nourishment provided by the maternal principle is present everywhere, and is part of the earthly, elemental character of the maternal. But whether this nourishment takes the form of wheat or rice, millet or tapioca, corn or barley, is a matter of secondary differentiation and is determined by the sociopsychic factor.

The world of the specifically human dimension, characterized as it is by a development of the conscious mind that has accelerated during the last few millennia, is relatively free and unfixated, and this freedom of the human psyche is crystallized in the ego-pole of the conscious mind, which acts as the executor of formative creation.

With the human and humane accentuation of the creative and formative process in the psyche, which emphasizes the individual and the ego, a new element of far-reaching creative freedom has entered human life.

The human drive for knowledge which is bound up with ego-consciousness is no longer passive, devoted simply to the defense of the human species, even if originally it may perhaps have evolved out of this tendency.

At any rate, it begins immediately, at the moment in history when this new capacity of the human species as a creative psyche achieves independence, to dissolve the primary psychic state of "being-in-the-world" by a process of philosophizing and abstraction. It begins to liberate itself from the graphic immediacy of our sensory apparatus and to form and produce a new dimension which is nothing less than a world of thinking in terms of concepts and logical laws. But not only that: the whole of human culture is in fact the product of this free activity of the ego, which—when it is creative—takes up into itself the prototype of the "Great Individual" and entrusts his achievement to the collective as a possession to be handed down to posterity. The immensely rich field of technology and agriculture and the unfolding of the later social and political developments in the history of mankind are all products of the free play and activity of the creative ego. Human cultures, in all their immeasurable abundance and variety, are not the result of given and preformed creation, like the social world of ants or bees; on the contrary, they are the expression of the continually shaping and forming potency of the human psyche, whose exponent is the acting, willing, sensing and intuiting, thinking and feeling ego, which represents the totality of man.

This shifting of the center of gravity to the individual and the formative activity of his ego is the precondition for the new creative world of man, which he is developing as a technological culture in the direction of a progressive loosening of the ties of his dependency on the environment. But it is the same ego, as the representative of the continuing creative potency of the human psyche, which, by virtue of its mythopoeic, religious, artistic, and philosophical powers, produces an inexhaustible flood of newborn psychic and spiritual worlds. And here we must emphasize, once again, in the light of the static nature of early man's culture over a period of hundreds of thousands of years, how very much the reverse of self-evident is the phenomenon, so self-evident to ourselves, that every corner of the earth's surface which has been discovered in the last few hundred years was, and still is to the present day, covered by the most manifold and widely differing human cultures.

It is the comparative freedom of the ego, the conscious mind, and the creative process which distinguishes the human psyche, as the place of active formative creation, from all those other types of existence which surround it and have preceded it in evolution. It is in the tension between the creative possibilities of the freely mobile ego and the deep layer of the psyche that the new creative and formative potential emerges, over and over again.

We can see to what a large extent the creative potency of the psyche is dependent on the accentuation of ego-consciousness from two phenomena (apart from the actual creative process itself, in the strict sense) which we must emphasize once more in this context. The first is the general psychic law that the psyche intervenes to compensate and regulate the constellation of ego-consciousness and is concerned in this way constantly to bring about a balance in line with totality. The second is the appearance of the "transcendent function," which emerges when the tension between the opposites of the conscious mind and the unconscious becomes too acute to be reconciled in a balance. In both cases, ego-consciousness by its attitude provokes into action the totality of the psyche and its center, the directing self.

As this potentiality for becoming conscious develops, in the final phase of the evolution of the creative process which unfolds and opens in the human psyche, the ego gradually catches sight of its own root, the self. But this self is also the center of the creative process, which brings forth fruitfully the product of creation and out of which, as form and as formless reality, the total experience of mankind bears witness to the numinous, creative Source.

2

Preanalytical philosophy and psychology took the view that the ego and the conscious mind were the authentic human dimension and at the same time provided the psychological basis for what they tried to define as human freedom. The human ego was, in fact, regarded not only as the far-ranging pole of world conquest and knowledge, but also as the representative of human totality as long as the unconscious deep level of the psyche remained unrecognized. As a result of the discovery by depth psychology of the relative dependence of the ego and the conscious mind on the complexes of the personal unconscious and the archetypes and instinctual structures of the collective unconscious, the "classical" psychology of freedom, based as it was on the conscious mind, was restricted, certainly, but not abolished. The emphasis was shifted to a more comprehensive psychic world, which includes the unconscious and the self; the conception of a closed psychic system based on the conscious mind had to be surrendered in favor of one of a relatively open psychic world. This meant that when the creative connection between the ego and the unconscious, in sickness and in health, became the centerpoint of interest, the creative freedom of the psyche, and of the directing ego-self axis within the psyche, was revealed as the basic principle of human existence.

Though the creative deep level of the psyche is related to the creative process in all forms of life, this in no way alters the fact that we have to perceive it as a new advance of the creative principle, in which the governance of this creativity has been handed over to the individual as the representative of the unity of the ego and the self.

Individuality is one of the essential specializations which distinguish the human species; its development is based on the affirmation of the creative individual, whether "great" or "small."

The principle of creativity which is inherent in the psyche produces an abundance of forms, which ascend in hierarchical layers from the biopsyche through the sociopsychic dimension to the personal unconscious of the individual and are linked up by the conscious ego with the specific creations of the conscious mind and elaborated into new creative forms. This is not the place to discuss the dynamism of the biopsyche and the instincts and their transformations; reference will be made here only to one particular factor, which is that the psyche apprehends both the so-called inner world and the so-called outer world *in terms of images*. This phenomenon already contains a fundamental and perhaps decisive element in the creative and formative process. Every archetype, every symbol, insofar as it has become an image, is already a creative psychic formulation, a mastering of the world by the creative psyche. The reality that lies behind these images is charged with an overwhelming, incomprehensible, and therefore destructive dynamism which impresses the psyche that is affected by it as a terrifying chaos and a menacing disorder. Every system within the psyche which apprehends reality in terms of images, whether on the level of our sensory experience or of the higher symbolic forms of psychic elaboration, always involves security and creative formulation, since it imposes order on the dynamic impact of anonymous outer and inner powers, and transforms them into a pattern that is accessible to us and psychologically comprehensible. This means not only that the unconscious process of image-formation, for example, as it is involved in the way our senses are organized, furthers—as with all living creatures—the preservation of life and the species by assisting our orientation in the world, but that the entire phenomenon of creativity in the psyche is governed by the constellation of order and form. Here the ego, in its capacity as "personal totality" and as the representative of biopsychic totality, is beyond question an essential factor in image-formation. It is not true that images already present and "available" are apprehended passively by the ego. On the contrary, image-formation itself depends, at any rate in its higher ranges, on the constellating and formative potency of the ego; if this is damaged, the result will be either a disturbance in the genesis or perception of the image—failure of the image—or a disturbance in the accurate co-ordination of these images with reality.

The ego is the representative of centroversion, the basic psychic function which strives towards the centered unity of the personality. It is an essential part of the structure of that creative pole of the personality which is incarnate in the ego. On it is based the ego's capability, as an "I am" and "I will," to erect and to apprehend the inner and the outer world in terms of images of totality and, furthermore, by virtue of its relationship with the supreme court of totality in the self, to pierce right through, beyond the images, to the essential core of the creative process. With the affirmation of the creative individual a new factor of far-reaching creative freedom enters life in the form of human culture. To some extent, these new creative processes can still be construed as a development of the instinct for self-preservation. Yet even the widening of the world of observation and action evolving in man extends far beyond anything that could still fall within the limits of the concept of the preservation of life. And the creative cultural potency of man in the fields of religion, art, philosophy, and, even to some extent, science, is closely connected with comprehending the meaning of life, but scarcely any longer, if at all, with its preservation.

The original link between the creative processes of the psyche and the religious dimension might in fact be regarded as a defense and incantation against terrifying powers that are hostile to life and in this way be attributed to the instinct for the preservation of life. Yet in the course of evolution the unique and characteristic significance of the creative power of the psyche becomes steadily more and more unmistakable. Even when a fragment of the instinct for the preservation of life is also fundamentally at work in the creativity of the psyche, the trend is still towards man's growing concern with the interpretation and the meaning of life, and this always involves a struggle for the opportunity to live the kind of life that is appointed and appropriate for man. In the normal sense of the term the preservation of life is always subordinate to the preservation of the species, and from this point of view the individual has no more than a statistical significance. Yet the question of meaning which is bound up with human creativity relates to man as an individual and to the preservation of his individual life as an existence creatively formed by himself. The phenomenon that the psyche, which aims at the individual, only fulfills itself in the individuation of the individual, corresponds to the fact that the individual only discovers the meaning of his life when he follows the creative tendencies of the psyche.

The basic archetypal schema of determinate images or forms is varied and modified by the differences in cultural education and the mobile requirements of man's adaptation to his locality and social grouping.

This means that the channel of tradition which extends from the family to the group no longer simply embodies biopsychically the experience of the species, but that the experience of the early history of the group is transmitted sociopsychically as a cultural possession. Yet this cultural possession is essentially molded as occasion arises by the newly won experience of "Great Individuals" who perform this task creatively on behalf of the collective.

In this way, through the significance of "tradition," the universal instinct for the preservation of the species becomes specialized and individualized. It is no longer concerned with the preservation of the human species in general, but with the preservation of a specific group tradition, e.g., of the tribe, the nation, etc. Yet this process of differentiation is carried even further, since, as the cultural development of the West shows us, the center of gravity now shifts towards the individual. This implies that this process of individualization, with its shift towards personal individuation, is not a special case confined to a particular culture, and certainly not to a "supercivilization." On the contrary, the whole development of the vital process is straining towards this process of the individualization of the single human being, in which in fact it finds its fulfillment. It can be either furthered or inhibited by collective processes of another kind, but it can no more be halted than the general evolution from the species to the group and from the group to the individual, since the ego as the bearer of the pole of consciousness and the center of individuality constellates the new tension in the creative psyche which has determined the evolution of the human race during the last few tens of thousands of years.

This means that the development of the human psyche has now reached a stage at which it is no longer sufficient for the productivity of creative man that he should elaborate the salient traditions of mankind and of his own narrower group and provide new material for a future tradition. The individual is now called upon to realize a new phase of the creative process, the phase which we know as "individuation," or in other words

357

becoming and creating one's own self. In the evolution of mankind this task was at first performed solely by the "Great Individuals," but in modern times, owing to the fact that the danger of collectivization and reduction to the level of the mass is so great, the performance of this task becomes the duty of every individual. Though the phenomenon of becoming one's own self is only beginning to enter man's consciousness in our time, it can be shown that man is by nature predisposed to be an individual, that is to say, to have a destiny.

The "human archetypes" of Mother and Father, Wise Man and Wise Woman, etc., which are of such decisive importance for individual and cultural development, are dependent on what I call "personal evocation." This means that for the purpose of actualizing these archetypes a fateful personal encounter must take place with a human being in the outside world who is the bearer of the image which is archetypally appropriate for a given stage of development. It is true that there is a structural archetypal schema, for example for the development of the ego and the conscious mind, and that there are archetypal phases which are inherent in the human psyche and which must be passed through in sequence,[12] but for the individual development of the single human being the general structural constitution is indissolubly connected with those persons in the human environment who evoke the archetypes concerned.

The fact that the human archetypes are dependent on a personal evocation implies as well that destiny, in the form of the personal, individual dimension, already has

12. Neumann, *Origins and History*.

its place in the constitution of human nature. This individual quality, towards which the human element in the psyche is oriented, is not simply based on the uniquely predetermined constitution of the single human being, his heredity, in fact, which is bound to realize itself in terms of a specific society, environment, and period, but is dependent, by its very nature, on fateful encounters in the form of relationships which are, as it were, prepared for him with other individuals who are fulfilling and suffering their own destiny. Society as the group, environment as the homeland, and period as the historical location make up what we may call the external co-ordinates of individuality; personal destiny, on the other hand—a good or a bad mother, a strong or a weak father, who activate the archetypal structures which determine the development of the boy or girl—all this is part of the unique constellation of destiny which influences the individual apart from and beyond his species and the social group. Conformity with the species does not mean simply "preformed form," i.e., the reverse of freedom, but also collective direction, i.e., totally uniform conditioned behavior. In the case of man, the prepared and a priori given collective constitution of the psyche has to be evoked by unique and non-repeatable personal encounters. The result is that, beyond the collective variants in the sociopsychic group dimension, a unique modification of the basic structure of humanity is activated, as occasion arises. The development of each single human being is in fact an uninterchangeable combination of given archetypal, biopsychic, and sociopsychic factors with unique individual experiences. Hence the life of every man, whether he is aware of it

359

or not, represents a synthesis between "the person and the myth."[13] In every case, the archetypal stages of the development of the ego and the conscious mind correspond with mythical phases which can be characterized by the modification of archetypal figures and constellations from the psychic background, such as the Great Mother, the Divine Child, the Young Hero, the Great Father, the Fight with the Dragon, the Marriage of Death, etc. And yet, indissolubly linked as it is with these figures, the development of the person as an individual continues to run its course, in its uniqueness, its earthly determinateness and, at the same time, its freedom.

In this connection it is perhaps necessary to make the point that the thrust forwards to a new phase of development never abrogates the validity of its predecessor. The tradition-bound sociopsyche of the group must always maintain its relationship with the biopsyche of the species, since otherwise the group itself will come to grief, and similarly the individual psyche of each person must not lose contact with the group if it is to avoid incurring the gravest danger. Yet in every case, connectedness also involves conflict. Just as no group can develop its own essential quality in any other way than by emphasizing certain archetypal constellations of the collective human psyche while at the same time neglecting others, so too the creative individual is also involved in a relationship of necesssary and inescapable tension with the highest values and traditions of his group, which he

13. Neumann, "Georg Trakl: The Person and the Myth," in *Creative Man.*

in part affirms and in part denies. But destiny means not only that the life of the single human person, embodying as it does the ego-self structure, leads to the individual becoming an ego and developing a conscious mind, but also that this life, in its totality as the self, presses onward to the fulfillment of the uniqueness of the individual, in his conditioned limitation and in his freedom.

The unity of person and destiny, like the unity of individuality and life, can best be demonstrated if we take as our example creative man in his capacity as the "Great Individual." However, creative man and sick man are both elucidations of man as such only because in both these cases the onward thrust of the ego towards the self and the fulfillment of individuality as a unity of ego and self is inescapable. The former "must" achieve unity because his ego-existence is over and over being directed in the creative process by his existence as the self and "must" recognize and come to terms with this fact; the sick man because his sick ego-life can only be restored to health if it recovers its connection with the compensatory healing and whole-making reality of the self.

One of the essential prerequisites for the possibility of experiencing this ego-self nature in man is what depth psychology calls "introversion," which means becoming aware, not only of the inwardness, but of the inner being of man.

Among living creatures other than man, life takes one single direction, which is turned outwards towards the world, and which we might describe broadly as extraversion. It is true that living creatures possess something "inner" that acts as a biopsychic determinant of their behavior. This, however, directs their relationship with the world without being mirrored, i.e., reflected, as such—since no ego-consciousness exists at this stage. The same preponderance of extraversion has a similar effect in the primitive phase of the evolution of man—in fact it still penetrates and profoundly influences the behavior of modern man. This means that even where something inner is at work, it appears in the form of something outer. We have only to think of the indestructible self-evidence of our sensory apparatus, which has the effect of an entity within us that pictures, and therefore structures, the outer world in a way fixed by law and characteristic of man—an entity, moreover, which for purposes of our direct experience is indispensable and can never be eliminated. What depth psychology describes as "projection" is only the continuation of this primary extraversion of the biopsychic life-processes.

It is not until something which we can already call "inwardness" is evolved in the higher animals that the possibility begins to emerge that this inwardness could be not only used but actually perceived by living creatures, though its function is always to "tone" or dispose them toward extraversion for purposes of courting, competing with rivals, breeding, etc. Phenomena which we should at first sight be glad to describe as simply "expressive" of inwardness (for example, birdsong) are in fact meaningful forms of extraversion which aim at specific effects and serve the purpose of the preservation of life and of the species. Even if these phenomena contain an element of creatively superabundant vitality which transcends the category of biological expedience, they are not an expression of the individual inwardness that is to be found, for example, in the most primitive love song. Even in a love song, the part played by the kind of "courting" that preserves the species must not be overlooked; yet this is now enclosed in a unique and reflective inwardness which expresses itself individually in a specific language and in a form that is already in part determined sociopsychically, i.e., through the medium of tradition and period, in the context of a specific social group.

The primary extraversion of living creatures which is still to be found residually among ourselves begins to be succeeded by something new at the point where the specifically human development of the psyche becomes manifest. With the emergence of the tension between ego-consciousness and the unconscious which is the basis of the new creative and formative phase of the human psyche, the polarization of the world into an outer and inner, a physical and a spiritual-psychic world, now begins to take visible form.

A process is now initiated in which the ego becomes Janus-faced, i.e., achieves a line of vision which is no longer unipolar or exclusively turned towards the environment in the sense of the outside world. So long as this Janus-facedness (though active and effective) remains unconscious, the so-called inner side will also appear as an outside. One essential consideration which helps to explain why man finds it so difficult to overcome the tendency in the vital process towards extraversion is to be found in the fact that one of the most fundamental qualities of the psyche is its capacity to form images, or in other words to transform dynamic force that is essentially non-pictorial into terms of "appearance," i.e., something ostensibly perceptible in the outside world.

The "so-called" inner dimension in fact appears to pre-modern man as an outer dimension; however, it is nevertheless generally removed into a special, "separate" world which is in direct contrast to external reality. To this world belongs the spiritual-psychic world of supernatural powers and demons, spirits and gods, who are, in themselves, essentially "invisible," but who appear in the world and have the capacity to incorporate themselves in parts of the world, and yet, in their "essential nature," are "not of this world."

Primarily, the emergence of images in the psyche possessed a purely directive significance; this was true irrespective of whether the image was an outer image of reality or what we should describe as an inner image. For example, whether early man was warned, as he entered a forest, by the outer image of a beast of prey or by the inner image of a "spirit," the intention and effect of the image in every case was that the man was alerted and put on his guard. In this case, whether the outer eye of the sense of sight registers an outer perception or the psyche, with its unconscious knowledge, detects a danger and transmits an inner image of perception to the inner, intuitive eye, the interpretation remains the same. Both images are experienced by man as outside and have a tendency and an effect towards extraversion. The result is a change in man's behavior in relation to the outside world.

As the polarization of the psyche and the Janus-facedness of the conscious mind increase and become more marked, reality itself begins to be seen as double-faced and is interpreted in terms of a physical outer and a psycho-spiritual inner world. However, in conformity with the law of projection, which even until today has lost none of its force, the inner dimension is still always seen as a secondary phenomenon, derived from a primary outer dimension. This means that even in modern times the psychic is still to a large extent regarded as a "reaction" of the vital process to an outer reality. We find this not only in the psychology of the conditioned reflex ("reflexology"), but also in the notion that the psyche is in some sense a "precipitate," i.e., the product of an evolutionary process. But this would imply that a vital process which is non-psychic is capable of having experience in the world, and that the precipitate of this experience becomes psychic. This conception is clearly impossible, since "having experience" is precisely, or presupposes, the psychic.

We in the West are living in the age not only of primary extraversion but also of the theory of evolution, and this postulates that man originated as a psychospiritual late development out of an earlier stage in which this psychospiritual element did not yet exist, or existed only in a rudimentary form. The history of evolution, as we know, is generally understood as a self-differentiating development which takes place in the environment of an outside reality, and in these circumstances the psychic is naturally evaluated as a late product of the coming to terms of the vital process with this outer reality.

It is probably clear by now that our metapsychological approach is attempting a different kind of interpretation, since we view the creative and formative principle as a primary manifestation of the vital process which has only come to its most particular and clearly marked expression in the human psyche. This formative principle is now seen by the gradually increasing consciousness of our Janus-faced ego in terms of two aspects. The first of these is quasi-"outer" and is equivalent to physical reality, whose ultimate principle is the formula of matter, which is identical with energy; the second is quasi-"inner" and is equivalent to the reality of the creative and formative principle, in which the living process is identical with the creative spirit in its dynamic, ineffable quality, ordering and directing life from within.

These two polar realities are primary. Neither of them can be derived from the other. Both are realities of the image, from which our conscious mind learns to formulate through abstracting and in this way overcoming the image, so that it can never, by so doing, in its stance of "over-againstness," which makes both outer and inner into objects, grasp and apprehend that unitary reality which is alive in and behind both these two polar aspects of reality.

As the evolution of the Janus-faced conscious mind continues, the bipolarity of the psyche begins to become evident, and the primary extraversion of the ego-potency is succeeded by an inner Copernican change, in which the phenomenon of the "inner" aspect becomes visible as a non-derivative, primary reality, toward which the ego necessarily turns, just as much as it turns toward the outer aspect. But the Janus-faced ego-consciousness remains an outgoing, conquering, and perceiving organ, and although by a process of abstraction it relativizes and sees through the reality of appearances, this by no means implies that the experience of the mere-ego is succeeded by an experience of the ego-self unity, which is the genuine basis and axis of the creatively formative human personality.

When the ego becomes conscious of the inwardness of the psyche, there is still no new development, apart from the fact that this leads to the birth of depth psychology, which like every other science comprehends reality by a process of comparison and confrontation, and approaches this reality in the same way, from outside, i.e., by treating it as an object, as is done—though with other methods—by the natural sciences.

However, it is an altogether different matter when man experiences himself as an ego-self structure, i.e., when he becomes aware, not of his inwardness but of his inner being. He experiences himself in his ego-self being as a creatively formative power which is alive in himself, in his ego and in his self; he is a part of this power as an ego, and as the self he himself is this power. In other words, an experience is emerging here whose basis is the total structure of the human psyche and not simply the conscious structure of the ego. But this implies that man is now gripped and transformed by a new psychic situation, to which there naturally corresponds a change in his conception of the world and a change in his experience of his being-in-the-world. So long as ego-consciousness was the center of his personality, the emphasis lay on the ego-apex, on the outreach of the ego-pole, on the primary extraversion and on experience as a development in time in the form of a history of evolution, at the end of which the human ego and the conscious mind are to be found.

This experience of his own, in which man apprehends himself as an ego-pole, constellates him in fact as an ego and as relative man, i.e., as only part of his total reality. As relative man, the individual experiences himself as a point along a line of evolution which leads from remote antiquity via the present to the future, and at the same time as the peak point of the Janus-faced situation, in which the ego finds itself between inner and outer and participates in both these aspects.

However, the fact that the creative process culminates in the individual and in his individuation means that man as an ego-self unity has a "destiny." This is tantamount to saying that the individual ceases to experience himself exclusively as "relative man." By arriving at an experience of his inner being and of his self-being, he achieves a new dimension of reality, in which he is able to experience himself also as what one might call "absolute man." Nothing is further from this experience than an inflationist failure to recognize the ego-like nature of man and of his existence as "relative man." He always remains also ego, always also a part of the inner-outer polarity and a point on the line of temporal succession which runs from remote antiquity to an unknown future. At the same time, however, something occurs which can at least be adumbrated in the light of the category of destiny. Here too the "Great Individual" is an illustration of everyman, who now, in his individuation, realizes the pattern of "creative formation" which is called both destiny and self-formation. Here all those categories come into play which I formulated in the context of my essays on creativity[14] and the realization of the "ego-self axis" of human nature. Both "meantness" ["*Gemeintsein*"], in the sense of a new anthropocentricity in which the individual recognizes himself as the meaningful center of his existence, and what we have called "actualization of eschatology" belong to this context; the realization, that is, of one's own life as an "absolute life" which is not oriented toward the future of a final state at the end of time but toward the fulfillment of the present as an "everlasting present." The experience of one's own numinosity, the numinosity of the ego as well as that of the self, forms the basis for this new state of "being-in-the-world," in which "relative man" is again and again re-formed and assimilated by "absolute man." This experience takes place in the midst of the world and of the problems of the age, and by no means in some remote "free space," since "to have a destiny" does not mean to exist outside time. Yet the concept of destiny which is familiar to us all is perfectly adapted to bring home to us the fact that in spite of everything the man who has a destiny has his own particular heaven above him and that his journey through life runs its course on an earth that belongs to him alone. At the same time the self-created form of destiny as a form that creates itself is both a created form of the age and an "enduring present." This involves no more contradiction than the fact that for us the music that we hear is at once a form or pattern shaping itself in time and an enduring present.

The ego that experiences itself as an organ of centro-

14. [Neumann here cites the entire volume *Der schöpferische Mensch*, published the year before this lecture was delivered at Eranos; see above, editorial note.]

version, a viceroy of the self, ceases to be fixated as the center of a closed system of the conscious mind. It experiences itself as a numinously open reality in relationship with that still more potently numinous and open reality which is the self.

This basic phenomenon, of being at the same time oneself and something "wholly other," leads, in its openness, to a further and still more essential experience. In individuation and in the creative process alike, it now becomes transparently obvious that the center of the creative and formative process is a reality which is itself formless. For the human being who turns his attention to the continually creative and formative process in the human psyche, openness toward this formless reality and the openness of this formless reality itself is the central experience. Analogous to this is the affirmation of the "formlessness" of the divine as a creative reality which, though itself a continuously form-making and image-making agency, is not to be worshipped under any particular form or image, because as an imageless and formless reality it always remains superior to its own creative and formative potency.

We here encounter the paradox, which is fundamental both for life and the psyche, that the imageless and formless reality, insofar as it is numinous, is incomprehensible and cannot be contained in any form or image, though on the other hand, by virtue of its nature as a formative agency, it creates forms and images and can be addressed and experienced by this creation, to whom it can appear equally well as a form and its image or as a formless, imageless reality. In the same way, the self can become a visible form and image, as a figure on the personal level, or as a divinity or epiphany incorporated in a symbol. But by its essential nature it can also appear as an open and formless, imageless reality, as an invisible directing agency, as a principle of order in the vital process or as an "archetype *an sich*" of psychic existence.

The image of God in the structure of man means precisely that the same holds good for the ego as for the self: both are form-creating and formless at the same time. The center of the "I am" and of the "ego-self" is formless and imageless openness, which is bound up just as much with the openness of the world as it is with the formless form-creating capacity of the psyche, which impinges on man from the open center of the vital process. At this point, however, the distinction between an inner and an outer aspect becomes just as inapplicable to man as it is to an unicellular organism which is directed by a center located in open space. In both of these cases a unitary reality appears which is operative before and after the polarization that takes place in the human psyche.

However, the experience of the formless center of the vital process which relativizes and dissolves form means infinitely more for the "inner being" of man than the cognitive glance of man's conscious mind, which, by relativizing and dissolving form in a seemingly analogous fashion, destroys the outer appearance of images. The formless "outer reality," to which the abstracting conscious mind of man thrusts its way, is comprehensible in terms of a formula for energy that can materialize. Yet in its capacity as matter it always remains an objective outer reality, which the comprehending conscious mind of man encounters as a subject. But when man as an ego-self unity experiences the creatively formative agency of the vital and psychic process as a formless form creator, he penetrates beyond the separation of inner and outer and of subject and object to a unitary reality which transforms the man who has overcome distance and who experiences this reality, and fills him with an altered feeling for existence.

The openness and formlessness of this central experience is distinguished by a freedom of the personality which is in marked contrast to the rigid structure by which the vital process is generally directed. But it is also not identical with the relatively arbitrary freedom of the conscious mere-ego, which can apply and turn its will and its interest in any direction it pleases. For on the rebound, this suffering and defensive ego recognizes that its freedom is restricted and that it is itself "conditioned" and "compelled." In contrast to this, for the ego-self totality the "fulfillment" of the creative process and of its own individuation always means both passivity and activity, to serve and to lead, to yield and to create at the same time. At this stage, the freedom of an ego that can behave arbitrarily, just as it pleases, is never the ruling factor, nor is the non-freedom that consists of being compelled by something alien. The truth is that in the experience both of the creative process and of individuation, the reality to which the ego in communion with the self surrenders and which it serves is the self as "oneself," and the fulfillment of the task to which the "wholly other" (that is also oneself) summons one never ultimately involves compulsion. "Openness" arises precisely because a space has been opened up between the ego and the self which gives access to the creative agency that is itself open and in no way previously formed or fixed, but something that realizes itself in a creative and formative process. This freedom from fixity is obvious enough in the case of the creative and formative process in art, but it is equally applicable to the process of creating and forming the self.

Here too the basic phenomenon is the formless creator of form, which on the one hand realizes itself in every human destiny—and in fact in every creature of any kind—as the mysterious One, yet at the same time in every case achieves form as a unique individual. But in these two aspects, i.e., in the infinite abundance of forms and in the formlessness that is superior to form, creativity becomes a conscious experience *in man alone*. Only in man's self-formation does this double nature of the self become transparent: as the individual center of human destiny it is a creative and formative form, yet at the same time as the creative and formative agency at work everywhere and in everything it remains itself formless. The experience of this paradoxical unfixable quality in the formative power of creativity is identical with the experience of the openness and unfixedness in human nature, and that represents an ultimate freedom. It is remarkable how closely these aspects resemble the essential characteristics of Zen, as they have been portrayed in many different accounts. And yet there is a vital distinction here, a difference both in what is affirmed and what is denied. It seems to me that we come to know no more than hints or allusions to what happens to Eastern man in the experience of Satori. This is because the annihilation of rationality and of the ego, which is one of the decisive ultimate goals of Zen, is probably not attainable, to the same degree, by ourselves. Individuation, after all, involves the inclusion of the ego as an essential pole of the ego-self axis, and destiny signifies just as much acceptance of the ego-self reality as an attempt by the creative and formative agency to realize itself in the uniqueness of the human psyche. In spite of this, however, a bridge between ourselves and the East is still to be found in a view of the world which may at first strike us as alien and at the same time paradoxical, but is nevertheless by no means alien to the experience of individuation.

In this connection, I should like to refer to a Hasidic story which has occupied my mind for very many years. It is a story told by a rabbi about a simple Jew, to whom the prophet Elijah had appeared. But the appearance of Elijah "signifies the real initiation of the individual into the secret of the doctrine."[15] The rabbi was asked how this could possibly be true, since the appearance of the prophet had never been vouchsafed to Master Ibn Esra, a man who was spiritually on an altogether higher plane. The rabbi replied that a larger or smaller part of the "allsoul" of Elijah enters into every child, according to his temperament and inheritance. And if the person concerned, when he is growing up, trains his part of the soul of Elijah, then Elijah will appear to him. The simple man to whom Elijah had appeared had realized his small part of the soul of Elijah, whereas Ibn Esra had not realized his much larger part.[16]

As I understand this story today, it means—in Jewish clothing—that what appears here as part of the soul of Elijah is the same as what we call the "self." This self in

15. Martin Buber, *Die chassidischen Bücher* (Hellerau, 1928), p. 690, note.
16. Ibid., p. 446.

374

a man is on the one hand the basis of his individuation and his destiny, but on the other hand the "smaller than small" and "greater than great" of the Indian *purusha* applies to it. This means that as something immeasurable and as a formless creator of form and images it is everywhere identical with itself.

From the standpoint of our metapsychological enquiry this soul of Elijah is valid not only for the Jew and not only for humankind but for everything that lives and everything that exists, and the formless reality is the basis not only of all individual existence but of each thing that has been formed, in all its diversity, since it is everywhere one and the same reality. This means, however, that everything which fulfills its own nature is equal in rank and equal in radiance, and the apparently nullifying effect which is the echo to any development of the vital process that culminates in the individual is actually the annulment of all differences in the equality of the formless center. But this equality applies just as much to the inanimate that fulfills its inanimate nature by existing, as it does to the vital process which fulfills itself unconsciously as preformed form, and to the human reality that fulfills itself consciously as a form creating form and images. And so, just as we have to recognize man in this sense as "absolute man," so in this line of experience every animal, every plant, and every stone becomes "absolute." But precisely from this point of view the Eastern aspect of the void that fills everything is only the complementary other side to the Western aspect of individuation.[17]

17. It must be said here that Zen, at any rate as represented by

In a time such as our own it seems almost absurd to talk about individuation and the development of the individual human person and, beyond that, to go on to assert that this principle represents an absolutely essential requirement for the process of development to man and in man. The truth is that we are all living in an age which is characterized by the diametrically opposite experience, or rather threat, of the extinction of the individual at the hands of the collective—the process, I mean, by which the individual is made anonymous owing to his reduction to the level of the mass. Nothing is more obvious or natural than to regard individuation as a kind of "escapism into inwardness" and its representatives as a group of human beings who are cut off, or who are cutting themselves off, from "what is really happening" and whose fate it is, inevitably, to die out. This problem has disturbed me profoundly; it becomes a burning question for me when I ask myself, "To whom am I really speaking, to whom, for example, is this way of thinking addressed, and the living concern that lies behind it?"

The historians of religion who lecture here are all professionals: they are reporting events that happened in the past. They may approve or disapprove of the subjects about which they have to inform us: that is quite simply irrelevant. Even a materialist can study mysticism as his special subject and report in an instructive way about his excursions into the history of human madness. Zoologists and physicists speak in harmony with nature and she will grant them or deny them her approval in their experiments. And you know as well as

---

D. T. Suzuki, tends to confuse the aspect of individuation in the West far too much with its ego-like quality.

I do that what is nowadays generally regarded as psychology, both in the West and in the East, has declared its allegiance in the same way to the ideal of this "natural science" and to exactitude, experiment, and statistics. Only the depth psychologist stands outside the security of the man of science, who does not need to expose himself. But unlike the priest, the depth psychologist has no church, sacraments, ritual, or dogma to stand behind him, either. For the theoretical knowledge of the fact that the experimenter is included in his experiment does not affect the individual, but the universal human structure of the investigator. Only the depth psychologist is unable to keep himself outside the game that is being played in him and with him.

Of course the depth psychologist also bases himself on experience, but it seems to me—in contrast, admittedly, to many of my colleagues—that this experience cannot adequately be communicated by tape recorders and the writing of "objectivizing" papers. For the bipersonal event which takes place between the analysand and the analyst is an event which involves transformation, and the depth psychologist himself is also included in this event. This means, however, that he does not stand over against the process in a scientific, objectivizing spirit, but is only able to objectivize parts and aspects of its reality after it has taken place. The event that really happens here is an example, on a small scale, of the truth which has been formulated, in general terms relating to the large scale, as follows: "The Tao that can be told of is not the Absolute Tao; the Names that can be given are not Absolute Names."[18]

18. Lao-tse, tr. Lin Yutang, in his *The Wisdom of China and India* (New York, 1942), p. 583.

This may sound like secretiveness and mysticism, particularly in the ears of a modern man. Depth psychology does take pains to arrive at formulations which are at any rate intelligible. However, if you have been able to follow my reasoning so far, you will understand that the development of humanity from polar, inner-outer knowledge gradually thrusts its way forward till the point is reached when it is no longer a question of an observing ego confronting an object in the outer and subsequently in the inner world, but where, though the experience of the ego in relationship with the self is certainly filled with a sense of its "inner-being" and with that of its fellow man and of the world, the possibility no longer exists in principle of expressing this experience objectively in terms of language.

It is at this point that, in the East, the testimony of art becomes relevant. In this we must include poetry, wash ink drawing, and painting, in which the secret of the form-creating formless reality finds expression in the inner being of the man who is in a close relationship with the world. In Western art too, it seems to me that, since the Renaissance and the baroque period, there is sufficient evidence to prove that a similar happening has been taking place, a dissolution of form in the direction of formlessness or, alternatively, a breakthrough of the formless background through the form of appearances in the foreground.

However, this formlessness in the background does not appear to Western man as the world or as nature to the extent that it does to Eastern man. To the East, it is the world, it is nature, as the open and formless creator of form and images, which reveals itself precisely as the background to man's introversion—and to his meditation, which originally penetrated into his depths as a subject. To Western man, it is the open and formless creator of form and images that is the self, which reveals itself as the background of his extraversion—and of his conscious mind, which originally penetrated into the depths of the object.

It is true that in the East the emphasis is laid on nature, but in the pictures of the Zen masters it is precisely man once again who appears as the incarnation of what we call the self. And inversely, though since the Renaissance and the baroque period, it is the apprehension of man as an individual, as an ego-self unity, that plays the decisive part, nature, too, along with landscape, from Leonardo da Vinci and Rembrandt through to Van Gogh, become transparent as a world of creative form-making formlessness, of light and of a space that permeates everything.

In spite of this, for Western man the center of the picture is occupied by the individuation of man as a unique incarnation of the self-revelation of imageless-ness. Anyone who has seen the sequence of self-portraits of Rembrandt will know that in the searching consciousness of his artistic creation Rembrandt was interested not in his "ego,"[19] his "I," but in the destiny that was being enacted in the human being who was himself. His real concern was to apprehend the power that was invisibly transforming him, the formless agency that in every phase of his life was changing and remodelling the character of his face. He was interested in making transparent the creative and formative quality that was the

19. Cf. D. Frey, "Das Fragmentarische als das Wandelbare bei Rembrandt," in *Das Unvollendete als künstlerische Form* (Bern, 1959).

living, really effective background behind the foreground of the "objective" human reality and of the "objective" world. But this background of formless openness and formless form-creating activity shines through a landscape in a Chinese painting in the same way as it does through the drawings, etchings, and pictures of Rembrandt. This formless and imageless quality of the background is just as clear and distinct in the void of the light and in the openness of Rembrandt's landscapes as it is in the translucence which permeates one of his human subjects, whether it is the sketch of a beggar or of a child, the Prodigal Son, the Jewish bride, or Christ on the cross.

It is certainly a transforming experience when we realize that in every stone and in every plant the same formless and imageless quality is translucent as in an animal or in a human being. But today it is humanity that is in peril, and with humanity everything that is living, but this does not apply to mountains and stones, stars and worlds, whose superior existence lasts and continues in a state of security and sheltered safeness that is unknown to ourselves.

So the individual turns out to be the most imperiled, the frailest and the most unimportant of all things, something which in the monstrous world of numberless quantities does not count, but something in which at the same time the unique event occurs that makes counting possible. The course of evolution runs from the experience of the outer to the experience of the objective inner world and to "inner being," from the biopsychic via the sociopsychic realm to individuation, from the "Great Individual" who, as an exceptional personality, anticipates development and points out the way, to the "meantness" of every single person.

The opening out of the human species leads from the small family of primitive man to the cultures of the various races and peoples which are spreading and covering the entire earth; it has led to monstrous collectives and to the ever-rolling juggernaut which reduces humanity to the level of the mass and has created problems that are still almost insoluble but that must be solved. Hunger, disease, and overpopulation on the one hand, technological development, concentrations of power, and wars on the other are the overwhelming external problems which this opening out of the human race has brought in its train. The countermovement to this development is provided by the paradoxical basic phenomenon of the incarnation of the formless form-creating agency in individuals created in the image of the Creator.

Just as the individual has learned how to exist, under the tyrannical rule of emperors and potentates, churches and dogmas, in poverty and exile just as much as in a state of recognition and apparent approval and acclaim, so too he will learn how to conceal his creative existence and his secret and to adapt under collective dictatorships of West and East, North and South. He is able to do this because, in contrast to the opening out of the masses in space and time, the simplicity of his inner being makes his fateful existence possible for him, since beyond his participation in the world and in history he realizes in himself as "absolute man" the formless form- and image-creating reality which occupies the place of the center in the human psyche.

INDEX

Abraham, 157, 212

abundance, of life, 131-32, 134, 198, 272, 332

Adam Kadmon, 90, 92, 204-5; as a God-figure, 117; and the man-world equation, 116, 120, 121, 122

agency, 341; directing, 328, 332

alchemy, 25-26, 39, 40, 64; and peace, 292, 293

alienation, 9, 98

anima, 146, 285-91; and animus, 82

anthropocentrism, 119, 120, 300, 369

anthropomorphism, 338, 339

anxiety, 184, 196, 205, 326

archetypal: figures, 33, 84, 186, 360

— field, 18-25, 27-35, 44-45, 47-48, 54-55; and the self-field, 47-48, 49, 56

— images, 23, 85, 86; in art, 186; in dreams, 32; formation of, 370-71; and the psyche, 353-60, 370-71; symbolic nature of, 66-67

archetype(s), 21, 78, 82-83, 88-90, 260-61; and archetypal images, 66-67, 86; *an sich,* 65, 371; and art, 41; and childhood, 150; and the collective unconscious, 22-23; and consciousness, 11; and creative man, 101; and the eternal problem, 148, 150-51, 156, 162; and the "Great Experience," 148, 186-88; and great works of art, 186-88; and individuation, 358-60; in Jung, 310; and knowledge, 11; and "personal evocation," 358-60; and the phenomenon of "latching on," 81, 84; and the psyche, 353-60, 370-71; as psychic nuclear structures, 39; symbolism of, 24-25, 148; and time, 20; transgressive character of, 22, 23, 28; of the "union," 92; unitary element of, 176-77; and unitary experience, 121; as "world enigmas," 150-51; world factor and psychic factor of, 25-26, 81-82, 85, 86; world of, harmony with, 310-12. *See also* archetypal; *and see* anima; child; circle; devil; dragon; father; Great Experience; Great Mother; Great Round; hero; incest; mandala; mother; rebirth; religion; self; shadow; Wise Old Man

art, 42, 65, 115, 173, 378-80; and

383

GPSR Authorized Representative: Easy Access System Europe - Mustamäe tee 50, 10621 Tallinn, Estonia, gpsr.requests@easproject.com

www.ingramcontent.com/pod-product-compliance
Lightning Source LLC
Chambersburg PA
CBHW032337280326
41935CB00008B/362